Changing Primary Practice

Changing Primary Practice

Robin Alexander
John Willcocks
Kay Kinder

The Falmer Press
(A member of the Taylor & Francis Group)
London • New York • Philadelphia

UK   The Falmer Press, Rankine Road, Basingstoke, Hampshire, RG24 OPR

USA   The Falmer Press, Taylor & Francis Inc., 1900 Frost Road, Suite 101, Bristol, PA 19007

First published 1989

British Library Cataloguing in Publication Data
Alexander, Robin
 Changing primary practice.
 1. England. Primary schools
 I. Title II. Willcocks, John III. Kinder, Kay
 372.942

ISBN 1-85000-632-6
ISBN 1-85000-633-4 pbk

Library of Congress Cataloging in Publication Data are available on request

Jacket design by Caroline Archer

Typeset in 11/13 Garamond by
Chapterhouse, The Cloisters, Formby L37 3PX

Printed in Great Britain by Taylor & Francis (Printers) Ltd, Basingstoke

Contents

Preface

This is the first of two volumes arising from the evaluation of Leeds City Council's Primary Needs Programme. Since this programme eventually included all the primary schools in one of Britain's largest LEAs, and the evaluation was a very complex affair, there are many people whose contribution or support needs to be acknowledged:

first, Leeds City Council, which commissioned, financed and housed the project;

second, the elected council members and LEA officers and advisers with whom we found ourselves working most closely;

third, the members of the project team whose names do not appear on this book's cover, but who played an important part in the gathering of data. They are listed in Appendix 1. Of these, we particularly acknowledge the contribution of the project's three successive research assistants: Steve Conway, Martin Ripley and Val Carroll;

fourth, the heads and staff of the 230 primary schools in Leeds. We gathered data of some kind from all these schools, and undertook fieldwork in eighty-five of them. But we were particularly grateful to two groups of colleagues: those in the thirty 'Fieldwork B' primary schools who readily submitted to being visited and studied over and over again during the three years of fieldwork; and the teachers in an additional ten classrooms with whom we undertook our most intensive and exacting study: the 1988 classroom observation and interview programme. Our commitment to confidentiality prevents us from naming any of these people, but we trust that they will accept our thanks nevertheless.

The writing of all our reports, and of this book, was a collective endeavour; so too were the planning and conduct of the research. However, as the originator and director of the project, Robin Alexander bears the ultimate responsibility for what took place and what appears here and in the companion volume.

Introduction

In 1985 one of Britain's largest cities launched an ambitious programme to improve the quality of education in its 230 primary schools. In 1986 the LEA invited this book's first author to submit proposals for evaluating the initiative.

The programme in question, aimed at meeting what were seen as the most pressing needs of the city's primary children and their teachers, was called the Primary Needs Programme (PNP). The evaluation project took the acronym PRINDEP — Primary Needs Independent Evaluation Project — and it is this project which has provided the material for the present two-volume study.

The content and relationship of the two books need to be explained. *Changing Primary Practice* incorporates material produced by PRINDEP between 1987 and mid-1989. During that period we wrote a sequence of ten reports, drawing on data gathered during the project's first two and a half years. Seven of these reports have been revised and reordered for the present volume. Together, as our title indicates, they explore the theme of change in primary education. In the second volume, to be published a year or so after this one, we draw on further PRINDEP data and the project's final report to present an account and assessment of the Primary Needs Programme as a whole, and to consider the implications of this particular initiative for primary schools and LEAs elsewhere.

The reports which form the core of Chapters 2 to 8 in the present volume were originally written for a mixed readership of primary teachers, heads, school governors, LEA advisers and elected city council members. This is not to say that they dodged complex issues — to have done so would have been to insult our readers' intelligence and betray our own — but they did seek to be reasonably accessible.

When preparing this first volume we debated whether, as well as editing the seven reports and providing each with an appropriate introduction, we should also recast them more in the style of mainstream research papers. We decided against doing so for three reasons: first, because we believed that studies like these should stand or fall on their substance rather than on their conformity to particular stylistic conventions; second, because we retained our sense of the value of this material to a mixed readership; third, because in planning the two volumes as a pair we knew that we could include further technical and bibliographic material later.

The use of 'changing' in the title of the book is deliberately neutral and ambiguous. The book charts some of the many ways in which primary schools and classrooms changed during the period when we were studying them; it explores and appraises some of the deliberate strategies employed by heads, teachers and the LEA to make change happen; and it also invites the question of whether changes of the kind explored are necessarily changes for the better. This last point is particularly important because policy-led changes are invariably premissed on an expectation (or, at any rate, a public claim) that they will produce improvements. Naturally, in embarking on our evaluation of the programme under discussion in these two volumes we ourselves could make no such assumption, though we do address the question of whether, on the basis of our evidence and analysis, it might be justified.

Moreover, the relationship between planned and actual change is a complex and wayward one. Change strategies do not always deliver the desired outcomes, and indeed can sometimes have consequences very different from those intended. The changes we observed were not necessarily those that the LEA wished for; and some of those it promoted most vigorously did not, to any great extent, occur. To seek to engineer large-scale change in classroom practice and school management is to enter a minefield, in which pre-existing attitudes, habits and competences are at least as significant as strategy in determining the success of a venture. Such themes, explored here in a local context, are highly relevant to the condition of primary education nationally, and seem likely to remain so for several years.

The 1970s witnessed challenges to primary schools on a number of fronts. The sometimes rather complacent orthodoxies of primary progressivism were questioned, in a probably accidental pincer movement, on ideological, empirical and conceptual grounds: by the right wings of both main political parties and by researchers and commentators of relatively liberal leanings. HMI surveys set an agenda of concerns from 1978 onwards, focusing chiefly on the content and management of the curriculum, from which they deviated very little in the following decade. The reiteration of these concerns (coupled with the habit of sometimes unthinking deference to their source) ensured that they acquired the status of an alternative orthodoxy within primary education: one which, by and large, teachers did not like very much yet felt obliged to acknowledge. But above all, laissez-faire in education gave away to increasing centralization and control, as successive Conservative administrations took full advantage of a large parliamentary majority to bring about changes which only a decade earlier few people would have contemplated. The culmination of this process — for the time being at any rate, since more change undoubtedly lies ahead — was the 1988 Education Reform Act, by common consent the most important piece of educational legislation for over forty years.

The Primary Needs Programme stands in an interesting relationship to the 1988 Act: one which, quite by chance, gives both PNP and PRINDEP's evaluation an added significance. Leeds LEA introduced the Primary Needs Programme in 1985. To begin with its messages, as we shall show, reflected a very local agenda — tackling the challenges of inner-city primary education, responding to the needs of ethnic minorities, catering for children with special educational needs in mainstream primary schools, and advancing the cause of progressive primary education in a city where the LEA felt that too many schools were old-fashioned and dull. By 1987, only two years into PNP, this agenda had begun to be squeezed by national events. The government issued the first consultation documents on the National Curriculum and on the other policies like opting out, local school financial management and open enrolment which by 1988 were to be enacted as law. Thus by 1989 primary teachers in Leeds were probably much more concerned about preparing for the introduction of the National Curriculum that September than about implementing their LEA's philosophy of primary education, and understandably so.

Yet in two respects PNP, far from being overtaken by events, may well prove to have been vindicated by them. One of these is our theme of planned change. Though the scale and means differed, both the Leeds Primary Needs Programme and the 1988 Education Reform Act were assertions of the power of central statutory bodies to bring about change in schools and classrooms from above. Leaving aside for the moment the question of whether power in each case was appropriately or justly exercised, or whether the educational goals being pursued were appropriate, the parallels in terms of political/administrative *strategy* seem worth noting. In particular, it might be predicted that the local experience of PNP would give the primary schools involved a training in the management of educational and professional change which would serve them well in the context of the requirements of the 1988 Act.

The other important test of the Leeds initiative is in the area of *pedagogy*. In its prescriptions for the curriculum the 1988 Education Reform Act was much more concerned with *content* and *outcomes* than with the *processes* by which these are achieved — expressed over simply, perhaps (for the two are really inseparable), an emphasis on the 'what' rather than the 'how'. Yet the successful delivery of the required standards in the National Curriculum depends on how the specified attainment targets and programmes of study are translated by teachers into the everyday classroom processes of planning, organization, diagnosis, teaching, learning and assessment. Indeed the programmes of study and attainment targets have no real meaning outside this act of translation: until then, they constitute nothing more than a paper curriculum.

The Primary Needs Programme, in contrast, focused firmly on classroom practice — and it did so in terms of principles which at first sight seem very relevant to the challenges facing teachers in the context of the 1988 Act. Teaching strategies, it was argued, should above all be *flexible*, since only through flexibility could the needs of all children in a period of educational and social change adequately be met. If the Primary Needs Programme has been successful in this regard, therefore, its teachers will have acquired further skills, complementing those in the management of educational change, to support them in their task of implementing the 1988 Act. At any rate, these hypotheses seem worth putting to the test, as we move through the two volumes towards both a retrospective appraisal of the impact of PNP and a prospective consideration of the lessons it holds for the future development of primary schools and primary teaching generally.

The studies which follow deal with change at several levels — in classroom practice, in school management, and in LEA policy — and in so doing they explore a variety of processes, from the minutiae of teacher–pupil interaction to staff professional relationships, school and LEA administrative procedures and a wide variety of strategies at the three levels for making change happen.

These studies build on a number of different lines of enquiry in primary education opened up in recent years: on classroom organization and pedagogy (Galton, Simon and Croll, 1980; Galton and Simon, 1980; Bennett, 1976; Bennett *et al.*, 1984; Mortimore, *et al.* 1988); on urban primary education (Tizard *et al.*, 1988); on professional roles and the management of educational change (Campbell, 1985; Taylor, 1986); on the culture of primary schools and primary teaching (Alexander, 1984a; Pollard, 1985; Nias, 1989; Nias, Southworth and Yeomans, 1989); and on the ideas of which modern primary education is constituted and which are such powerful influences on practice (Dearden, 1968; Entwistle, 1970; Alexander, 1984a; Blenkin and Kelly, 1987; Blyth, 1984, 1988).

Though, as Blyth's (1989) review shows, the serious study of primary education, as least on its present scale, is a comparatively recent phenomenon, works like those cited here already constitute a 'tradition' which it would be cavalier to ignore, and our own indebtedness to these and other colleagues will be apparent. At the same time we trust that we manage to take the quest further and to offer distinctive as well as familiar perspectives. For example, these two volumes are unusual in the way they combine empirical and conceptual analysis: more commonly the two modes are kept firmly apart, not least by the peculiarly British habit of treating research and empiricism as synonymous and relegating conceptual exploration to second division status; and the volumes are perhaps unique in the way they encompass an entire local system of primary education, from classroom to staffroom, and from staffroom to town hall.

There is one final stylistic point: the core of each of Chapters 2 to 8 is a report which was written, as we explained above, for a local audience at a particular time. Our frequent use of the present and perfect tenses reflects this. When we came to edit the reports for this book we felt that preserving the present tense could be misleading, in as far as there would be an increasing time lapse between the events discussed and readers' encounters with them. We would not, in other words, wish to convey the impression that the 'now' of 1987–89 persists into the 1990s (even though it frequently does). So we started changing all the tenses. Unfortunately, that was even less satisfactory. Verbs are so fundamental to language that to tamper with them in this way can dramatically distort the sense of the words to which they relate. In any case, as anyone who has tried this will understand, we found ourselves becoming tied in impossible grammatical knots. We therefore reverted to the original tenses. Each of Chapters 2 to 8 starts with a new introduction, specially written for this book. Then comes the body of the report, fairly lightly edited and with its original tenses intact. It should be read as existing, as it were, between quotation marks. We hope that readers will agree that this is a more satisfactory way of dealing with the problem.

1
Changing Primary Practice:
Context, Policy and Evaluation

Context: The City

On the map it is Leeds rather than the misleadingly named Midlands which is somewhere near the centre of the British mainland. At the same time, in its dramatic, hilly landscapes, its confident use of local building materials like millstone, brick and faience, its stark contrasts of affluence and poverty, its cultural diversity and vitality, its traditions of religious and political dissent, and its independence verging occasionally on chauvinism, it is unmistakably northern.

With a population of nearly three-quarters of a million, Leeds is the largest city in Yorkshire and the third largest in England. In fact, the Leeds Metropolitan District comprises two quite distinct areas, the city and those parts of the former West Riding of Yorkshire which were incorporated during the 1974 local government reorganization. The latter constitute a much larger area than the city, though the city contains the greater proportion of the population. A consequence of this amalgamation was to accentuate still further the existing cultural and environmental contrasts in Leeds. The old West Riding areas include solid and self-sufficient market towns like Otley, Wetherby, Morley and Pudsey, mining communities to the east and south-east, affluent and scenic commuter villages, separated by unspoiled dales countryside, to the north-east and north, and the rural-urban Bradford-Leeds hinterland to the west.

The city itself contains even greater contrasts. Rather more of the Victorian centre than of many comparable cities survived the planning megalomania of the 1960s, and the monumental municipal buildings, elaborately detailed shopping arcades, grandiose business premises and sprawling university bear witness to the commercial success and civic pride of the last century, as do the parks and villas to the north and north-east of the city centre (Leeds claims to be the greenest city in Europe). Though tower blocks have supplanted chimneys on the city's skyline, churches — the spiritual complement to the Victorian mill — are everywhere still prominent; some blackened and delapidated, some converted into offices or bingo halls, others newly sandblasted and restored, but all still evoking the Protestant ethic as powerfully as any Weber or Tawney.

By the late 1980s a new phase of major redevelopment had started, post-modernist in style, and thus adding further to the city's visual heterogeneity. As in London, Liverpool, Salford and several other cities, the redundant river and canal frontages were being rapidly transformed into new commercial premises and enclaves of high-cost housing.

Away from the centre, where people live rather than shop or work, there is the inevitable domestic counterpoint: large areas of terraced and back-to-back Victorian artisan housing, some of it well cared for in stable communities, some of it in transient areas deteriorating rapidly, some of it undergoing yuppification, much of it already bulldozed and replaced by the vast, anonymous estates of the 1930s and 1950s or by 1960s/1970s tower blocks or again, more recently, by low-rise precincts on a consciously more human scale. Further out are the leafy Victorian former suburbs of Roundhay and Headingley, now solidly professional, and beyond them the newer estates and mini-mansions of the northern and eastern boundaries between the city and the former West Riding. Like many cities, however, Leeds is not symmetrical and this pattern is not repeated in every direction, particularly on the considerably less affluent south side.

The population is even more diverse: well-established families and communities descended from the vast influx of workers who moved into Leeds and the jobs in its woollen mills in the first half of the nineteenth century and expanded its population in that short space of time from 50,000 to a quarter of a million; a sizeable and influential Jewish community dating back to the nineteenth century; more recently established ethnic minority communities, mainly of Afro-Caribbean and Asian origin, which form about 9 per cent of the total population but up to 90 per cent in some parts of the city; and the usual admixture in any large city of geographically mobile and transient professional groups.

Context: The Schools

The 230 Leeds primary schools are housed in buildings of all ages, shapes and sizes. The oldest was built in 1716, the most recent was opened in 1989; in between are the numerous archetypal late Victorian elementary schools, the rambling buildings of the 1930s and 1950s, and various kinds of architectural response to the post-1960s progressive vision — fully open-plan, semi open-plan and barely open-plan.

Though in size Leeds primary schools range from village church schools of twenty or thirty children to large inner-city schools of between 500 and 600, and both extremes are minorities, the average size, at 191 children, is rather larger than in neighbouring LEAs and indeed than the national average. The overall primary school population (1988 figures) is some 48,000 pupils and 2400 teachers.

The system contains various organizational patterns. The central area has mainly 5–9 first and 9–13 middle schools (and it should be noted here that in Leeds, unlike many LEAs, the middle schools are administratively and culturally quite distinct); while the former West Riding schools — despite the fact that middle schools originated in the West Riding — are mainly 5–7 infant, 7–11 junior and 5–11 junior/infant.

The two traditions — city and county — are still, nearly two decades after reorganization, distinct in certain respects, in terms of both loyalties and educational outlook and practice. In some of the former West Riding schools the inspiration of progressive luminaries like Clegg, Tanner and Schiller is still asserted. Whether, if still alive, these would be prepared to endorse the classroom practice justified in their names is another matter. Perhaps the issue is as much one of mutual suspicion and disparagement between town and country as of genuine divergence of educational principle, since in primary education progressive ideals tend to be espoused across the board. Thus those confronting the challenges of the inner city see themselves as inhabiting the only 'real world' in primary education, compared with which the task of teachers in what they mockingly term 'leafy-lanes' schools is deemed in every sense peripheral and elementary; while staff in the latter feel on the one hand that they are neglected, unappreciated and underresourced, and on the other that they are the true standard-bearers of the progressive primary tradition.

In parenthesis, the influence of the rural shires in the rise and — currently — the continuing defence of primary progressivism is worth noting in this context (Cunningham, 1988). Its arts and crafts nostalgia has never sat particularly comfortably with urban realities, as Robin Tanner himself discovered during the brief period when he worked in Leeds (Tanner, 1987).

While this is to some extent a simplification of the various cross-currents, it does at least serve to point up two further salient features of the context within which the initiatives discussed in these two volumes were located, in addition to that of extreme diversity in provision. The first was a professional climate shot through with a certain amount of suspicion and antagonism; and the second was the prominence in all matters primary, in

Leeds as elsewhere, of 'informal' primary ideology (Alexander, 1984a, 1988; Blyth, 1988; Simon, 1981). Both had an important part to play in the inception and development of the Primary Needs Programme.

Context: The LEA

Throughout the period under review in these two volumes Leeds City Council was controlled by Labour, with a large majority, and had been since 1980. But much of the administrative machinery for primary education had been established during the period when the council was either Conservative-controlled (1967–1972) or 'hung' (1974–79). We do not intend to enter the somewhat contentious arena of attributing responsibility for the various aspects of the legacy which the LEA sought, through PNP and related policies, to transform. Suffice it to say that by the mid-1980s there were some in positions of power in the LEA who felt that primary education in Leeds was in need of a considerable injection of ideas, energy and resources. For instance, the DES and CIPFA statistics of education for the period prior to PNP show Leeds in a consistently low position in the national league table in terms of per capita educational expenditure and primary school pupil-teacher ratios. In the four years before the introduction of the Primary Needs Programme in 1985, for example, Leeds was always in the bottom 25 per cent of LEAs in terms of unit costs for primary education, and for the previous five years never higher than the lower half. Similarly, between 1976 and 1985 the primary school class sizes in Leeds were well above the average for both metropolitan districts and the country as a whole.

Alongside low spending and large classes was a third element. While, inevitably in an LEA of this size, there had been a constant turnover of staff, it had tended to take the form of movement between schools in the Authority, particularly those in the inner city, rather than into the LEA from elsewhere. For many years, indeed, the only way teachers from other parts of the country could gain permanent employment in Leeds schools was by entering with temporary contracts which might later be made permanent, and the 'ring fence' policy on new appointments which was applied during the period of falling school rolls reduced mobility still further.

By the early 1980s many schools were staffed by heads and teachers who had been there for two decades or more and showed no signs of wanting to move. Added to this, strong local and family ties tended to ensure that a fair proportion of such staff were also locally educated and trained. Such a limited degree of professional mobility, the more notable considering the size of the LEA, produced a powerful perception among some of the city's political leaders that the system had become stagnant and parochial. (It must be acknowledged that 'immobility' is in this context an unfavourable synonym for 'stability' — a characteristic which is generally applauded. The perception, however, is not ours.)

Support services for teachers were also, compared with many LEAs of comparable size, somewhat thin. The LEA's advisory service had, prior to PNP, just one senior primary adviser and three specialist primary advisers for 230 primary schools: advisory coverage of primary schools was achieved through a system of general 'pastoral' advisers who oversaw primary, middle and secondary schools. Though teachers had access to a wide range of in-service courses, many of them at the teachers' centre, some of them run in local higher education institutions or on a consortium basis with neighbouring LEAs, this provision was not supplemented by the kind of highly specific targeting of school and teacher needs which a developed and specialist advisory support service, in theory at least, allows.

The Primary Needs Programme: Origins

These kinds of perceptions about the state of primary education in Leeds were significant determinants of the direction eventually taken by the Primary Needs Programme. To begin with, however, they competed with two more specific concerns. The first of these was the task of providing for children with special educational needs in mainstream primary schools in the context of the 1981 Education Act and of subsequent DES circulars, guidelines and regulations (especially DES, 1983). The second was the situation of children in the inner-city primary schools, and particularly those experiencing high levels of social and material disadvantage. Certain key members of the City Council held the view that any increased investment in primary education should be directed at boosting the circumstances and prospects of these children rather than at multiplying the advantages of the socially and/or materially better-off.

Both 'needs' found their way not just into the programme's name, but also into its basic strategy for determining which schools should be accorded priority when extra resources were allocated. Schools were introduced into PNP in three phases, the first starting in September 1985. Two simple procedures were used. The first, in response to the criterion of educational need, was an analysis of schools' scores on the Authority's 7+ and 9+ reading screening tests (see Chapter 3). The second, in response to the criterion of social/material need, was an examination of schools' figures for free meals. To special and social/material needs were added needs arising from the Authority's commitments in the fields of multi-ethnicity and gender, thus producing a set of four categories of pupil need within and around which PNP policy and provision were framed and which we explore in detail in Chapter 2.

Initially, the special needs emphasis was pre-eminent. Its highlighting in the advertisements and job specifications for the key staff appointed to the Phase 1 schools led many to believe that PNP was exclusively a special needs programme, and that the extra staff were being recruited solely to cater for children with learning difficulties in the light of the requirements of the Warnock Report (DES, 1978b) and the 1981 Education Act in respect of integration and statementing. No sooner had this view been propounded by the LEA and internalized by its teachers than it was replaced by one both more comprehensive and more elusive. For competing with the principle of meeting the needs of specific groups of children was a sense among some elected council members and LEA advisers that here at last was an opportunity to reform the whole character of primary education in the city; to use extra resources, and especially extra staff, to rejuvenate classroom practice in accordance with progressive primary ideals and undo the damage caused by years of stagnation and underresourcing.

Thus, while phrases like 'special needs' and 'children with learning difficulties' dominated early PNP material, they quickly yielded to the language of general educational reform: 'retrenchment' and 'the dark decade' (the old regime); 'enrichment', 'revitalization', 'bringing in new blood', 'raising morale', and, most typical and ubiquitous, 'establishing a quality learning environment rich in stimulus and challenge' (the new).

Behind this apparent shift in direction lay political and administrative manoeuvrings which will be explored more fully later, as will the way the special needs emphasis reasserted itself as time went on. There were two consequences of immediate note, however. The first was the generation of a certain amount of confusion among some teachers as to exactly what the Primary Needs Programme was all about — confusion which persisted for a surprisingly long time. The second was the crystallizing of the purposes of PNP into a single broad aim:

> to meet the educational needs of all children, and in particular those children experiencing learning difficulties;

and three rather more specific goals by which this aim would be realized:

> developing a curriculum which is broadly based, with a stimulating and challenging learning environment;

> developing flexible teaching strategies to meet the identified needs

of individual pupils, including specific practical help for individuals and small groups, within the context of general classroom provision;

developing productive links with parents and the community. (Leeds City Council, 1985a)

Though the language seems bland, it remained constant over many council documents of the period, and its underlying signals are quite clear: the original commitments to special needs and social/material disadvantage are honoured, but both are to be subsumed within a general framework of progressive practice. In the latter respect, the three goals manage to pack in all the main principles of Plowden, together with the characteristically Plowdenesque combination of persuasiveness and ambiguity.

The Primary Needs Programme: Provision

Be that as it may, the practical face of PNP was not in the least bit ambiguous. Substantial funds were earmarked to bring schools into the programme in three phases, starting, respectively, in September 1985 (seventy-one schools), January 1987 (fifty-six schools) and September 1988 (103 schools). The main areas for expenditure and development were additional staff, increased capitation, refurbished buildings and in-service support. While full details of numbers and expenditure under each of these headings will appear in Volume 2, we provide here sufficient to indicate the scale and relative emphases of the programme.

Additional School Staff

The key appointment was the 'PNP coordinator' — an experienced teacher appointed at a relatively senior level in each school to serve as a change agent stimulating and leading curriculum and professional development in pursuit of the four PNP goals. Coordinators worked to specifications set by their heads, within a general framework provided by the LEA. A small number were appointed to the more specific brief of multi-racial coordinator. Chapter 5 explores the various ways in which PNP coordinators across the city fulfilled their roles, the strategies they used, the educational and professional tasks they undertook, and the problems they and other staff encountered in the process.

While every school in the programme had its PNP coordinator (and a few had more than one), the grade of the appointment varied according to the size of the school and the extent of its 'need' as indicated by the measures referred to above (Scale II or III under the Burnham salary scales, Main Professional Grade, with or without incentive allowance, after 1988). So too did the extent of additional staffing beyond the coordinator. In the first phase a large number of Scale I experienced and probationary teachers were appointed to the programme, with smaller numbers being appointed in subsequent phases. These worked in a number of ways, though most operated in what were termed 'support' roles. In addition, there were specialist appointments involving work in or attachment to schools: for example, nursery nurses, Home-School Liaison Assistants (later redesignated Home-School Liaison Officers) and (three years into PNP) teachers of English as a second language. Finally, in 1987 most PNP Phase 1 and 2 schools were allocated one or more Ancillary Assistants, each employed for between ten and thirty hours per week, but most between ten and fifteen hours. These appointees were mainly staff redeployed from other council departments as a result of financial cuts, and were not PNP funded. The numbers of PNP appointments are shown in Table 1.1.

Table 1.1. Appointments to the Primary Needs Programme, 1985–89

	1985–86	1986–87	1987–88	1988–89	Total
School-based staff					
Coordinators	53	28	18	4	103
Scale 1/MPG	54	36[a]	35	88[b]	213
Probationers	6	29	5	14	54
Nursery Nurses	17	4			21
Home School Liaison Officers		10		2	12
Ancillary Assistants			120		120
Support staff					
Coordinator	1[c]				1
Head of Primary Schools Centre		1[d]			1
Primary Support Teacher (Equal Opportunities)		1			1
Teacher in charge Multicultural Resource Centre	1				1
Administrative staff	2[d]	1[d]			3
				Grand Total	530

Notes: a Includes five half-time appointments.
b Includes twenty-eight half-time appointments.
c For one year only.
d Until 1987–88, when absorbed into central administration.

The original intention of the Authority was that schools would maintain their staffing at the enhanced PNP level. At the time of writing, however, delegation of financial responsibility from LEAs to schools under Sections 33 to 51 of the 1988 Education Reform Act and subsequent government circulars appears to restrict LEAs' scope for staffing schools at the generous level of PNP Phase 1 (DES, 1988a): while the usual enhancement was one or two extra teachers, in some schools it was much higher (up to ten above normal establishment). (This matter will probably be clarified by the time Volume 2 is published.)

Increased Capitation

The LEA allocated a considerable sum for enhancing PNP schools' capitation to enable them to expand their resources of books, equipment and materials. Schools prepared bids specifying and costing their requirements which were then checked and approved by advisers before going to the appropriate Council subcommittee. Part of Chapter 4 is devoted to an analysis and discussion of the curriculum priorities reflected by this expenditure, which from the start of PNP to 1989 amounted to some £461,600.

Refurbished Buildings

PNP incorporated a Minor Works Programme of refurbishment to some of the least prepossessing buildings in each phase. Each school, having different problems, was tackled differently, but the refurbishment package could include some or all of the following: new furniture; provision of display boards and curtains; repainting; carpeting; lowering ceilings in older buildings; removing walls to create larger, open areas.

It is a basic tenet of progressive primary belief, and thus of the Primary Needs Programme, that the physical character of the school environment has a powerful impact on the child's learning (Cunningham, 1988; Bennett *et al.*, 1980). However, in discussing refurbishment towards the end of Chapter 2 we note that its impact is probably impossible to measure, and certainly not in terms of cost-effectiveness. Yet we also suggest that other indicators, not least the judgments of the teachers concerned, deserve to be given due weight in attempting to assess such impact. The number of refurbished schools in each phase, to May 1989, was as follows: Phase 1 — sixteen, Phase 2 — six, Phase 3 — three.

In-Service Support

The generally centrist character of the Primary Needs Programme has been referred to already. One of the ways it was reinforced was through an extensive programme of in-service courses at which members of the LEA's advisory staff delivered to teachers their versions of good practice. The number and variety of such courses were considerable, and most took place in the new Primary Centre. This was another PNP investment: the first centre occupied the top floor of an inner-city primary school; subsequently it took over a redundant 1960s school on the edge of the city, thus gaining a large amount of space in an attractive building.

The early programmes of courses were labelled 'PNP', and many were designed exclusively for staff in PNP schools. Soon, however, in common with several other aspects of the programme, they merged with the LEA's mainstream primary provision. The latter part of Chapter 4 considers the curriculum priorities reflected in teachers' attendance at some of these courses, while in Chapter 6 we analyze and discuss in detail the style and impact of this approach to professional development, concentrating on a pivotal series of courses on classroom organization which were among the many monitored by PRINDEP during the second year of PNP. The follow-up to this study, in which the teachers who attended the courses were observed and interviewed in their classrooms, forms part of Chapter 8.

Centralized courses are but one of many forms of in-service support. In addition, schools undertook their own programmes, often using the PNP co-ordinator, either as an agent or as an enabler of professional development (see Chapter 5). One of the most potent procedures for professional development we encountered was that of teachers working together in the classroom, a practice many endorse but few are able to implement because it requires staffing above the normally tight level applied to primary schools. PNP provided this opportunity, and some of the results (and problems) are explored in Chapter 7.

Related Developments

Disentangling the Primary Needs Programme from other policies and pro-grammes within the LEA has not always been easy. The picture was fairly clearcut to begin with, but as more schools came into the Programme, and as originally specific appointments and initiatives were modified or merged, the boundaries between PNP and general primary policy became increasingly hard to discern. The LEA itself asserted that this was both inevitable and proper, and that PNP and the Authority's policy on primary education should be treated as synonymous.

This no doubt desirable evolution creates certain problems for a commissioned evaluation, to which we shall need to return later. It also makes it essential that we make a point of mentioning some of the parallel developments in the LEA which, while not officially part of PNP, bore most heavily upon it.

First, and most notable, was the expansion of the LEA's primary advisory service. As noted above, the pre-1985 complement of specialist primary advisers was just four, of whom one was a senior adviser. The LEA then started rapidly to expand its primary advisory service, the exercise coinciding with a restructuring of the LEA's administration as a whole. The result was a Department of Primary Education with advisers, advisory teachers, administrative officer and clerks, all headed by a Director of Primary Education. By the start of the third phase of PNP, in September 1988, the primary department's central staff included, as well as the Director, seven primary advisers and eight primary advisory teachers. Most of the latter, it should be noted, did not operate in the usual manner of such appointees by being mainly classroom-based, but as, in effect, additional advisers, each with a responsibility for a group of schools and/or a cross-LEA brief for some aspect of curriculum or policy.

Thus, from being relatively peripheral figures — if only because they were so few in number — advisers and advisory teachers became a highly significant element in the LEA's primary programme. In particular, although not part of PNP in terms of funding, they were PNP's chief agents in terms of interpretation and implementation. The strategy was a strongly centrist one. Its consequences for practice and for school–LEA relationships, and the question of whether in the circumstances it was the most productive way to proceed, we shall explore later.

Second, the LEA undertook a major primary school rebuilding programme. Thirteen schools have been, or are being, rebuilt since the start of PNP in 1985, at a total cost of £18 million. There are also plans to begin rebuilding a further nine primary schools before the end of 1992, at a projected cost of £16.6 million. The design of all these schools involved close consultation among the architects, heads and the advisory service, and physically enacted the latter groups' view of primary education.

Third, the LEA's initiatives in primary education ran alongside others in special needs. As in many LEAs, the traditionally divided worlds of special and mainstream schools were reflected in separate administrative structures, a feature which persisted after the 1981 Education Act and was consolidated through the LEA's 1987 administrative restructuring. This meant that the new Special Services Department was involved in mainstream primary education to the considerable extent that the 1981 Act required, while being administratively and physically separate, answerable to a different Director, and subject to different departmental goals. In this respect Leeds appears to have been little different from other LEAs. Noting, somewhat critically, the persistence of the structural separation of mainstream and special needs administration and support in LEAs nationally, HMI commented that 'in no LEA was there any evidence of the special needs support service becoming an integral part of an advisory team working towards common goals' (DES, 1989b, p. 5).

Thus some of the initiatives most prominently associated with the Primary Needs Programme, particularly during its first phase, were in the area of special needs — the procedure for identifying and monitoring children in the various DES categories of need and the associated training course for teachers for example, together with a number of teaching packages and programmes (see Chapter 2). Moreover, the 7+ and 9+ reading tests, the LEA's only measures of attainment at the primary stage, were also administered by Special Services rather than the primary department. This was because their original function had been as a screening device for identifying children with learning difficulties. (Chapter 3 discusses our analysis of the results of these tests over a six-year period.)

Alongside these LEA initiatives there were two national developments which also had considerable repercussions for primary schools. One was the change in the funding of INSET introduced (as Grant-Related In-Service Training or GRIST) in April 1987, and renamed the LEA Training Grant Scheme (LEATGS) under the 1988 Education Reform Act. Apart from curtailing full-time secondments (which Leeds had made exceptionally heavy use of until 1988), the LEA introduced an experiment in school-controlled INSET which contrasted sharply with the strategy of centralized courses through which the Authority's messages about good primary practice in general, and PNP practice in particular, had until then been conveyed. At the time of writing the experiment of devolved in-service budgets is about to be extended beyond the initial 30 per cent of schools, and some comparisons of the two approaches will feature in Volume 2.

The other national development was the 1988 Education Reform Act, a piece of legislation having profound consequences for schools and teachers throughout England and Wales. We have noted in the Introduction how the challenge of preparing for the September 1989 arrival of the National Curriculum supplanted PNP and indeed most other concerns from early in the 1988–89 school year. At this stage one can only speculate about the precise impact of the Act on the ideas and practices of which the Primary Needs

Programme is constituted, though two areas of concern beyond the obvious one of the curriculum were identified in the Introduction (management and pedagogy), and to these must be added staffing. All of these will be explored in detail in this book and its companion volume.

There were other contingent developments. Throughout the period of our evaluation of the Primary Needs Programme, the LEA was involved in schemes for phasing out middle schools and reintroducing a single 5–11 primary system. The proposals engendered — as school reorganization proposals invariably do — a certain amount of opposition, and in their first version were rejected by the Secretary of State. Naturally enough, they added to the sense of professional destabilization experienced by teachers involved in the Primary Needs Programme. Finally, in a similar vein and bringing us full circle, there was the industrial dispute over teachers' pay and conditions which coincided with the first year of PNP and aggravated the difficulties in its implementation, particularly for heads.

The Cost of the Primary Needs Programme

A summary will indicate something of the scale of the initiative: see Table 1.2. More detailed figures appear in the second volume.

Table 1.2. Summary of Expenditure (pounds sterling) on the Primary Needs Programme, 1985–89

	1985–86	1986–87	1987–88	1988–89	Total
Extra school staff	1,217,000	2,301,000	3,109,000	4,623,000	11,250,000
Extra support staff	52,000	53,000	35,000	38,000	178,000
Increased capitation	119,023	125,704	97,762	79,120	461,609
Refurbishment/minor works		600,000	650,000	650,000	1,900,000
Major works			8,200	17,200	25,400
Total	1,388,023	3,079,704	3,899,962	5,407,320	13,775,009

Evaluating the Primary Needs Programme: Issues

Following lengthy negotiations between the LEA and Leeds University, the contract for a four-year evaluation project was signed and PRINDEP was set up in the summer of 1986. By then, as is so often the case with commissioned evaluations, many of the critical decisions about the programme being evaluated had already been taken. Its philosophy and strategy had been agreed, Phase 1 schools had been identified, PNP staff had been appointed, the in-service support programme had been planned, and the entire programme had been running for a year.

It was already clear that the challenges involved in attempting to evaluate PNP would be formidable. That expectation was amply fulfilled, and we shall be providing later a full discussion of the strategy and methods adopted, together with an analysis of their implications. At this stage, however, it is necessary at least to signal some of the more problematic issues. These can be grouped under three headings: political, methodological and conceptual.

Political Issues

It is by now a truism to assert that all evaluation is political. Its context is an arena of competing values and agendas, each of which is associated with varying degrees of power, so that the question is less whether an agenda is valid than whether and how it is enforced. A commissioned evaluation has to decide where it stands in relation to the various value constituencies, and even if it pursues a line of studied neutrality, it is almost invariably at risk from two kinds of assault: being manipulated by one or other of these constituencies in order to buttress their sectional interests and ambitions; or being marginalized or even sabotaged because it delivers unpalatable findings (House, 1973; Adelman and Alexander, 1982).

In the present case the political dimension was particularly acute: two strongly hierarchical cultures — in the primary schools, and in the LEA as a whole; a programme premised on the view that schools were not always performing adequately and that 'power-coercive' strategies (Bennis *et al.*, 1976) might be the most effective way to produce change; a context of uneasy relations between employers and employees over matters like pay, conditions, school reorganization and the Primary Needs Programme itself; and a high level of personal investment in the programme by certain key individuals and groups, with status and careers bound up in its being perceived to be successful.

Overarching and influencing all these were local and national party politics: the power struggles within and between parties, the point-scoring, vote-catching, negotiation, compromise and personal ambition; the knife-edge of reconciling policy ideals, resources and political support; the tension, and sometimes conflict, between national policies and local aspirations and circumstances, between Conservative government and Labour council, between DES and LEA.

Methodological Issues

The Primary Needs Programme presented many methodological problems to an evaluation team, of which three were paramount. The first was its sheer size: what started as an already large initiative, involving seventy schools, soon expanded into one involving 230 schools, 2400 teachers, 48,000 children and £14 million. The second was its openendedness and elusiveness. Where did the programme start and finish? Were we evaluating PNP or primary education more generally? How, in such a context, could one control all the variables? Indeed, could one even say what the variables were? The third was its changing character. PNP started as an idea, or rather — as we showed above — several ideas in some degree of competition. It became a practical programme enacting some of these ideas, but then it began to change: partly as a result of experience, partly as a result of policy shifts, partly because of external events (notably government legislation) and partly, it has to be said, in response to the evaluation process itself.

Together, these factors of scale, elusiveness and instability add up to a methodological problem which can be expressed quite simply. Evaluation involves the use of procedures and the application of criteria in order to judge the worth and/or effectiveness of something. But by what means, and in terms of what criteria, do you evaluate something which refuses to stand still or keeps changing its shape?

Beyond these three hurdles were problems to do with methodology in a stricter, more technical sense: sampling; the construction, piloting and administration of instruments like questionnaires, interview protocols and observation schedules; the handling and processing of very large quantities of data; and the proper use of such data, separately and/or in juxtaposition, as a basis for findings and judgments offered in reports (Burgess, 1985; Hammersley, 1986).

Conceptual Issues

However far professional researchers and evaluators may have progressed in their private conversations and writings, not least in relation to political and methodological issues like those identified above, the lay concept of programme evaluation still tends to be dominated by three assumptions.

One is that an evaluation should deliver hard proof of the success or otherwise of the programme in question. The second is that such proof is best demonstrated through numbers rather than words. The third is that this measurement process necessarily involves a before-and-after testing programme.

The first of these expectations is, up to a point, legitimate, in as far as those commissioning an evaluation have a right to anticipate that their money will yield something conclusive and useful. The other two assumptions are more questionable in any context, but especially so in the present case, given the constantly changing character of the Primary Needs Programme. However, since the one thing an evaluator cannot afford is to be dismissive of clients' expectations, they have somehow to be addressed and if alternatives are offered, they have to be convincing.

There are further issues to be resolved. Can a programme evaluation evaluate everything? If, as in this case, that is manifestly impossible, what should be selected, and on what basis? If evaluation is in the end a judgmental process, who will do the judging? Will the evaluation offer descriptive data to enable others to judge for themselves, will it make its own judgments, or will it do both? And by what criteria will the programme be judged? By those embedded as goals or principles in the programme itself? By those of the many participants, all of whom may have different criteria? By those of the evaluation team? By a combination?

How one resolves all the questions and dilemmas listed so far — political, methodological, conceptual — is partly a matter of practical circumstances, for evaluation, like politics, is very much the art of the possible. But those involved in evaluation can never afford the politician's luxury of being guided entirely by pragmatic considerations. There is room for realism in evaluation, but not for cynicism.

The decisions one takes in relation to organizing and conducting a large-scale evaluation, then, turn partly on practicalities but more fundamentally on one's basic perceptions or defintions of the evaluation process and of the phenomena being evaluated. This needs elaborating. Evaluation is a process of acquiring knowledge, gathering evidence, clarifying and applying criteria, delivering information and offering judgments. How one goes about these tasks depends on the kinds of material one is prepared to count as valid evidence and the rules to which one subjects oneself in the search for knowledge which one is happy to stand by. Hence, for example, all the methodological debates about sampling and the statistical analysis of quantitative data.

But the validity of an evaluation method depends not just on its proper construction and application; it also depends on its appropriateness, or its congruence with what is being evaluated. In order to judge and achieve such congruence one needs, therefore, a proper conceptualization of both elements in the evaluation enterprise, the evaluation procedure and its object or focus. In the present case the foci were educational policies and processes, at the three levels of LEA, school and classroom, with particular emphasis on the last two. Our response to this further conceptual challenge will emerge as we proceed through the studies in these two volumes. At this stage, however, one very important aspect of our conceptualization needs to be asserted from the outset. It is the view that teaching is as much about ideas as it is about action; that the teacher's thinking is as significant a determinant of the quality of children's learning as are the teacher's movements round the classroom; and that the 'practice' of teaching is properly conceived as a fusion of knowledge and understanding, interpersonal commitment and competence, situational skill and judgment, and on-the-spot capacities for rapid diagnosis and decision-making.

Those outside teaching, and not a few inside it, would see nothing remarkable in this statement. Yet the world of primary education has long been dominated by a notion of professional 'practice' as somehow free of much more than fairly rudimentary cognitive skills and processes, let alone rigorous intellectual exploration. It is a notion we encountered frequently, in one form or another, in the course of our evaluation. In its most extreme manifestation (which is very common), the definition acquires an aggressively territorial loading, signalling not so much a world of action in which people sensibly keep their feet on the ground as one from which ideas must at all costs be excluded.

One immediate consequence of the latter stance for evaluation is that those subscribing to it tend to expect an evaluation project to concentrate on gathering data about behaviours rather than about the motivations and justifications which inform such behaviours and which, if explored, might help to illuminate and explain them. Another is that they will expect evaluation not to examine policies and prescriptions as such, but only the extent to which they are carried out. The second of these consequences is partly a function of the political arena in which all evaluation commissioned in a hierarchical context is undertaken: put simply, there may be some who expect the evaluation to support, even endorse, the policy and policy-maker, rather than question them.

Our response has to be to adumbrate and hold to our basic stance on teaching and evaluation, regardless of any professional or political pressures to which we may be subjected. We happen to subscribe to the view that the proper understanding of educational processes and outcomes demands that one attends to ideas as well as to action, and both therefore feature prominently in our evaluation studies. But we do not expect this view to have an easy ride: the atheoretical view of practice is so much more powerful and pervasive. It is also self-justifying and self-reinforcing, since merely to entertain the possibility of an alternative is to engage in the very activity — theorizing — which is rejected (for the development and justification of this line of argument, see Alexander, 1979, 1984a, 1984b, 1988, 1989).

Principles

Such an array of challenges made it essential that the independence of the evaluation project be asserted and demonstrated from the outset and that notwithstanding the extensive consultation which would be required, PRINDEP would in the end have to make its own decisions about what to evaluate and how.

The other principles adopted in the face of these circumstances can be summarized very briefly. First, the programme was to be mainly formative, though with summative judgments and recommendations offered in the final report. Its principal function before that would be to raise issues and questions, and provide information and insights, in order to help those involved to study, understand and develop their work. Second, while the evaluation would need to be wide-ranging, it would also have to be selective. A 'total' evaluation of a programme on the scale of PNP would be impossible within the resources allocated. Third, the evaluation would need to be flexible and responsive, able to explore issues and practices as they emerged. Moreover it would have to accommodate shifts in LEA policy and even in the basic definition and direction of the programme being evaluated. Fourth, the evaluation would have to be methodologically diverse and eclectic. Fifth, its material would be presented in a way which prevented individuals and institutions from being identified. Sixth, it would be open: there would be no secret or restricted reports, but instead everything published by the project would be disseminated widely across the LEA and would be freely available to all. Seventh, these reports would need to be presented in a style which made them accessible to a very diverse readership, both lay and professional, without prejudicing the complexity of the issues and arguments which needed to be addressed.

Evaluation Themes and Methods

Our first task was to identify the issues to be explored and set up the frameworks and procedures. Two series of meetings were organized. The first, with

LEA advisers and officers, with elected Council members, and with officers of the teachers' unions, negotiated the scope and style of the programme as indicated above. The second series, with teachers and heads from PNP Phase 1 schools (already nearly a year into the programme) yielded important insights into the way the programme was developing. These latter groups also completed questionnaires which explored their individual roles, experiences and perceptions in relation to the first year of PNP.

From this process emerged the first two reports — preliminary rather than interim — and a set of six major themes for the evaluation. These were:

children's needs: definition, differentiation and provision;
curriculum: content, development and evaluation;
teaching strategies, especially collaborative teaching;
links between school, home and community;
the management context of PNP schools, and changes in staff roles and
    relationships;
professional development and in-service provision.

The origins of the first four of these will by now be readily apparent. They were derived directly from the goals of the Primary Needs Programme itself ('broadly-based curriculum ... identified needs of all pupils ... flexible teaching strategies ... productive home–school links ...'). The other two were clearly a sine qua non of the programme's successful implementation. That much was acknowledged by the LEA in its use of a particular managerial strategy, that of the PNP coordinator as change agent, and in its substantial in-service programme and expansion of the advisory service. But it also came through very strongly in the preliminary questionnaire returns, as we mentioned in our second report:

> The introduction of a major innovation challenges existing practices both in the classroom and in the wider school community. Where the innovation includes, as PNP does, extra staff and unfamiliar roles, it offers a particular challenge to schools' management capacities — to the ways decisions are made, to the ways in which individual jobs are defined, to patterns of communication, to styles of leadership, and to the quality and kinds of personal relationships on which successful management depends. There is evidence of a considerable degree of tension in some schools and it is possible that some traditional management styles may be inappropriate to cope with this or with the complexities of PNP in general. Alternatives will need to be explored, but this is a long-term issue, not amenable to overnight transformation ....

and

> Inservice support is essential, given the extent of the change implied by PNP. But 'inservice' means far more than courses at the Primary Centre or the local university or college. In a more fundamental sense it is about how heads and staff see themselves as professionals, and the importance they attach to their professional development. Since it is a commonplace that there can be no educational development without professional development, this too must be a priority for the evaluation programme. (PRINDEP Report 2, pp. 11–12)

The six themes were to be explored using a variety of methods within the context of four main methodological strands. First was the study of *representative practice*, which we termed 'Fieldwork B'. This involved a sample of thirty primary schools selected by computer analysis of such basic features as size, location, catchment area, pupil age-range, county/denominational status, age/type of building and so on. Ten were in PNP Phase 1, ten in Phase 2, and ten were at that stage not yet in PNP and therefore provided a control group. Technically this process does not make the *practice* representative, even though the schools may be, but it offers reasonable indicators in this regard. Studies in these schools proceeded in parallel so that a comparable range of data was generated from each school. This element provided data for comparative studies of each PNP phase, for interim studies of the six PRINDEP themes, and for the longitudinal study of change and development in primary schools across the city.

Second was the study of *interesting* or *significant practice*, which we termed 'Fieldwork A'. This involved the accumulation of data from schools which might not appear in the representative sample but which were nevertheless a necessary part of the total picture. Whether the practice in these schools was representative was not the issue: it was chosen for inclusion in the evaluation programme because we or others (whether advisers or teachers) deemed it worth studying. Among these schools were many whose approaches were quite distinctive in some way, or which were pursuing unusual or minority policies. What they had in common was that their activities were stimulated or facilitated by PNP staffing and resources. At the time of writing the number of schools in which Fieldwork A of some kind had been undertaken stood at fifty-five, making a total, with the thirty Fieldwork B schools, of eighty-five schools (out of 230) in which the project team had worked.

The third methodological strand was *survey*. Survey methods, usually in the form of postal questionnaires, enabled us to find out more about practice and reaction across the LEA as a whole than was possible through Fieldwork A or B. Surveys covered various populations — heads, PNP co-ordinators, other staff and so on.

Fourthly, we collated and analyzed *basic school and LEA factual and quantitative data*, drawing where possible on the LEA's own material. This included staff numbers, appointments and responsibilities in all schools and the advisory service; pupil numbers, groups and attendances; special needs and statementing figures; scores in the LEA's 7 + and 9 + reading tests over the period 1983–89; INSET courses and teacher attendances; the finances of PNP, including both the global costs for major items like staffing and building refurbishment, and the specific uses of moneys under the smaller budget headings like increased capitation.

In addition, there were miscellaneous procedures such as interviews with parents and with some of the key actors in the creation and develop-ment of PNP.

The project generated various purpose-designed instruments: interview schedules for use with teachers, heads, parents, advisers, officers and elected council members; questionnaires for completion mainly by school heads and staff; and observation schedules: three for classroom interaction, one for staff meetings, another for in-service courses.

Throughout, as we stressed in our discussion of conceptual issues earlier, we adopted the stance that 'practice' is constituted of thinking as well as action and that the ideas informing the Primary Needs Programme were as worthy of study as were the patterns of behaviour by which it was mani-fested.

The Studies in Chapters 2–8

The studies which follow draw on data from the first two full years of the evaluation project, January 1987 to December 1988. During this period we gathered data from both Fieldwork A and B schools, supplemented by survey material on certain issues, in order to gain a purchase on each of the six project themes of Pupil Needs, Curriculum, Teaching Strategies, Home–School Links, Management and Professional Development. Together these were to be the subject of a series of six interim reports. These were preceded by two brief papers based on the preliminary studies and enquiries, and were followed by three further interim reports. One of these was an analysis of 7 + and 9 + reading scores over the period 1983–88, and the other two, published in 1989, reported on a three-stage study, in a sense the culmination of the project up to that point, of teachers and children at work in PNP classrooms.

The complete sequence of interim reports, using their titles and numbers, is listed below. Those edited for publication in this volume are asterisked.

> Report 1 (November 1986). *Reactions to the PNP Inservice Support Programme*
> Report 2 (November 1986). *One Year into PNP: The View from Phase One Schools*
> Report 3 (May 1987). *Home–School Links: First Findings*
> *Report 4 (May 1987). *Teachers Teaching Together: Emerging Issues*
> *Report 5 (November 1987). *The PNP Coordinator: Opportunities and Ambiguities*
> *Report 6 (November 1987). *PNP INSET: A Closer Look*
> *Report 7 (July 1988). *Children in PNP Schools: Defining and Meeting Needs*
> *Report 8 (October 1988). *The PNP Curriculum: Policy and Management*
> *Report 9 (October 1988). *Reading Standards in PNP Schools*
> *Report 10 (June 1989). *Changing Classroom Practice: Decisions and Dilemmas*

In preparation or planned at the time of writing:
Report 11 (late 1989). *Classroom Practice: Teaching and Learning*
Report 12 (early 1990). *Home–School Links: Further Developments*
Report 13 (mid-1990). *The Primary Needs Programme: Final Report*

Of the ten reports available at the time of writing the first three have not been used. The first two were very much preliminary soundings, while the third was based on limited data and is therefore held over to be discussed in the context of its follow-up study (Report 12) in Volume 2. Report 11, at the time of going to press, is still in preparation. It is a substantial and concentrated study of the activities of children and teachers over a typical fortnight in a number of PNP classrooms. The enquiry combined systematic observation and interview and generated a large amount of quantitative and qualitative data. The analysis and discussion of this material will form an important part of Volume 2, as of course will the project's final report (Report 13) with its review of the Primary Needs Programme as a whole, its conclusions and recommendations.

The reports used here have been reordered. That might seem a somewhat perverse decision, but it seemed to us that, except in cases where chronology was particularly significant, our main guiding principle should be the book's coherence. These studies explore the book's theme of 'change' in a variety of ways. We look at a wide range of strategies for generating change, and examine their impact and effectiveness. We seek to chart some of the many changes which actually took place; and we focus on each of the three main levels to which a proper understanding of change in local primary education dictates attention: the LEA, the school, and the classroom.

2
Redefining Children's Needs

Introduction

The concept of 'needs' is central to teaching: we educate children in accordance with what we judge their needs to be. But the word has for a long time had extra resonances in primary education as the unassailable pivot of the child-centred movement, strongly endorsed in key official publications like the Plowden Report (CACE, 1967) and, nearly sixty years ago, by Hadow (Board of Education, 1931). So by naming its initiative the Primary *Needs* Programme, Leeds LEA gave the concept its own seal of approval and signalled a focus with which few would be likely to disagree.

Nevertheless, the concept of 'needs' is not without its problems. On the one hand, psychologists and physiologists have delineated a range of human needs from 'basic', 'primary', 'biological' and 'organic' to 'secondary', 'higher' and 'social' (classically exemplified in the work of Maslow, 1954, and, more recently, Kellmer Pringle, 1980); but on the other hand, philosophical analysis has shown how difficult it is to sustain the argument that more than a handful of such needs are intrinsic; and how, in any case, discussion of needs too often fails to make basic and necessary distinctions between 'needs', 'wants' and 'interests' (Dearden, 1968; Hirst and Peters, 1970, provide good examples of these kinds of clarification).

Each of these lines of analysis can be — and sometimes is — taken to extremes. Thus, on the one hand, one hears a stolid insistence that all claimed needs are absolutes, that children need what we say they need, that this is the way children 'naturally' are, and that's the end of the matter; on the other, a remorseless chipping away at all needs claims, in the manner of Shakespeare's Goneril and Regan ('What need you five and twenty? Ten? Or five? . . . .What need one?'), until it can be shown that nobody, neither king nor child, really needs anything. Alternatively, some adopt what they see as the sensible middle position, accepting that since needs are social constructs they should be discussed and argued over rather than be assumed to be 'given', yet at the same time recognizing that the enterprise is in the end a humanitarian rather than a logical one.

None of this sense of the problematic nature of needs statements clouded the inception of the Primary Needs Programme, despite the apparently punning reference to Maslow in its title; and in a sense perhaps it did not have to, since the LEA's concern was simply to exercise its prerogative of constructing a policy for its primary schools in which certain defined needs were paramount and of then ensuring that these needs were met. However, as this chapter shows, the very fact that the needs were defined from above made it inevitable that at the operational levels of the school and classroom there would be considerable variation in how they were understood and responded to.

The chapter is based on the seventh project report. In Part 1 we outline the policy background, and then move on to examine how schools responded to the main categories of need within that policy. In doing so, we draw on a combination of what we have termed Fieldwork A and Fieldwork B data — that is, material gathered both in representative sample and other schools, together with material from the annual questionnaire surveys. Scattered through Part 1 are examples of viewpoints or practices which we originally included (bearing in mind the formative function of these reports) for staffroom discussion purposes as well as for illustration. The analysis and discussion are constructed round a conceptual framework (represented as the grid on page 69) which indicates our two levels of exploration, the LEA and the school, and what we take to be the four necessary components or stages in the process of formulating a need and translating it into classroom practice: definition, identification, diagnosis, provision.

Part 1: Policy and Practice

The Concept of Needs in PNP

From the earliest planning stages of the Leeds Primary Needs Programme the LEA's policy documents have contained a clear and straightforward list of basic objectives, and apart from very minor and insignificant variations in the wording these objectives have remained the same in all official statements since. An early version, dating from a June 1985 Education Committee document, stated:

1.2   the proposal is intended to be the first phase of a three year programme, aimed at providing additional resources to

        meet the educational needs of all children in the Autho-
        rity's primary schools, and in particular those children ex-
        periencing learning difficulties.

1.3   The proposed programme aims to continue the Authority's
        support of Head Teachers and their colleagues in all primary
        schools:

1.3.1 developing a curriculum which is broadly based, with a
        stimulating and challenging learning environment

1.3.2 developing flexible teaching strategies to meet the iden-
        tified needs of individual pupils, including specific practical
        help for individuals and small groups, within the context of
        general classroom provision

1.3.3 developing productive links with parents and the com-
        munity. (Leeds City Council, 1985a)

Although particular mention is made in paragraph 1.2 of children who experience learning difficulties, the major emphasis in this part of the statement is on those educational needs which may be said to be shared by all children: the broadly-based curriculum and the stimulating and challenging learning environment of paragraph 1.3.1 are for everybody.

Paragraph 1.3.2 turns from needs which all children share to needs of a different order which are peculiar to particular individuals or groups. The demand here is for a teaching approach which will allow teachers to vary their way of working with different children in accordance with their differing needs. This proposal quite clearly indicates that teachers will need to be able to identify and recognize the specific personal needs of their pupils before they can hope to respond to them: the flexible teaching strategies of paragraph 1.3.2 are *to meet the identified needs of individual pupils*, and this implies an identification process, however informal it may be.

Other PRINDEP reports examine the broadly-based curriculum and flexible teaching strategies in some depth. This present report is concerned with those educational needs which are not shared by all children. It seeks to discover how the LEA defines the needs and identifies the children who have them, and it explores the ways in which teachers, as part of their everyday responsibilities, identify children within each of the LEA's broad areas of need, how they diagnose the precise needs of the children so identified, and how they make provision for them.

In spite of their emphasis on *individual* needs, it is not to be expected that the Authority's policy statements will or can give much in the way of detailed guidance about what the needs of individual children might be, and how they should be met; such needs are in their very nature personal and idiosyncratic, and hence a matter for individual teachers and children to explore in collaboration with each other. In its concern for the needs of particular *groups*, however, the Authority has made its views and its priorities clear from the outset. We have already seen, in the committee document quoted above, one such group singled out for special mention: *'those children experiencing learning difficulties'*. Indeed, so strong was the initial emphasis on this particular group in such public documents as the PNP coordinator job description of June 1985 that the early stages of PNP were characterized by a certain amount of confusion about the extent to which the programme was purely and simply concerned with special educational needs; and the way in which this situation was resolved is charted in Chapter 5.

However, some initial confusion was perhaps inevitable in view of the proposal that:

> 7.1.1 Existing Scale 3 teachers, who are currently Special Educational Needs Coordinators in target schools of Group 5 and above, should be confirmed as Primary Needs Programme Coordinators at their present schools on their present grade, with security of tenure at that school.
>
> 7.1.2 Existing Scale 2 or Scale 3 teachers who are currently Special Needs Coordinators in target schools of Group 4 and below, should also be confirmed as Primary Needs Programme Coordinators at their present school, at their present grade, with security of tenure at that school. (Leeds City Council, 1985a)

Although it was mistaken, the assumption which some people made at the time that PNP was signalling nothing more substantial than a change of name is not difficult to understand.

The detailed explanation of the basis upon which *target schools* were to be selected throws further light on the Authority's interpretation of particular group needs:

> 3.1 It is proposed that those primary schools included in the first year of the programme (the 'target schools') should be identified by application of criteria which would include the results of existing reading screening procedures at 7 + and 9 + , combined with an assessment of social need (using data on free school meals and pupil absence rates). The use of the criteria is discussed in the Appendix . . . .
>
> 3.3 Information is being collected of the number of primary

school children from the minority ethnic groups, and their mother tongue languages. It is proposed to use this data to identify those schools which will be assigned teaching staff for the specific needs of these pupils . . . .

Appendix . . .

1.3   By examining the results of standardised tests and other procedures, and using percentiles it will be possible to ascertain which schools have the largest concentration of those pupils with serious learning difficulties.

1.4   Additionally, social factors such as pupil absence rates and the number of pupils' free school meals, will be taken into account.

1.5   The assessment of these educational and social factors will provide a valid analysis of need, enabling decisions based on objective data to be made as to which schools should be identified for additional support. (Leeds City Council, 1985a)

This statement contains certain key phrases indicating the Authority's awareness of three quite different groups of children who were seen as having needs peculiar to themselves: '. . . pupils with serious learning difficulties . . . '; '. . . children from the ethnic minority groups . . . '; '. . . [children experiencing] social need . . . '. The criteria proposed for inclusion in the last of these three groups were frequent absence from school and entitlement to free school meals, although in the event the absence criterion was dropped, and the sole index of social need became free school meals. In short, social need was equated with poverty.

It should be pointed out at once that the Authority's term 'pupils with serious learning difficulties' was not intended to imply that the pupils in question had been or were about to be allocated to one of the DES clinical and formal categories of special need. Indeed, the point was made quite explicitly, and at some length:

Appendix . . .

2.1   The use of the number of pupils requiring statements has been examined as to its suitability for inclusion in the overall criteria.

2.2   The statementing process, by its very nature, is concerned with only a small proportion of the total pupil population. It is not necessarily a sound indication of broad educational

2.4   need in the school and it may well be that its use will distort the overall assessment of educational and social need . . . .

2.4   . . . at this stage, there is considerable doubt as to the appropriateness of the 'statementing' factor for inclusion in the overall criteria to be used for identifying the target schools. (Leeds City Council, 1985a)

Statemented children form only a small minority of those pupils who seem to demand some kind of special attention if their teacher is to have any realistic hope of understanding and meeting their particular needs in the classroom. As well as those who are eventually statemented, there are those who will never reach the attention of specialist agencies but who nevertheless seem to their teachers to have special needs which are in some way different from those of other children. In its selection criteria the Authority acknowledged a basic difference between these two groups of children, and thus the list of three groups recognized as having needs peculiar to themselves becomes a list of four: children with special educational needs in the broadest and most informal sense of the term; statemented children; children from ethnic minorities; children experiencing social need.

The Authority's view of the needs of children from ethnic minorities was set out in greater detail in a document submitted to the Education Committee in October 1985:

4.9   'Multi-racial Education'
An important aim of the Programme is the provision of a learning environment relevant to a multi-racial society, and a primary education service which meets the specific needs of children from the minority ethnic communities.
This aspect could include

4.9.1 the multi-racial educational curriculum

4.9.2 the role and utilisation of those staff appointed specifically for multi-racial educational work

4.9.3 the identification of those factors which influence the learning experiences of minority ethnic children and teaching and curricular strategies to meet these. (Leeds City Council, 1985b)

Paragraph 4.9.2 of this document refers to 'staff appointed specifically for multi-racial work', and the Authority's commitment to the needs of pupils from ethnic minority groups is clearly signalled in the funding of a very large number of posts both from the PNP budget and from other sources. At about the same time as the document quoted above the relevant committee approved the appointment of a number of Multi-Racial Coordinators: 'There will be in each school a senior member of staff (at Scale 1, 2 or Scale 3 level) responsible to the Head Teacher, for seeking ways of preparing all children for life in a multi-racial community . . .'. (Leeds City Council, 1985c). The job specification was long and carefully worded, and emphasized two somewhat different aspects of the role: on the one hand the preparation of all children for life in a multi-racial society, and on the other the particular needs of ethnic minority groups. The Multi-Racial Coordinators were to: help teachers develop flexible teaching strategies and to respond with sensitivity to the needs of children from minority ethnic communities; cooperate with ESL team members to continue the language support for children whose need is extension work within the class setting and so on.

Once PNP was under way the Authority appointed a team of Home-School Liaison Assistants (later to become Home-School Liaison Officers) who were themselves all representatives of ethnic minority groups, and whose training and initial work in the Authority have been charted in the third PRINDEP report, *Home–School Links: First Findings*. Nor is the Authority's provision for the needs of pupils from ethnic minorities yet complete. At the time of writing (July 1988) the Authority is advertising for twenty-five Bilingual and Cultural Support Assistants under Section II of the Local Government Act of 1966. Their role will be to work in primary schools alongside teachers, nursery nurses, Home-School Liaison Officers and teachers of English as a Second Language, to help children whose first language is not English.

In February 1986 the deliberations of the PNP Monitoring and Evaluation Group, a formally constituted subcommittee of the Education Committee, took a new direction when it found itself considering proposals from the Leeds Women's Committee regarding equal opportunities for girls. In consequence the group made four additions to the aims of the Primary Needs Programme:

2.1.1 to develop in each primary school a non-sexist learning and social environment;

2.1.2 to actively encourage implementation of anti-sexist practices in primary schools;

2.1.3 to ensure that the full potential and abilities of both girls and boys are fully realised;

2.1.4 to end sex stereotyping both in curricular and non-curricular activities. (Leeds City Council, 1986)

A small group of officers was established to coordinate the implementation of these aims, with the following terms of reference:

3.2.1 preparing comprehensive guidelines for schools actively encouraging the positive promotion of equal opportunities for girls;

3.2.2 initiating and developing programmes of in-service training and education, which are both school and Authority based;

3.2.3 advising on the methods for evaluating the relevant aspects of the Primary Needs Programme. (Leeds City Council, 1986)

In addition, an experienced teacher was seconded for an initial period of one year (later extended by a further year) to support and advise schools on the promotion of equal opportunities for girls. This adds a fifth and final category to the list of groups recognized by the Authority in its official policy documents as having particular needs for which the additional resources of the Primary Needs Programme were especially intended. In its complete form the list provides a framework for what follows in this report, and, in the order in which the categories will be treated here, it reads as follows:

children with special educational needs;
statemented children;
children from ethnic minorities;
gender;
children experiencing social and/or material disadvantage.

However, an account of the Authority's concern with the differing needs of children would not be complete without reference to the Profile of Need and Provision in Mainstream Schools, a questionnaire devised by the Director of Special Services and the SEN Adviser, and distributed to schools during the educational year 1987–88. The results of this major enquiry have not yet been fully analyzed, and cannot be reported here, but the enquiry itself represents a serious and systematic attempt to gain a clearer understanding of educational needs and the provision that should be made for them. In the words of the original proposal:

1.1 At the present time there is no coherent system or structure for describing or assessing the specific needs of mainstream schools in the context of provision for children who have special needs . . . .

1.4 The current practice of using Statements as a means of providing additional resources has created a number of problems not least being a significant increase in the number of requests for assessment of pupils. This alone has created an enormous administrative problem for the Special

Needs Section of the Special Services Division. However, a major problem has been the emphasis on individual children which has tended to divert attention away from the school, its organization, structure and philosophy and in many instances this has prevented the development of appropriate strategies within a whole-school framework.

1.5   It is therefore considered essential to adopt a more appropriate model, firstly in order to assess and analyse the particular needs of schools and subsequently to consider the resource implications based on agreed needs....(Leeds City Council, 1987a)

Meanwhile, the main focus of the present report is the individual school and the groups of children within it. The study is based on data gathered from three sources. PRINDEP's long-term involvement in a representative sample of thirty Leeds primary schools has by now yielded a mass of information on the ways in which, at classroom and whole-school level, and with or without the additional resources of PNP, teachers are striving to meet the differing needs of individual pupils and of particular groups or categories. For this report the information already to hand was augmented by data from special structured interviews which were carried out in each of the thirty schools in the summer of 1987, together with data from PRINDEP's annual questionnaire surveys of all PNP schools.

In addition, the net has been spread wider to include illustrative material both from the sample schools and from elsewhere in the Authority. This material, which is presented in the form of display paragraphs or boxes, is neither a catalogue of good practice nor a chamber of horrors. It was chosen simply because of its individual flavour and quality, with two purposes in mind. First, it is intended to illuminate the major points made in the report, although the main text is complete in itself, and at a pinch the reader in a hurry could ignore the boxes altogether without losing the thread of the argument. Second, the boxes contain some challenging and at times even startling material which, either alongside the main text or on its own, might provide a useful trigger for discussion and the evaluation of current practice elsewhere. The schools mentioned in the boxes have been disguised to the extent of giving them new names, simply because people have talked to us on the understanding that although they might be quoted, neither they nor their schools would be identified.

Children with Special Educational Needs

An obvious starting point for the present enquiry was the field of special educational needs. This was not simply because children who have been officially allocated to one or more of the DES clinical and formal categories of special need come very readily to mind when teachers are invited to comment on pupils' differing needs, although this is undoubtedly so. In addition, however, the Authority's set of procedures leading to a formal statement of needs demands of teachers a detailed consideration of long- and short-term educational goals as well as proposals for ways of achieving them.

How Special Educational Needs are Defined

INRS (the Individual Needs Recording System used in Leeds) cannot be described in detail here. It is enough to say that, in relation to individual children who are causing concern, it requires teachers to consult with colleagues and outside agencies where appropriate, and to make a cumulative written record of: specific areas of concern; objectives; strategies through which these objectives are to be achieved; progress subsequently made; revised objectives; modified strategies and so on.

INRS is organized in five stages. At the first stage a class teacher need not consult anyone else before going through the actions listed above. If the strategies she devises to meet her objectives are successful, the child will not need to progress to the later stages of INRS, and will no longer be considered to have special educational needs. At the second stage the teacher works in collaboration with her special needs coordinator or with some other colleague or colleagues within the school to reconsider objectives and devise new strategies. At the third stage the setting of objectives and the formulation of strategies are carried out in consultation with the Educational Psychology and Family Advisory Service (EPFAS) or some other outside agency. Again, if things go well, the child progresses no further through INRS and the procedure comes to an end. The fourth stage represents the point where the statementing procedure is set in motion and all the formal documentation is prepared. At this stage the expectation is that the child will be statemented, although this does not invariably happen and he or she may be referred back instead. The fifth stage signals the issuing of a formal statement. The numbers of children involved and the pattern of areas of concern inevitably change with the passage of time, but a summary of the situation in the PRINDEP representative sample of thirty schools towards the end of the summer term of 1988 is given in Table 2.1.

Table 2.1. Special Educational Needs: Areas of Concern — Numbers of Children Recorded on INRS in a Representative Sample of Leeds Primary Schools

Column code:	A	B	C	D	E	F	G	H	I	J	K	L	M	N	O	P	Q	R	S
INRS stage:		One			Two			Three			Four			Five			All stages		All phases
PNP phase:	1	2	3	1	2	3	1	2	3	1	2	3	1	2	3	1	2	3	
Educational attainment	54	52	25	136	29	51	21	9	28	11	5	2	7	3	1	229	98	107	434
Behaviour	12	13	12	16	2	4	12	2	8	8	2	2	2	0	1	50	19	27	96
Language	5	9	2	11	14	11	3	3	5	7	0	0	1	1	1	27	27	19	73
Social skills	3	8	4	12	3	1	4	2	1	8	1	0	3	3	1	30	17	7	54
Speech	4	21	6	6	2	1	2	0	0	2	0	0	1	3	1	15	26	8	49
Approach to learning	4	10	7	9	1	1	2	5	3	3	0	0	1	0	0	19	16	11	46
Motor skills	3	7	1	4	2	1	4	0	0	1	0	0	3	2	3	15	11	5	31
Physical	4	0	1	1	0	0	2	0	1	4	0	0	3	2	0	14	3	2	19
Attendance	1	3	1	10	0	0	1	1	0	0	0	0	0	0	0	12	3	1	16
Hearing	0	8	1	3	0	2	1	0	0	0	1	0	0	0	0	4	9	3	16
Health	0	1	2	1	1	0	0	1	1	0	0	0	0	0	0	1	2	3	6
Vision	1	0	0	1	0	1	0	0	0	0	0	0	1	1	0	3	0	2	5
Unspecified	1	0	0	1	0	0	0	0	0	0	0	0	1	0	0	3	1	0	4
Totals	92	132	62	211	53	73	52	23	48	44	9	4	23	15	8	422	232	195	849
Number of children	68	110	43	160	37	53	32	15	38	24	6	2	13	8	6	297	176	142	615
Total number of children on roll:																2320	1730	1680	5730

The table highlights a dramatic difference in the relative numbers of children recorded on INRS in the three PNP phases, the figures ranging from 297 out of 2320 children in the Phase 1 schools (13 per cent) to 142 out of 1680 children in the non-PNP schools (8 per cent). The table also confirms that only a small proportion of the children who become the subjects of the INRS consultation process are eventually statemented.

Columns A, B and C of the table show the numbers of children from Phase 1, Phase 2 and non-PNP schools respectively who were causing concern in each of the areas listed and who were consequently recorded on Stage 1 of INRS. Columns D to O give similar information in relation to each of the remaining stages of INRS, while columns P to R amalgamate the figures for all stages, and column S gives a grand total for each area of concern. It should be noted that many children were listed under more than one category simultaneously, so that the overall number of children involved at each stage is less than the total of the numbers recorded under each category separately.

The areas of concern which present themselves most frequently in primary classrooms throughout the Authority are apparent in this table. Across the board, problems with educational attainment are unequivocally the major cause for concern, accounting for more than half of all INRS transactions. Indeed, taken in conjunction with the closely related categories of language, speech and motor skills, they account for just over two-thirds of all INRS transactions in Phases 1 and 2 and for more than 70 per cent in non-PNP schools. A good way behind, yet still looming large, are problems relating to behaviour, approaches to learning, and social skills. Taken together, these account for almost a quarter of all INRS transactions, and this proportion scarcely varies from one PNP phase to another.

There can be few teachers who are not familiar with at least some of these problems and difficulties, and during the PRINDEP structured interviews all the respondents acknowledged the existence of children with such problems in their schools. In talking about them, they used a wide range of terms. By far the most common descriptive tags were 'slow learners', 'children with learning difficulties', and a number of other expressions pointing to general or specific learning problems. Less common, but still frequently used, were terms indicating some kind of emotional or behavioural disturbance:

Children with behaviour problems....
Emotionally disturbed....
Children with social and emotional problems....
Temporary emotional or behaviour problems....

Almost as common were terms denoting problems with speech and/or language. No other terms were used by a substantial proportion of respondents. Four people referred to children with hearing problems, and three to physical problems of one kind or another.

How Children with Special Educational Needs Are Identified

At least in principle identification in this context is a twofold matter. It necessarily involves a decision that a particular pupil is in some way so different from the other children in the class that he or she must be thought of as having needs that cannot be met through everyday classroom routines or techniques. This may be termed the *identification of the child*, and it is a process which may take place very quickly or involve a dawning awareness over several weeks. Following this, or possibly alongside it, there must at some level be an exploration of the particular difficulties experienced by the child in his efforts to cope with the everyday demands of the classroom. This will lead to the *diagnosis of the special needs themselves*.

In the interviews reported here respondents were asked how and by whom the children were identified, and also what special needs they had. Often the identification procedure involved consultation, and the head, the special needs coordinator, the PNP coordinator, the health visitor, the educational welfare officer and the doctor were all mentioned in this context. Techniques for the identification of the children varied a good deal. Two out of every five respondents reported that the procedure went no further than Stage 1 of INRS; that is to say, the class teacher identified the problem herself without consulting colleagues. On the whole, less consultation was reported in non-PNP schools than in PNP schools.

Other respondents gave a fuller account of the steps taken by class teachers and others during the process of identification and diagnosis, mentioning the keeping of detailed notes and records, the monitoring of classwork and the use of tests. It was not unusual for several different techniques to be mentioned by one person. A little under half of the respondents said that the children's scores on such standardized measures as the 7 + and 9 + reading tests used by the LEA were helpful in identifying the need of some pupils for special help.

About a third of the respondents answered the question rather differently, talking not of the procedures used but rather of the basis or evidence upon which the identification was made, and simply mentioning problems or symptoms:

> Problems of coordination . . . .
> Delayed language development . . . .

Behaviour problems . . . .
Mismatch between ability and level of work . . . .
Social problems . . . .

Box A. Special Educational Needs and the Computer

Hart Side is a Phase 2 primary school fairly near the city centre. As a major component in their approach to special educational needs, the head, special needs coordinator and computer coordinator have worked alongside the other members of staff to develop their own version of a computer-based individual record system (POWYS) which lists stages of development in various curricular areas. In its original form this system has been used for some time as part of the Authority's annual review system of children in special schools.

A preliminary modified version was piloted on six children from each year group in the school, and successive revisions have added and removed details until the system is as precise, comprehensive and manageable as possible. Its usefulness is by no means restricted to children experiencing difficulties, since its content is highly relevant to the developing skills of all children.

No testing is involved before information about a child's development is added to the system; the record starts at the point where the child is known to be. In relation to individual children the system provides a detailed and up-to-date record of achievement and progress, and for the school as a whole it gives a continuing picture of the changing pattern of special educational needs.

However, POWYS is not simply a highly structured record system. In Hart Side it is also a vital tool for professional development, and has been the focal point of weekly evening meetings held by the staff to break down learning skills into their component parts and to work out a fully coordinated approach to special educational needs.

These needs are generally tackled through individual programmes of work, and the special needs coordinator spends half her time working with children who have been recorded on the various stages of INRS. The children work within their own classrooms on the same general topics as their classmates. With the aid of POWYS a very detailed programme of task analysis is possible.

Advisory support cames from EPFAS in the form of a fortnightly visit. It is considered important to identify problems as early as possible, and through POWYS and the INRS procedure a number of children needing special help have been identified in the nursery.

How the Children's Special Educational Needs Are Diagnosed

Most comments about the special educational needs of children fell into one of three categories, with many respondents giving answers in more than one category. Most common of all was the expression of a child's need for a particular kind of management strategy:

> More attention . . . .
> Working with family to modify the child's behaviour . . . .
> They need to be watched . . . .
> To be integrated with their peers . . . .
> Discipline situations . . . .

and so on. About three-quarters of the responses were of this kind. Also very common, and offered by half the respondents, were further mentions of problems or symptoms:

> Behaviour . . . .
> They can't cope with the basic skills . . . .
> Problems with reading . . . .
> They have learning difficulties . . . .
> Maths/number problems . . . .

Less common, and offered by a third of the respondents, were responses pointing to the children's need for a particular type of teaching strategy:

> One-to-one teaching . . . .
> Withdrawal in small groups . . . .
> Structured learning . . . .
> Work pitched at their level . . . .
> Speech programmes . . . .

Provision for Children with Special Educational Needs

A variety of special teaching arrangements was in use. The most popular of these was the use of withdrawal groups, but there were also many others:

> Withdrawal groups . . . .
> Individual attention from support teacher in class . . . .
> Withdrawal of individual children . . . .
> Head goes into the class to help . . . .
> Individual help from class teacher while support teacher works
> with class . . . .

Attention in small groups (location of groups not stated) . . . .
The child's mother helps him in class . . . .
Extra language input from school secretary . . . .
Work sent home for parents to help with . . . .
I sometimes isolate them so they can concentrate . . . .
Children are grouped by ability . . . .

More than a quarter of the responses mentioned special curricula:

Special programme of work devised in consultation . . . .
Special programme of work devised by PNP/SN coordinator . . . .
Work cards made especially for them . . . .
Their own timetable . . . .
Some directed teaching (METRA, Aston Index, etc.) . . . .
Special reading schemes, etc. . . . . .

A few respondents indicated that their special provision involved a change of level rather than a change of content in the class curriculum.

Not all the responses mentioned special teaching arrangements or curricula, and it was clear that teachers and indeed whole schools are mounting a wide range of provision from the very formal and tightly organized to the homely and ad hoc:

A whole-school approach to children with problems . . . .
Special large-print books/work cards for children who need
  them . . . .
Behaviour modification programmes . . . .
Consultation and cooperation with parents . . . .
Voluntary help from the community . . . .
Staff cooperation . . . .
All staff (even dinner staff) are informed of special needs . . . .
A little more of my time . . . .
Give them little jobs . . . .

Outside Support and Resources to Meet Special Educational Needs

As would be expected in view of the fact that many of the children under discussion were part way through the INRS procedures, the most widely quoted source of outside help and support was EPFAS. It was mentioned by more than two-thirds of the respondents, and although two individual comments were framed in rather critical terms, the criticism was aimed at the amount of help EPFAS was able to give rather than at the quality of the help when it was given. In addition, just under a third of the respondents paid tribute to EPFAS courses of one kind or another, notably the Leeds In-Service Special Educational Needs (LISSEN) course. A sixth of the respondents mentioned speech therapists, while medical agencies and non-EPFAS visiting teachers were each mentioned by four respondents. There were also a few sources of help and support which were each mentioned by only one or two people:

> Help from our neighbouring junior school . . . .
> Visits from the child's social worker . . . .
> EWO . . . .
> Unit for partially sighted children involved . . . .
> Advisers come in occasionally . . . .

On the whole, respondents were relatively content with the amount of outside help they were receiving, although several wanted to qualify their comments:

> We could use still more help . . . .
> OK, but it would be better if LEA provided cover to release the special needs coordinator . . . .
> More money would be nice but we are not exactly hard done to . . . .

Where schools had experienced the extra resources provided by PNP, respondents invariably reported improvements in the provision they were now able to make for the particular needs of children who were experiencing difficulties in school:

> PNP has given us the time to tackle problems properly . . . .
> It has made smaller groups possible . . . .
> Extra staffing has released the part-time teacher . . . .
> Some members of staff are changing their teaching methods . . . .
> Extra staffing has helped . . . .
> Teachers have been able to start teaching together . . . .
> There is the coordinator's expertise to draw on . . . .
> There is now much more parental involvement . . . .
> The INSET has been particularly helpful in alerting inexperienced teachers to the needs of bilingual children . . . .
> We have been able to set up a reading workshop . . . .
> It has encouraged the staff to raise their expectations of what these pupils can do . . . .

Statemented Children

We have already seen that a relatively small proportion of children with special educational needs go through all stages of the INRS process and are eventually the subjects of formal statements of educational need; in the present sample less than one in twenty of the children recorded on INRS were statemented, and these children accounted for only one half of 1 per cent of the school population.

Although the proportion of statemented children was very small in all phases, it was highest in Phase 1 schools (with a mean incidence of 5.6 per thousand) and lowest in non-PNP schools (with a mean incidence of 3.6 per thousand).

Box B. Special Educational Needs in an Inner-City School

Yewbarrow is a Phase 1 school. It is situated in an area of extreme social and material disadvantage, and among its pupils are many with severe social and behavioural problems.

At the time of the PRINDEP visit the school had only one statemented child, who was spending the mornings in a special school and returning to Yewbarrow in the afternoons. The head was attempting to reach a satisfactory agreement with the Authority about whether an extra part-time member of staff could be appointed to undertake the necessary supervision of this child, or whether this should be undertaken by the existing PNP staff.

Of the six children on Stages 2 and 3 of INRS, four presented severe behaviour problems, and their teachers were tackling the situation with systematic behaviour management techniques including the use of reward charts. To maximize the effectiveness of this approach, parental cooperation was secured wherever possible. As part of the programme children were sometimes withdrawn from their classes and a room had been set aside specifically for this purpose.

At Yewbarrow school special educational needs are the full-time responsibility of both the special needs coordinator and the PNP coordinator, the former dealing with children on Stage 2 of INRS and beyond, and the latter with those on Stage 1. Before PNP, provision in this area was limited to a nominal half day a week timetabled for the deputy head. In the head's view the arrival of PNP has totally transformed the extent to which special educational needs can be tackled.

The areas of concern in relation to statemented children were much more evenly balanced than among the larger group of children with special educational needs, although there was a comparatively high incidence of statementing for poor educational attainment in Phase 1 schools.

How the Needs of Statemented Children Are Diagnosed

The mechanics of the identification procedure need no elaboration here, for on the rare occasions when children are statemented it is at the very end of the INRS process already described in the previous section.

The ways in which teachers perceive the needs themselves, however, cannot be taken for granted from the earlier section, for the point has already been made that: '2.2 The statementing process, by its very nature, is concerned with only a small proportion of the total pupil population. It is not necessarily a sound indication of broad educational need in the school . . .'. (Leeds City Council, 1985a). To put it another way, although statemented children come from the larger group of children with special educational needs, their own needs do not reflect those of the larger group either in their spread or their intensity. It is this very difference that leads to their being statemented while the other children are not.

As would be expected in view of the variety of disorders listed, the range of perceived needs was very wide. Some respondents articulated the children's needs in an indirect way by means of a simple restatement of the presenting problem:

> Immature language . . . .
> Immature behaviour . . . .
> Their learning capabilities are different from their peers . . . .
> The possible diagnosis is cerebral palsy . . . .

The majority of the rest either emphasized the children's need to be taught in a particular way:

> Extra teaching in the form of individual tuition . . . .
> Small group sessions . . . .
> Lots of oral work . . . .
> Activities outlined in Oregon and Portage schemes . . . .

or their need for a particular style of management:

> More attention . . . .
> A one-to-one relationship . . . .

Opportunities to relate to others . . . .
A stable environment . . . .

Although ranging from the general to the highly specific, these responses have in common a clear reference back to the teacher's own responsibility for the child. In effect each is saying, 'This child needs me (or my immediate colleagues) to offer a certain kind of treatment or relationship'.

Other responses with a similar implication related specifically to the need for physical assistance:

Physical help, with PE and at playtime . . . .
Additional help for motor skills . . . .
Immediate attention should he have a fit . . . .
Encouragement to use apparatus as normally as possible . . . .

A few comments referred to needs which would involve specialist treatment outside the range of competence of the respondent and his or her immediate colleagues:

Speech therapy . . . .
Special boots . . . .
Immediate medical attention if he has a fit . . . .
Braille skills . . . .

In summary, the teachers in this sample of schools tended to articulate children's special educational needs in terms of immediate courses of action, without necessarily putting into words their long-term aims and objectives for the children in question. This does not imply that they had not considered the outcomes they were hoping to achieve: to make such a response as 'speech therapy' or 'special boots', for example, implies a specific outcome so strongly that to state it in words would be virtually tautologous.

Provision for Statemented Children

The official PNP literature indicates an expectation that the identified needs of children will be met through the medium of *flexible teaching strategies*, and we have just seen that a high proportion of respondents actually equated their statemented children's needs with particular ways of teaching. It is not surprising, therefore, that when respondents turned their attention from needs to provision, most of them mentioned special teaching arrangements; in general, provision matched the children's perceived needs very closely:

The child is withdrawn for individual work . . . .

Withdrawn for small group attention . . . .

The PNP coordinator works with them individually in the classroom . . . .

NTA works with child in the classroom . . . .

Extra teaching time . . . .

Half time . . . in unit for blind and partially sighted children . . . .

Visiting specialist teacher . . . .

Work sent from school for him to do in hospital . . . .

Particular attention during maths, at which he excels . . . .

Closely allied to special teaching arrangements was a behaviour modification programme for a physically handicapped child.

In general, schools were not attempting to provide special curricula for statemented children. Only one respondent described a situation where a child had a completely tailor-made curriculum: 'Individual work through-out; he can't cope with the curriculum as experienced by the other children . . . '. In all other cases, whatever the disability, a standard curriculum was in operation, modified as little as was consistent with the need to make it appropriate for the statemented child or children in question:

They have the mainstream curriculum with support . . . .

Half time in mainstream to give broad curriculum and social contact with sighted children . . . .

As many practical experiences as possible, to develop
language . . . .

Basically the same, only scaled down: altered to fit their needs . . . .

Respondents from Phase 2 and non-PNP schools tended to report modified curricula rather than special teaching arrangements for their statemented pupils; special teaching arrangements were more common in Phase 1 schools.

Outside Support and Resources for Statemented Children

Respondents were invited to indicate which services of the Local Authority or other outside agencies had helped or were helping them in their attempts to make adequate provision for their statemented pupils. They mentioned:

EPFAS;
the educational psychologist;
specialist teachers;
speech therapists;

the peripatetic teacher of the deaf;
the physiotherapist;
the hospital;
LISSEN courses;
extra capitation;
small language apparatus on loan.

One in six of the respondents stated flatly that the help they were receiving was not adequate. A smaller number said that it was adequate or reasonable. The majority made no comment on the matter, although several indicated that 'it could be better, but help is always there if you ring and ask'.

There was a marked imbalance between the number of kinds of outside help mentioned by respondents from the three groups of schools. From Phase 1 schools there were twenty accounts of various kinds of help and support, while from Phase 2 schools there were six, and from non-PNP schools four. Again, it must be remembered that the Phase 1 schools had many more statemented children to deal with.

In the PNP schools opinion was divided about the extent to which PNP had made it easier to meet the needs of statemented children. Some respondents had experienced very positive changes:

Teachers are now more aware of special needs . . . .
It has made small group support possible . . . .
We can now do individual teaching . . . .
It has provided extra time for observation and testing . . . .
There are now more people to talk over problems and plans . . . .

Others were by no means so enthusiastic:

We still have no PNP coordinator . . . .
PNP has made no difference; [the child] would have received exactly the same help anyway . . . .

Children from Ethnic Minorities

Because of the Authority's concern to develop multicultural education in all its schools, and its wish to promote a greater awareness of the particular needs of children from ethnic minority groups, and encourage and enable schools to make whatever provision might be necessary to meet these needs, respondents were specifically asked whether they thought that children from ethnic minority groups in fact fall within the range of those who have needs which are different from those of other children.

Just under half of the sample answered no, either as a generalization, or in relation to the situation in which they personally found themselves:

No; the families involved are of high socio-economic status . . . .
Not in this school: we have two Asian families but the children are third and fourth generation . . . .
Too much emphasis is put on multiculturalism . . . .
We treat everyone equally here . . . .
Not really applicable; they're very westernized families . . . .
We do have one boy but I think he would be most put out if we treated him differently . . . .
They are all from supportive socio-economic backgrounds and do not need any preferential treatment . . . .

Some of these responses give clear expression to a particular view of children from ethnic minority groups, namely that:

if their families have been settled in England for some time and are relatively prosperous, then their needs will be just the same as those of indigenous white children;

if their needs did differ from those of indigenous white children, this would necessarily imply that they should be treated preferentially.

By no means all the respondents held this particular view. In all, about a third of them expressed the opinion that particular needs might arise directly and specifically from membership of a minority culture, irrespective of an individual family's circumstances. Among the PNP Phase 1 and Phase 2 schools the ratio of 'yes' to 'no' responses was almost exactly half and half; in the non-PNP schools, where on the whole there were fewer pupils from ethnic minority groups, there were also proportionately fewer 'yes' responses. Even then several respondents made it clear that they were answering 'yes' in principle only, since there were no such children in their own schools. These responses are particularly interesting in view of the Authority's intention that anti-racist education should be practised in all educational institutions:

1.1 The Education Authority has a responsibility to make sure that all individuals are . . . prepared for life in a multi-racial and culturally diverse society.

3.2.3 Anti-racist education is not a separate topic that can be grafted to existing practices but it should permeate all aspects of the work of every educational institution . . . .(Leeds City Council, 1987b)

How the Needs of Children from Ethnic Minorities Are Diagnosed

Most of the respondents who attempted to define the particular needs of children from ethnic minorities expressed them in terms of language acquisition:

> Language . . . .
> Language and vocabulary . . . .
> Mainly language, but ours are from English-speaking families . . . .

One respondent emphasized the complexity of the need in this area, pointing to the fact that a child whose first language is not English may need something more than just help with English: 'Bilingualism must be understood; it can sometimes be a definite advantage . . . '.

Other responses were more general and at the same time more contentious in that they were directly concerned with the relationship between minorities and the majority within which they find themselves:

> Help with social situations . . . .
> Integration . . . .
> To be accepted by the majority . . . .

Finally, there was a recurrence of the view that pupils from ethnic minorities have particular needs only if their families come from a low socio-economic level. One respondent characterized their needs as: 'in this school, none; they all come from professional backgrounds'.

There was a marked difference between the way in which respondents generally spoke of the needs of children from ethnic minorities and the way in which they had described the needs of their pupils with special educational needs. It will be recalled that when speaking of special educational needs they usually described *proposed courses of action*, often in some detail. Very rarely did they make explicit the outcomes they were intending, since in the main these were self-evident. They concentrated on means rather than ends. In relation to children from ethnic minority groups the situation was exactly reversed. In the present enquiry, respondents who believed that these children have needs peculiar to themselves nearly always spoke of desired *long-term outcomes* rather than of proposed courses of action — of ends rather than means.

Although striking, this difference is scarcely surprising. In discussing special educational needs, respondents had been considering problems to which, in the main, there are classroom-based solutions. Even the most severe difficulties of pupils in coping with ordinary learning tasks present a

Box C. Verbatim Extract from an Interview with a Phase 1 Class Teacher

[Branstree Primary School is in a very mixed social area. About half of its pupils are from ethnic minority groups.]

I think the main need is for the teachers to be aware of what is lacking within the home. We don't just teach children to read and write. We really try to make them into an all-round person, so I think the role of the teacher is to make the children aware of what is available to them in our society today and, to a certain extent, to provide these things for them. I also think that the role doesn't stop there.

We need to talk to parents about the things that we're trying to do in school because only then will the children get the full benefit. If you compare them with indigenous white children, the parents don't provide the things that we normally say all children should get — parental support for the things they do in school, for outings, for reading, for other things that they might need for colouring, painting, etcetera. They don't provide these things for the children because they see education in much narrower terms — in terms of reading and writing and tables, and that's it.

I've heard teachers saying — not only in this school — that Asian children are not imaginative, that they're not creative. Now, how can a child come into a situation cold, and be creative and imaginative when they haven't had the facility or the things to use within the home, first hand?

Of course, I'm not saying that all indigenous white children have these things at home; they don't. But I think for many Asian children there's an acute lacking that we as educators really need to stress.

The teacher quoted here is herself a member of one of the Asian minority groups. Does that fact change the impact or validity of her comments? Should it?

legitimate challenge for a teacher's professional skills. On the whole, respondents had a clear notion of the options open to them, and a realistic idea of their chances of success. In discussing children from ethnic minority groups, respondents were understandably a little less sure of their ground. They were now dealing with a different situation, less exclusively concerned with the professional skills of teaching. Here the responsibility of teachers is not to make good some deficit, but rather to reach and then disseminate an understanding of what it means to live in a society in which valid alternative cultures coexist, and to use their skill and authority as teachers not only to ensure that all pupils are educated to the full extent of their potential, but also to protect the status of minority cultures and encourage mutual toleration. Important as these tasks are, they are not all very easily translated into sure-fire practical classroom activities; the ends are clear enough, but the means can be dauntingly elusive.

Provision for Children from Ethnic Minorities

The lack of detail about proposed courses of action is echoed in the accounts of current provision. As would be expected, those respondents who were of the opinion that children from the ethnic minorities have no particular needs of their own were, virtually by definition, making no special provision for them. In all, about a quarter of the respondents explicitly stated that this was the case:

> No special provision is present . . . .
> There is a small group for whom English is a second language but
>   as yet we haven't made any special teaching arrangements . . . .
> We have several Asian families but they cause no problems so no
>   special provision is made . . . .

In the last of these responses there is an unsettling implication that the only problems which need tackling in relation to minority groups are those the minority groups are thought to cause rather than those they experience. To counterbalance this, another respondent proposed a course of action which placed the principal need outside the children altogether: 'Before we can educate the children for a multicultural society we have to educate the teachers . . . '.

A number of schools were directly and positively tackling the language needs of children from ethnic minorities, and there was a range of kinds of provision in operation. Some respondents spoke of special teaching arrangements:

> The ESL team supports us in planning, and in teaching within the
>   classroom . . . .
> New arrivals go to Mrs B . . . .

> We have withdrawal groups run by the peripatetic language
> teacher . . . .
> Lots of conversation practice — with the head, the secretary, the
> class teacher or an articulate mum . . . .

Several respondents spoke of the curriculum. One such response was very straightforward and specific: 'More time on the naming of objects, etc . . .'. Outside the context of special help with language, however, talk about the curriculum was couched in rather general terms so that it is not always possible to guess how the ideas expressed might be translated into practice:

> Culture is brought into the classroom and all children in a class
> look at different cultures when the need arises . . .
> The curriculum should reflect the need of these children to be
> accepted by the majority, by minimising rather than high-
> lighting cultural differences . . . .

In the PNP schools special teaching arrangements were far more common than special curricula, while in non-PNP schools the balance between the two was much more even.

Outside Support and Resources for Children from Ethnic Minorities

The introduction to this report has briefly summarized the very considerable investment of money and resources made by the Authority in this area. Here we are concerned with teachers' perceptions of the help they are receiving in their attempts to get to grips with the issues involved and with their own attitudes towards these issues.

When asked specifically about the help or support they were getting from outside the school, they mentioned more often than anything else a large number of courses offered jointly by the multicultural advisory teacher and the equal opportunities support teacher. These courses were challenging in their content and highly interactive in their style, and hence made considerable personal demands on organizers and participants alike. They were open to teachers from non-PNP as well as PNP primary schools.

In general, PRINDEP's respondents had little to say about any other help or support they were receiving in their attempts to make adequate provision for the needs of children from ethnic minorities. As already indicated, the work of the ESL team was singled out for special mention, as

Box D. Working with Parents in a Phase 1 School

About nine-tenths of the pupils at Grey Knotts Primary School are from ethnic minority groups, and a major feature of the school's ethos is a firm belief that the needs of its pupils can be understood and met much more effectively if there is a continuing positive relationship with parents as well as children. Consequently there are many activities and initiatives in this general area:

> an open-door policy, both figuratively and literally, since the head's door stands open all the time unless she is talking privately with someone;
>
> open house all morning once a week in the reception class;
>
> shared reading sessions for second and third year children once a week;
>
> parents are invited to class assemblies once a week, and may stay on afterwards to talk with their child's class teacher or with other members of staff;
>
> all morning mothers' and toddlers' group once a week;
>
> occasional minibus outings for parents, e.g. to an emporium in Bradford specializing in goods from the Indian subcontinent;
>
> a community room in the school where parents can talk with the Home-School Liaison Officers or other members of staff;
>
> home visits from the Home-School Liaison Officers, not only to sort out problems but also, for example, to explain shared reading and invite individual parents to take part;
>
> home visits from the Ethnic Minority Coordinator;
>
> the Portage scheme, involving two nursery nurses supervised by the PNP coordinator for special educational needs.

were grants from the School Curriculum Development Committee to develop multicultural work in two schools. Three people said they were receiving no help or support at all in this matter, and one respondent expressed strong regret that the current multicultural advisory teacher was coming to the end of her secondment.

Only two respondents thought that PNP had made much difference in this area: one said that it had given teachers more time to tackle the needs of children from ethnic minorities; another that it had provided extra members of staff to cope with the problem.

Box E. Extracts from a PNP 'Racism and Sexism Awareness' Course Exercise

Can you identify *inadequate or wrong information* and *possible hidden assumptions which are racist/sexist in effect* behind these statements? What point would you make in replying to them?

1. 'I treat all children the same — in our school we make no difference between children, black or white, girl or boy.'
2. 'I can't talk about attitudes towards racism/sexism with my colleagues. Some of them would find it personally offensive, and raising such issues directly can be counter-productive . . . .'
4. 'Positive discrimination either means lowering standards or giving unfairly preferential treatment, or both.'
5. 'You can't expect teachers to adopt a multicultural/non-sexist approach until the Authority provides enough of the right materials . . . .'
7. 'I can't teach Muslim ways, because I can't sympathize with the way they regard and treat their women.'
8. 'We don't do multicultural education in our school because we have none of them . . . .'

Box F. Draft Policy Statement from a Phase 1 School with a Very High Proportion of Pupils from Ethnic Minority Groups

1. We will provide an atmosphere of understanding and tolerance — within the diversity of the school population we will create a caring community and family atmosphere.
2. We will aim to provide equal opportunity for all children.
3. All children's cultural backgrounds will be respected and valued and used as an integral part of the school learning situation.
4. Teachers at all times will promote positive pupil self-esteem and high self-expectation.
5. Discriminatory influences which may inhibit learning, achievement and development will not be tolerated.

Gender Issues

Definition of Gender Issues

Because of the Authority's concern to promote awareness of the particular needs of girls, and its wish to encourage and enable schools to make whatever provision might be necessary to meet them, respondents were asked for their views on the proposition that girls and boys have differing needs, and were invited to give details of any special provision they were making in this area. A high proportion rejected the idea of special provision altogether:

> Too much emphasis is put on equal opportunities . . . .
> I don't understand what all the fuss is about . . . .
> It's not a priority; other things are more important . . . .
> We have no policy on equal opportunities . . . .
> The problem has not reared its head at this age . . . .
> We treat everyone equally here . . . .

This last response was made by respondents from no fewer than eight of the thirty schools. Others indicated that they and their colleagues had reached no firm conclusions but were still considering and discussing the matter:

> Not sure; we should have the same expectation of boys and
>   girls . . . .
> We're becoming more aware of girls' needs . . . .
> They could well have [needs of their own] . . . .
> Of course, girls must have special needs — but only as much as
>   boys do . . . .

One of these comments highlights an important aspect of the subject under discussion. If the sole focus is the needs of girls, something may be achieved but something will be missing. The long-term goal must be to develop the awareness and increase the opportunities of all of us, male or female; and if we start with the needs of girls, this is simply because the needs of girls have been almost totally neglected in the past.

A few respondents were quite sure that girls, as a group, do have needs which are peculiar to themselves:

> Yes . . . .
> Yes, in our school in particular . . . .
> Yes, at 11 +, for physical and emotional reasons which are
>   obvious . . . .

Box G. A Statement of Policy Drawn up by the Staff of a Non-PNP School

It is our intention that boys and girls should derive equal benefits from the education that is given to them. We propose to achieve this aim by the following steps:

1. equal treatment of children in school;
2. presenting a variety of role models to children so that they do not feel that their opportunities in later life are restricted by their sex.

Equal Treatment

1. Include activities which have a traditional bias towards one sex (such as baking and woodwork) in the curriculum for all children.
2. Where choices are offered to children in the classroom, encourage them to make non-traditional choices.
3. Avoid unnecessary segregation of girls and boys.
4. Give boys and girls equal experience of doing different types of jobs around the school.
5. Make sure that girls and boys are able to make equal contributions in class discussions, particularly if the subject under discussion is conventionally of interest to one sex rather than the other.

Role Models

1. Ensure that books in use, and displays around the school, show boys, girls, women and men in non-traditional roles as well as traditional ones.
2. When we talk to children, make reference to fathers as parents and mothers as wage-earners.
3. When we invite adults into school, try to ensure that they do not all reflect conventional roles for women and men.
4. As teachers, try to develop interests which children might otherwise associate with the opposite sex only.

Box H. An Approach to Gender Issues in a Phase 1 School

With the head's support and cooperation, three interested teachers of three different age groups at Mellbreak Primary School undertook a series of observation sessions of their pupils' free choice activities to discover whether there were any differences in the choices made by boys and girls, or in the ways they played. Observation sessions lasted for half an hour and took place over a period of several weeks. Every five minutes, the names of the children using each activity were recorded.

Left to themselves, more girls than boys were using the home corner and creative toys, while more boys than girls were using cars, trains and constructional toys. There was a good deal of repetitive activity, both in the sense that children tended to choose the same activities and materials time after time, and also in the sense that on the whole they were using the equipment in the same way each time they worked with it.

Faced with these findings, the teachers began to explore the effects of different kinds of intervention. They found that children were more likely to participate in particular activities if their teacher encouraged them to do so, and this was especially so if she sat and worked with a group herself. It also became clear that children tended to work more cooperatively and to talk more about what they were doing when they were not organized in friendship groups.

The findings of this study led the three teachers into a good deal of discussion with their colleagues elsewhere in the school, and led to an increased interest in gender issues among the staff as a whole.

How Needs are Diagnosed in Relation to Gender

As a simple way of illuminating their thinking on gender issues, those respondents who had not rejected the topic outright were invited to comment on the particular needs of girls. Among the responses were the following:

> They should be encouraged to take an interest in the subjects that
>   girls traditionally are not interested in . . . .
> They need to be treated equally with boys . . . .
> Girls and maths needs looking into . . . .
> To play with construction toys . . . .
> Active encouragement . . . .

Equal access to the curriculum . . . .

Encouragement to try things — but one must be aware of the parents' culture . . . .

Equality: things like boys taking up all the playground with their games . . . .

There were more comments about the particular needs of girls from Phase 1 than from Phase 2 schools, and more from Phase 2 than from non-PNP schools.

Box I. Part of an Overall Strategy in a Phase 1 School

When PRINDEP visited Red Pike Primary School, the PNP coordinator emphasized that much of what she had to say was her personal observation and opinion. She pointed out that the staff in the school reflected many different attitudes towards girls, but they were working hard to formulate a whole-school approach towards gender issues. She also stressed that the policy of equal opportunities for girls was still very much in its infancy, and a great deal remained to be done to ensure that all staff pursued the aims of that policy . . . .

A wide range of initiatives was in operation, and at the time of the PRINDEP visit a further plan was being considered. This was a design technology project for which the school hoped to get an SCDC grant to buy better construction toys. The aim was to teach three quite separate things in a structured way: problem-solving; spatial awareness; cooperative working. The first two of these were seen as particularly important in the light of the Cockcroft Report and girls' underachievement in maths. In was anticipated that the Science Coordinator would take charge of the project to ensure that girls gained experience in a wide range of structural and three-dimensional materials.

In considering these responses it is worth referring to the earlier comparison between the ways in which respondents spoke about children with special educational needs on the one hand, and children from ethnic minorities on the other. It will be recalled that the needs of the former group were characteristically expressed as proposed courses of action, or as means rather than ends, while those of the latter group were more often expressed in the form of desired states of affairs, or as ends rather than means. We have suggested that this difference relates to the extent to which individual problems can be precisely defined, and credible and realistic classroom-based solutions implemented.

In relation to gender issues, respondents were again dealing with a matter which did not seem to all of them to be directly related to their traditional task of handing on acquired skills or information, but which depended on their own sympathy for, and understanding of, a major contemporary issue and the ways in which they could do something positive about it. In their comments on the particular needs of girls, they tended to say things which were much less easily categorized as either proposed courses of action or long-term objectives. This may be partly because some of them were still in the middle of their thinking and discussion in this area, but there may also be a sense in which gender is an area where courses of action and desired outcomes, or ends and means, cannot be so readily distinguished.

Provision in Relation to Gender

Respondents spoke of a range of ways in which they were tackling gender issues:

> Staff try to be aware of unnecessary discrimination . . . .
> Lines of children will be mixed although registers will remain separate for ease of filling in Form 7 . . . .
> There is a computer club for girls . . . .
> We are going to stop having such things as milk boys and dinner girls . . . .
> We ought to be making more opportunities for girls to play with Lego and boys to play in the Wendy house, but we haven't yet tackled it as a staff . . . .
> It's left to individual teachers' awareness; it does need clarification . . . .

No respondents reported special teaching arrangements in this context, but a few mentioned the curriculum:

> All children bake and sew . . . .
> Girls are encouraged to take more of an interest in maths and technology . . . .
> Girls do netball and boys do football . . . .
> Boys and girls take sewing . . . .

Box J. Verbatim Extract from an Interview with a Class Teacher at Mellbreak

Occasionally the [gender] issue comes up very obviously and it's easy to pick that up and actually make the children conscious of it. But in lots more subtle ways you're looking all the time at your organization — at how you plan and how you respond — so that you are more aware of the possibility of treating the boys and girls differently simply because they *are* boys and girls. My emphasis has been to try and treat the children differently because of their different needs, and not because of their gender.

The specific thing I've looked for is how I group them . . . . The children themselves constantly go back into the boy/girl groupings, and I think you have to find ways of getting them to mix naturally, rather than just because teacher said so, so that it's there in the fabric of the day for them. Sometimes you need to actually overcompensate, I think.

With the Technical Lego for example, which we've been using in the classroom in the last couple of weeks, I've sometimes deliberately put two girls together who I think would be put down by being with a boy who's had a lot of experience with it at home already and who would be just obviously more experienced with it — not necessarily more capable, but simply because he gets the practice. Then again I might group a boy and a girl where I think the girl would benefit from being with a child who's got more [experience]; and I might deliberately put some of the boys who think that they are better *because* they're boys with somebody who's going to do better than they do — to show them that it's not to do with what gender they are . . . .

[Question: What is the long-term objective in all that you do about gender?]

I think if you want to state it in big terms, it's to give each child a full recognition of their own potential — quite regardless of gender in one sense, but also taking gender into account — to know that, whether they be boy or girl, there are skills and achievements that they can have that shouldn't be limited by gender.

For example, I think it's important to encourage the boys that they can be gentle and kind, and that they don't have to be macho in the playground, and all of those issues. I think that's just as important — in fact in terms of discipline in the school it's probably more important than the more obvious things that one might want to do for the girls. I

> think there's been a tendency for the gender issue to become a kind of feminism issue in some areas, whereas I think it's a *human* issue. I think it's about people [about each one] achieving his or her potential. It's not just standing on the bandwagon.

Outside Support and Resources in Relation to Gender

Respondents mentioned only one source of help or support in their attempts to clarify their ideas about gender issues or to make appropriate provision for the particular needs of girls, and this was the primary support teacher seconded by the Local Authority. Every respondent who mentioned this teacher spoke with unreserved enthusiasm of her work: of the books she had lent to school staffs, the talks she had given in schools and the equal opportunities courses she had run in conjunction with the multicultural advisory teacher.

Most of the references to this source of help came from PNP schools, and it is clear that, although there is a long way to go, PNP has made some impact in the area of equal opportunities for girls. However, it should be emphasized that the primary support teacher interpreted her role from the outset as not restricted to PNP schools, and her courses and other forms of advice have been open and available to teachers from all primary schools in the Authority. It must not be supposed that non-PNP schools are necessarily lagging behind in their thinking on gender issues.

Social and Material Disadvantage

How Social and Material Disadvantage Are Defined

We have seen that, at the outset of the Primary Needs Programme, schools were selected by the Local Authority for inclusion in Phase 1 on the basis of only two criteria: mean scores on the 7 + and 9 + reading tests administered to all primary schools in the Authority, and the numbers of children receiving free school dinners. This second criterion is an unmistakable measure of social disadvantage, and its inclusion can be taken as an indication of the Authority's assumption that the extra educational resources of PNP would in some way be of particular relevance to socially or materially disadvantaged children. With this in mind, respondents were invited to comment on the particular needs of this group of children, and on any special provision they were making for them in the classroom.

It proved a difficult area of enquiry; respondents had problems in formulating their responses, and the responses were correspondingly resistant to analysis. The difficulty seems to be twofold.

In the first place, social disadvantage is not infrequently found alongside either special educational needs or membership of ethnic minority groups, or both. This is not to say that the three terms are in any way synonymous or that the conditions to which they refer are never found in isolation from each other. Nevertheless, many teachers whose classes contain a high proportion of children with special educational needs and of children from ethnic minority groups are likely to be very familiar with the problems of social disadvantage as well. Although it is necessary to deal with the themes separately in a report like this, some teachers find that in daily life they are interwoven to the point of being inseparable. This being so, it can be very difficult for a teacher to speak about the last topic in isolation from the other two, simply because in her everyday work she deals not so much with the abstract implications of this or that condition, but rather with the very practical and pressing immediate problems of this or that child.

The second aspect of the difficulty lies in the relationship between the nature of social disadvantage and the professional role of the class teacher. We have already suggested that special educational needs on the one hand, and ethnic and gender issues on the other, necessarily have quite different kinds of significance for teachers. It is not surprising that, in teachers' conversations with PRINDEP, social and material disadvantage proved the most difficult topic of all. Here we were back again with a deficit to be put right, rather than with a problem of acknowledging and learning not to be threatened by natural differences between groups of people. However, the deficits of social and material disadvantage are, in both their scale and their nature, well outside the range of practical competence of a teacher to put right. If we ask what a child from a family which is poor, hungry, homeless and ill-clad needs, the list of answers is obvious, but no class teacher can hope to meet those requirements in her role as a teacher.

The legitimate feelings of helplessness engendered by such a situation shone through many of the answers given by respondents in the present enquiry. In some of the non-PNP schools the discussions were of academic interest only:

> We've no real problems in this category, or at least none we've identified . . . .

> We have no children from that background . . . .
> We do have one or two families, but you wouldn't notice them.
> We treat them all the same . . . .

At the other end of the scale, and particularly in some Phase 1 schools, the situation under discussion directly affected many of the children:

> Yes, we have many such children at this school . . . .
> Most children here are in that category . . . .
> We have lots of children from poor families, but we don't feel special provision has to be made at school . . . .

How Social and Material Disadvantage Are Identified

The identification of socially and materially disadvantaged children was occasionally made from medical records or through contact with health visitors or educational welfare officers. In general, however, it was carried out in a very informal way:

> Teachers spot them . . . .
> Parents tell us . . . .
> Poor clothing . . . .
> The family background is well known to the school . . . .

Box K. Verbatim Extract from an Interview with the Head of Branstree Primary School

In principle, I think Home-School Liaison Officers are an absolute must . . . . [X] has been exceptionally good in every way . . . . We desperately need a parents' room just to be able to communicate. Right the way across the curriculum, not just the ethnic minorities area but in all areas, we need to be able to communicate with our parents and to invite them in. Without that facility we're very limited. Our Home-School Liaison Officer cannot visit all 500 families; it's just a physical impossibility.

How the Needs of Socially and Materially Disadvantaged Children Are Diagnosed

In discussing the needs of the children, respondents were clearly aware of the limitations of their role and tended to restrict their comments to practical courses of action which, while not in any basic way tackling the major problems of disadvantage, might at least alleviate some of its day-by-day manifestations:

> Extra food at dinner time . . . .
> Opportunities they don't get at home . . . .
> Books . . . .
> More outings . . . .

A few respondents formulated the children's needs in more general and ambitious terms:

> Something to aim at . . . .
> Respect as people . . . .
> A chance to achieve . . . .
> Giving them a sense of their own worth . . . .

Others suggested that the principal need was for affection and attention:

> Someone to talk to . . . .
> Love . . . .
> Time spent with an adult . . . .
> Close relationships . . . .
> A cuddle now and again . . . .

Responses of this kind were not necessarily intended to imply that children from socially or materially disadvantaged families invariably *lack* love, affection or attention, but were rather reflections of the respondents' determination to foster greater acceptance, self-esteem and success for these pupils in the classroom.

Provision for Socially and Materially Disadvantaged Children

The point has perhaps already been laboured that any provision which might effectively tackle the problems of social and material disadvantage is well outside the professional scope or responsibility of an individual child's class teacher or school. In terms of the categories used in earlier sections of this report, no special provision was being made for this particular group of

---

Box L. Verbatim Extract from an Interview with a Phase 1 Class Teacher

[Great Gable is a Phase 1 primary school situated in an area of extreme poverty and deprivation. It has been extensively refurbished as part of the Primary Needs Programme.]

> Parents came in last year to work with their children, even during the refurbishment itself....They noticed the before and after, how quiet it was now that the chairs weren't clattering and scraping on the floor; and they noticed that it seemed warmer. Now they notice that the new ceiling means the noise doesn't carry around. They notice all that, but it's not really been the determining factor in their coming in. The real deciding factor is the atmosphere that one creates and how you go about getting the parents in in the first place. That's far more important than the fact that we've got a carpet....
>
> I have visited everybody at their home. There are some children who have no wallpaper and no curtains. I'm very careful how I put over how we look after the carpet because I wouldn't want them to think I was telling them that what they had at home was wrong. But it must be nice for them — yes — to experience a carpet and to experience curtains, to be able to sit comfortably in school....I think I'd just be very careful about that particular point....
>
> The children do love it; they are appreciative....What I hope we're providing is that while they're at school there's a very loving, caring, homely, warm atmosphere and that....they feel safe here....
>
> It does have an impact on their behaviour....They do look after it; they're careful to look after things....

---

children: there were no formal special teaching arrangements and no special curricula in operation.

Respondents were tackling the matter individually, in an entirely informal manner, and the best that can be offered here is a more or less random selection from the practices they listed:

Encouraging parental involvement....

The school subsidizes outings and trips . . . .

The dinner ladies sometimes give them more dinner . . . .

We make allowances for tiredness, etc . . . .

The gym club enables us in a very quiet way to provide pumps, tracksuits, etc. for children who need them . . . .

The teacher and the NTA make opportunities to talk to these children during the day . . . .

Crayons might be provided for work at home . . . .

Children come and read to the head as a special treat; they can't take their reading books home because they wouldn't be returned . . . .

Respondents in PNP schools were asked whether PNP had made any impact on the provision they were able to make for socially and materially disadvantaged children. The prevailing view from Phase 2 schools was that it was too soon to say, although one respondent believed that the smaller groups which had been made possible by the appointment of extra staff were in themselves helpful in this context. Respondents from Phase 1 schools echoed this view, and several made particular mention of the extra time which can now be spent with these children as a result of a more generous allocation of staff to the school.

Another Group with Particular Needs

Before we move on to the conclusions to be drawn from the material presented here, a brief comment needs to be made about another group of children. Towards the end of their interviews, respondents were invited to consider whether there were any other groups who had particular needs over and above those shared by all pupils within the school. The only sizeable group of children not already discussed consisted of children variously termed 'gifted', 'bright' and 'high fliers'.

How Gifted Children Are Identified

These children were generally identified by class teachers, although in some cases parents had taken the initiative by speaking of their child's giftedness at the time of his or her admission to school. In no school was there an official procedure for identifying giftedness; it was invariably a matter of the individual teacher's awareness or professional judgment.

How the Needs of Gifted Children Are Diagnosed

The needs of gifted children were couched in rather general terms:

> They should be encouraged more . . . .
> More personal learning . . . .
> To be extended . . . .

The undoubted difficulty of formulating the needs of these particular children was disarmingly expressed by a respondent from a Phase 1 school: 'I'm not sure what their needs are, but we must be meeting them because standards are high . . . '. Another respondent restructured the question so that it dealt with the needs of the teacher: 'The teacher needs to be aware that the child's emotional development is not always equal to his academic development . . . '.

Provision for Gifted Children

The nature and the extent of special provision for gifted children varied a good deal:

> We haven't done anything about them yet . . . .
> The staff order specialist books for bright children . . . .
> We borrow books from the High School . . . .
> Special equipment has been bought for them (Stage V of SPMG) . . . .

Some schools had modified the curriculum to cater for the particular needs of this group of children:

> Special work: problem-solving activities . . . .
> Special maths programme worked out by Mrs V . . . .
> Individual programmes . . . .
> No distinctive curriculum: it's just extended . . . .

Other schools were relying on special teaching arrangements:

> They are withdrawn by the head . . . .
> Withdrawn by the deputy head . . . .
> We put them to work alongside older children at their level . . . .

Respondents from PNP schools were invited to comment on the impact of PNP on the provision they were able to make for gifted children. As before, the verdict from some Phase 2 schools was that it was too early to say.

Apart from that, the unanimous response was that the extra staffing had made it possible to release teachers to give these children attention, either individually or in small groups.

Part 2: Issues and Implications

The Analysis So Far

The remainder of this report considers some of the more important issues raised by PRINDEP's preliminary exploration of how children's needs are defined and met in the PNP context. First, however, let us remind ourselves of the framework within which the discussion takes place.

The notion of 'needs' is central to any educational activity or programme, but PNP doubly underlines that centrality, in its name and in its resource investment. We have seen how, within a policy which claims to meet the needs of all children in Leeds primary schools, certain categories of need have been given particular prominence. These are:

children with special educational needs;
statemented children;
children from ethnic minorities;
gender;
children experiencing social and/or material disadvantage.

The first two categories have been separated in our discussion so far because statementing entails particular procedures and provision. However, in as far as statemented children are a group within the larger category of special needs, and are the subject of the same general policy and LEA departmental arrangements, we bring them back together in our observations below, though separate points need to be made about arrangements for state-mented and non-statemented children with special needs, those conventionally referred to as the 2 per cent and the 18 per cent.

To these we have added for discussion purposes a sixth category, that of exceptionally able or *gifted children* because, although it does not appear in LEA policy, a number of teachers mentioned such children when we asked them to indicate any other groups with specific needs warranting particular attention.

We have also seen how, in the case of two of the LEA categories of need (ethnic minorities and gender) this targeting of specific groups of children is interwoven with a more general commitment to foster in all children related kinds of awareness concerning multiculture and gender, and that in turn these form part of a wider package of commitments extending across all Council departments, not just education.

Our data sources have been various. Cumulative information from our representative practice Fieldwork B sample was supplemented by special interviews on this theme in the same schools, interviews and observations in a number of Fieldwork A schools, annually collected survey data from all PNP schools, and analysis of LEA documentary material. Using these data, we have been able to chart in general terms policy and practice at two levels, the LEA and the school.

Our interviews were structured round what we see as the four logically related components of any policy on needs: definition, identification, diagnosis and provision. That is to say, we sought to discover at both LEA and school levels:

1. the view held of the nature of a particular need, or how it was *defined*;
2. the means used to *identify* children falling into the defined category of need;
3. the methods used to *diagnose* the precise nature of those children's needs, within the general definition; and
4. the resources, teaching methods, curriculum and other *provision* made available to enable the diagnosed needs of such children to be met.

Not all four of these components or headings applied to every category of need: for example, as we pointed out, identification procedures are hardly necessary in the case of girls or children from ethnic minority groups — membership of these two categories is self-evident — but they are certainly required in the case of more subjectively defined categories like special needs or social disadvantage.

Having said that, we feel that definition, identification, diagnosis and provision are not only logically contingent aspects of any needs policy, but also minimum practical requirements. In other words, to be complete and useful, a needs policy should specify, at the very least, the nature of the need, how children having such a need can be identified and their specific requirements diagnosed, and the most appropriate forms of educational provision to enable their diagnosed needs to be met. Our discussion below, however, will show that policy and practice at the two levels are very variable, so that, for example, a particular need may feature quite prominently in the LEA's or a school's policy statements while classroom provision may be left somewhat to chance; or, in respect of a different category of need, elaborate identification and diagnosis procedures may be coupled with rather vague or even conflicting notions of the needs the procedures are directed towards. Put more simply, educational needs imply both ends and means, a clear view of both the desired outcomes and the specific courses of action necessary for achieving them.

Our focus in this report can be summarized, therefore, in terms of the simple grid in Table 2.2, applied in turn to each of the LEA's defined categories of pupil need. The grid represents the main areas of our analysis in each case, but it can also be used as a straightforward device for checking the comprehensiveness of any policy relating to any categories of child need, those discussed in this report or others, at any level from LEA to the classroom.

Table 2.2

	Definition	Identification	Diagnosis	Provision
LEA				
School				

The LEA's Specific Categories of Need: Some Issues

Children with Special Educational Needs, Including Statemented Children

In terms of the framework above, this appears to be the most comprehensively developed of the LEA's needs policies, at both Authority and school levels. It starts with the advantage of definitions and procedures enshrined in law — the 1981 Education Act and subsequent Regulations and DES Circulars, particularly Circular 1/83 which sets out in detail the framework within which the assessments laid down in Section 5 of the Act are to be carried out.

Thus at LEA level the working definitions were nationally determined. The Authority then developed INRS as the local vehicle for teachers to identify children falling, or possibly falling, into the various special needs categories, and to begin the process of more precise diagnosis. INRS is an extremely comprehensive instrument whose application introduces considerable rigour and thoroughness into the identification and diagnosis stages. To enable teachers to use it correctly and to help in the processes of devising educational programmes and evaluating children's progress, the Authority mounted a special in-service programme, LISSEN, which our study of the PNP in-service support programme shows to have been very highly regarded by teachers. In addition, the psychological service, remodelled into EPFAS, provides specialist guidance and support and centrally monitors both general trends and individual cases. Statementing introduces a wider array of medical and social, as well as psychological, expertise. The procedures themselves are subjected to internal evaluation.

This whole special needs package (which extends into middle and high schools) has acquired national recognition (see Wolfendale, 1987), not least because the Leeds initiatives stand in marked contrast to the known failure of a number of other LEAs to implement the 1981 Act in full, a fact which has led to the inclusion of various special needs sections in the Education Reform Act (see also DES, 1989a). That might suggest that there is little more for PRINDEP to say, particularly in a report not exclusively devoted to special needs. There are, however, certain issues meriting discussion.

The main one concerns INRS as a procedure for, in terms of the PRINDEP dimensions of needs policy, *identification* and *diagnosis*: in this context Table 2.1 deserves close scrutiny. It will be noted that overall the number of statemented children, 0.5 per cent of those in our sample schools, is well below the Warnock notional 2 per cent, and that there is no statistically significant difference in the numbers of statemented children in the PNP Phases 1 and 2 and non-PNP schools. The total number of children perceived as having special needs of some kind represents 11 per cent of the children on roll in our sample schools, well below the Warnock notional 20 per cent. The basic question to be posed, then, is whether the INRS system is in fact picking up all children with special needs in Leeds primary schools.

Before considering this question we report, briefly and with minimal comment, suggestions made to us concerning what one might term a 'maverick' professional use of INRS, namely that 'getting children on to INRS' may in certain quarters be seen as a lever for securing extra staffing and thus lead to an artifical inflation of INRS numbers. This was one risk which the Authority itself anticipated, and on which its Profile of Need and Provision (mentioned earlier) may provide more precise information. We have no proof as yet that this is anything other than professional folklore, but it seems worth mentioning because it does point up the possible potential for abuse of a basically reliable and comprehensive scheme, in certain circumstances.

Now to more substantive issues. It will also be noted that our ranking of the categories shows how children's educational attainment and behaviour dominate the areas of concern and that in respect of these two the differences between PNP Phases 1, 2 and non-PNP are dramatic and clearly of some significance. If one takes all five INRS stages together, the percentages of children in the PRINDEP representative sample being perceived by the schools to have special needs of some kind are: PNP Phase 1, 13 per cent; Phase 2, 10 per cent; non-PNP, 8 per cent. If we add that the last figure is distorted upwards since exactly half of the non-PNP children on INRS were in just one of the sample schools, and that the proportion across the remaining non-PNP schools was about 3 per cent, the difference between PNP and non-PNP schools becomes even more marked.

The obvious response to such differences is that they vindicate the whole idea of PNP, especially the staggered phasing procedures and the differential allocation of resources: the Phase 1 schools, by this analysis, have conclusively proved themselves to be those with the most need. However, the matter is not so simple. It should be remembered that INRS, for all its considerable sophistication of approach, is in the end a subjective procedure (and therefore open to the kinds of manipulation reported above as figuring in local folklore). It is not a fail-safe, standardized, objective testing process but a checklist designed to prompt and structure teacher observation and diagnosis. The critical factor, therefore, is the teacher using INRS as much as INRS itself. So some of the PNP/non-PNP discrepancy can be accounted for by the head-start which PNP teachers had with LISSEN and INRS. The fact that at the time of our enquiry there were more Phase 2 than Phase 1 children on INRS Stage 1 bears this out: Phase 2 schools were at that time just beginning a process started earlier by Phase 1 schools which will inevitably produce some evening-out of the figures later on.

Moreover, there is in most problem identification procedures a correlation between the apparent extent of a problem and the resources available for identifying it. The obvious example is when crime figures appear to rise as police numbers, and therefore detection rates, increase. In the present case Phase 1 schools have by far the greatest share of the enhanced staffing made available under the Primary Needs Programme, and Phase 3 has smaller numbers of extra staffing spread much more thinly across the very large residue of schools which were not in the two earlier phases.

Having extra staff facilitates closer attention to individuals and groups: the greater the degree of individual attention, the greater the likelihood of spotting problems which a busy class teacher responsible for thirty-three children may miss. Most children, as any teacher knows very well, are adept at disguising whether they find work too difficult or too easy, but where two teachers are working together, or a school specifically uses extra staff for diagnostic and/or assessment purposes, children who have learning diffi-culties, or are underachieving, will be less likely to slip through the net.

We are certainly not suggesting that differences in staffing levels account for the whole of the PNP/non-PNP discrepancy: anyone visiting schools across the Authority as a whole (as PRINDEP does) gains immediate and ample evidence that the scale and severity of the attainment and behaviour problems confronting teachers vary enormously and that many of the toughest challenges do indeed occur in Phase 1 schools — but it must be one element to be borne in mind in making sense of the figures.

The discrepancies, and the notion of a link between staffing and identification/diagnosis, also raise a question about those schools *without* enhanced staffing. How many children in non-PNP schools have special needs which are simply going undetected? As the table shows, children in the clinical categories leading rapidly to statementing are identified and statemented in similar proportions in each PNP phase. But what of children with special needs not severe enough to warrant statementing — the 'Warnock 18 per cent'? What proportion, in all schools, but perhaps especially those of the non-PNP schools having such low INRS numbers (3 per cent), are remaining undetected simply because their teachers are so stretched by their other responsibilities that they do not notice them?

That this is possible is reinforced by an occasional tendency in some of the interviews for a teacher to define a child's special needs *in terms of the teacher's (rather than the child's) problems*. If no such 'problem' is manifest, the child may then be assumed to have no need for other than the mainstream educational diet. But, of course, the externalized teaching 'problem' is not necessarily an exact indicator of the child's learning need.

All this points, as does so much in PRINDEP's accumulating data on PNP, to enhanced staffing as perhaps the single most powerful and produc-tive part of the PNP initiative. But it is not, as we shall see later, a panacea. Enhanced staffing, of itself, solves nothing: the critical issue is how it is used.

Another important point in relation to INRS is that to get a more exact bearing on the adequacy of the mechanisms for identification and diagnosis one would need to compare teachers' INRS ratings of children's needs with other indicators of their ability. PRINDEP decided, as a matter of deliberate policy discussed at some length with officers, advisers and teachers, not to institute a formal testing programme as part of its evaluation of PNP, but to collect and analyze all available LEA data on educational outcomes, including the Authority's own test data. Opinion is divided over the value of the 7+ and 9+ reading tests, but at least they constitute a fairly uniform indicator of attainment. PRINDEP is analyzing reading scores from two years before the start of PNP to when we cease fieldwork. The issue of the relationship between reading scores and PNP (or in this case INRS) is a complicated one, but one theme signalled by the discrepancies which emerge may be the ideological conflict that we have had cause to refer to elsewhere, between the advocates of highly specific programmes for targeted children and those who see all children's needs as best met through enriched general classroom provision — the belief that 'all children have special needs' and that 'good primary practice' will amply provide for them.

It can also be mentioned here that the anomalous school in the non-PNP part of our Fieldwork B sample (the one referred to earlier as providing half of the INRS numbers for the non-PNP sample schools and thus distorting the overall figures from about 3 per cent to 8 per cent) can be explained in several ways. One explanation, germane to the general question above about the reliability of specific indicators of need (like INRS) or of attainment (like reading scores), is that the needs of the school as a whole were incorrectly diagnosed at the beginning of PNP and the school ought to have been in Phase 1 or 2.

One final point about special educational needs as a major Authority needs category has to do with provision. Teachers in our sample refer positively to the range of support and resources available at LEA level and mention a variety of practices in the school. So in this area of need, PRINDEP's grid for checking or summarizing the comprehensiveness of a particular needs policy is fuller than for any other of the LEA's designated categories of need.

However, one aspect of provision causing increasing concern in the schools has been mentioned to us many times during the 1987–88 school year. Originally the LEA defined PNP coordinators as essentially special needs coordinators. Subsequently, as the 'good primary practice' version of PNP gathered strength, coordinators were given a redefined role reflecting that view, and special needs became just one of the several areas of concern they might (or might not) attend to. More recently, schools tell us, their requests for the entitlement of extra staffing to implement agreed programmes for statemented children have been met by the response that this is the job of PNP coordinators, that the latter constitute the entitlement for statemented children and that no further support is available.

No doubt there will be some dispute over whether the policy has really changed, and if so what it now means, but we mention this perception held by many schools to indicate that after a brief period of apparent resolution of the initial special needs/primary needs controversy, it appears to be re-emerging.

Children from Ethnic Minority Groups

At present (in July 1988) a detailed and up-to-date Council survey is nearing completion, but at the time when PNP began, children from ethnic minority groups formed about 9 per cent of the primary school population of Leeds. These children tend to be concentrated in certain schools, where they can form anything from a substantial minority to a majority (up to 92 per cent) of the children on roll. This means that for many primary schools the education of children from ethnic minority groups is simply not part of their everyday reality.

In common with many other cities having a culturally and ethnically diverse population, Leeds has evolved policies at all levels and covering all departments (not just education) to meet what it sees as the aspirations and needs of members of ethnic minority groups and to enhance relationships between such groups and the white population, especially through anti-racism and multicultural awareness. These policies have been backed by substantial resources, so that our needs policy grid can show, in respect of race and education, a clear commitment under *definition* and a variety of LEA initiatives under *provision*, from multi-ethnic coordinators, advisory teachers, a primary adviser with multicultural responsibilities, Home-School Liaison Officers, second language teachers and other staff appointments to various courses to enhance professional skills and understanding and the staff and resources of a multicultural centre. Moreover, the staff investment is of a kind which also shows attention to our dimension of needs *diagnosis*, especially in specific areas like second language learning. So far, so good. But when we move from the LEA to the school level, the situation becomes more complex, variable and open to question. Our investigations highlight a number of issues for discussion by both the LEA and the schools.

The interview programme whose data inform part of this report focused more on the needs of children from ethnic minority groups than on multi-cultural education for all. However, the two are contingent, for one of the most basic needs for any ethnic minority group must be freedom from racial discrimination, and this freedom, or need, is enshrined in law. Thus the existence of minorities entails obligations and needs for majorities also, central among which is the need for all children, regardless of cultural origin or affiliation, to understand and respect the notion of pluralism itself and the situations of the various minority and majority groups which produce it.

So, despite the starting point of our questions, discussion soon extended into the wider issue of multicultural education; in this, though we found several who argued strongly for multicultural awareness as a necessary part of the multi-ethnic needs package, there were others who tended to assert that if there were few or no children from ethnic minority groups in their own school, then for them multicultural education was simply not an issue.

However, we wish to stress most strongly that our evidence does not show this to be simply a geographical problem of inner city and so-called 'leafy lanes', or a matter of 'out of sight, out of mind.' We emphasize this because we have become aware of a tendency for some to polarize the two contexts. It is a polarization which seems deeply unhelpful to all concerned. Moreover, and ironically, it displays the same characteristic — that of stereotyping — which proponents of multiculturalism are themselves most concerned to eradicate. In the present case, therefore, the situation is much more complicated than mere geography. It is true, as some of the quoted responses show, that there are some who see multiculturalism as a non-issue because they are not presented with any 'problem' in relation to the teaching of children from ethnic minority groups. But it is equally true that it was in an all-white school that we found some of the most committed and articulate policies and innovative practices in multicultural education. So it is ultimately a matter of the attitudes and understandings of individual heads and teachers, and of the extent to which these are translated into collective debate, policy and provision.

We commented earlier that whereas in talking about special needs many of our respondents were clear about both goals and courses of action, or the entire PRINDEP policy spectrum from *definition* to *provision*, in the present case there was rather more vagueness about provision, even though long-term goals might be clear enough. The vagueness was particularly marked where implementing multicultural commitments was concerned, as opposed to meeting the specific needs of children from minority groups, where schools usually had a range of provision at the classroom level. This would suggest that the LEA may wish to give more attention not only to the dissemination and discussion of multicultural policy as such — since clearly its impact has been patchy — but also to practical ways of implementing it.

With regard to policy, our point about individual consciousness indicates that it is not enough merely to have a policy and expect teachers to quote it on demand. That reduces the issue to one of playing verbal or political games. Attitude change requires knowledge, understanding and insight, of the facts and issues in question, and of oneself, and at a deep and sophisticated level. This was clearly recognized in the multicultural awareness courses we reported earlier.

Such courses, however, have been necessarily brief, and far from universally subscribed. This raises the question of the balance of LEA resourcing in this area, which while very substantial is concentrated mainly on one dimension of the task, that of meeting the social and linguistic needs of children from ethnic minority groups. The other dimension, that of promoting multicultural understanding and commitment among all teachers, and of providing them with guidance and support for school and classroom programmes to engender the same understanding and commitment in children, has been more modestly resourced. For a task of such complexity and universality, a multicultural centre, a multicultural advisory teacher and a programme of courses, however good (and they evidently are), can only be a starting point, and in any event they have as yet reached a relatively small proportion of Leeds primary teachers.

Similarly, at school level many schools have policy statements in which multicultural goals are prominent. With few exceptions, the schools in our sample which are most convincingly translating such goals into effective practice are those with enhanced staffing. The reason for this has to do with the nature of the need in question. Where special educational needs were concerned, enhanced staffing enabled very specific tasks to be undertaken — like identifying and assessing in connection with INRS, or devising and implementing programmes for particular children. But in the present case the prime and prior need is the professional development of staff, and for that, as PRINDEP Reports 4 and 5 clearly showed, enhanced staffing and especially what we called TTT (teachers teaching together) are very powerful tools (see Chapters 5 and 7).

With tight staffing, the amount and quality of school-based staff development possible are more limited, however well-intentioned and committed the participants. Moreover, in such cases success is most likely if the problem to be tackled is a relatively clear, straightforward and instrumental one. Exploring the dimensions of multicultural education is of a wholly different order of challenge. It is true that staff need information, but they also need time to confront and discuss the difficult, contentious and often threatening issues involved, and time and resources to establish the best possible climate for doing so.

The issue is one of making better use of resources to ensure that the two linked dimensions of this category of need — the needs of children from ethnic minority groups, and the needs of all children for an understanding of their pluralist society — are attended to, and that in particular all teachers, wherever they teach, are given constructive help in relation to the second dimension. In saying this it is important to be reminded of the earlier point that multicultural education in the more general sense is a necessary part of the process of meeting minority group needs, not an additional or peripheral activity. We are acutely aware, however, of the sensitivity of this issue in schools, communities and the political arena, and recognize that in relation to this aspect of LEA policy very careful and delicate judgments have constantly to be made, within both the Council and its schools.

Equal Opportunities and Gender

Here again the starting point is a Council policy covering all departments, and some degree of resourcing for education under PNP, though the resource allocation for equal opportunities in primary schools is on a far smaller scale than for any other of the LEA's needs categories. There are three obvious consequences of this. First, a relatively small proportion of primary teachers will gain access to the central provision available (i.e. the courses on gender awareness and equal opportunities and the advice of the support teacher). Second, however good the central provision (and we noted teachers' enthusiasm for these courses), on its own it cannot be expected to do more than begin the long process of consciousness-raising and professional re-education which national evidence suggests is needed. Third, the onus for dealing with this issue then is placed squarely on individual schools.

It is not just the resourcing which is different from, say, special needs. In the case of gender issues and the needs of girls, as with multicultural education, the LEA has a general policy commitment but nothing is enforced, whereas in the case of special needs the legal requirements provide the lever for policy to be backed by firm requirements and procedures.

So essentially it is up to the schools. They respond, as we show, in very different ways. Some see no problem at all, though most are aware, at least, of gender stereotyping as a current issue. Others see a problem but are not quite sure what to do about it beyond the two usual gestures of non-segregated registers and queues. Others go beyond this to penetrate the deeper levels of teachers' and children's gender-influenced assumptions about human capacities and relationships. In doing so, as our work in non-sample schools showed, teachers act out their commitments either in relative isolation, or, if they are lucky, with the support of a few colleagues.

The exceptionally wide variation in the degree and kind of attention given to this area of need in the schools is to be expected, given the historical and cultural background to this issue, yet of all the areas of need it is the one where there is the strongest case for consistency, given that the need in question is essentially a universal one. Girls, after all, constitute half the population of every primary school, and gender parity is the right of all children.

The interviews seem to show, though with exceptions as always, a sliding scale of gender awareness and action: rather more in PNP Phase 1 than in non-PNP schools. One reason for this is undoubtedly the impact of the equal opportunities support teacher and her courses and equally, perhaps, the effectiveness of the Authority in conveying its messages about gender, one PNP phase at a time. Another, however, is likely to be resource-related. The non-PNP school with a clearly articulated equal opportunities policy (see Box G) is a case in point. Here the commitment was evident, and as much as possible was done to ensure that it became a practical reality, but the tightness of staffing drastically limited the extent of professional and curricular development activity that the policy needed in order thoroughly to permeate both daily classroom practice and longer-term planning.

In other words, as with cultural pluralism and its educational implications, so with gender. We are dealing here with another issue where the prior and paramount need is professional consciousness-raising, and that simply cannot be achieved by central policy statements and a modest provision of courses alone. It is, again, an issue of profound complexity, and one, furthermore, which fundamentally challenges our most deeply ingrained assumptions and habits of thought. Each teacher, because of her or his unique experiences, values, sensitivities and capacities, is at a different point of development in relation to this issue. So the problem is an individual one, for which the natural collective forum is the school, and this implies staffing at a level which will enable a school to cope with this fairly subtle kind of professional development as well as all its other day-to-day challenges.

We noted earlier that whereas with special needs, teachers were fairly clear about both definitions and goals on the one hand and provision or courses of action on the other, when they spoke of ethnic minority needs their views of practical provision were much vaguer. In the case of gender, it will be observed, means and ends frequently appeared to be confused, and this underlines the need both for more support for school-based clarification of the issues and for more positive guidance on practical classroom strategies.

All this suggests that however commendable its basic policy, the Authority may need to look carefully at the levels and kinds of resourcing it provides in order to ensure that the policy is translated into school and classroom practice. It may also wish to consider whether the patchy and indeed sometimes negligible response to the gender policy at school level warrants not only resource redistribution but also much clearer guidelines as to practice.

Social and Material Disadvantage

This is the final official category of need within PNP. As we have indicated, it is also the target of by far the largest proportion of PNP funding, since the enhanced staffing (the most expensive of the various PNP initiatives) and refurbishment have had their greatest concentration in the schools with large numbers of children in this category.

Working through the PRINDEP grid components at each of the two levels, LEA and school, we see how anomalous and problematic this category of need becomes. The initial LEA *definition* had to do with the simplest of indicators — free school meals. The response was then to provide each school scoring high on this indicator with substantial human and material resources to maximize its chances of success in coping with the need in question.

The Authority gave no further pointers, however, on procedures for the *identification* of individual cases, or on ways of *diagnosing* their specific educational needs, nor on school and classroom *provision*. The definition was generalized and broad, the identification procedure basic and universal, and the provision of an enabling rather than a programmatic kind. Thus there is a marked contrast with the strategy adopted by the Authority for meeting the needs of SEN children, where systematic identification and diagnosis procedures are backed by clear guidance as to classroom programmes to be pursued in individual cases.

The contrast does not necessarily imply criticism, for the two kinds of needs are obviously very different, especially in the sense, as we have emphasized, that so many of the problems experienced by these children not only lie outside the school but are beyond the school's capacity to do much about. So schools find themselves adopting an essentially compensatory role. At that level schools use mainly rule-of-thumb methods for *identification* and *diagnosis* and thence for determining *provision*. It can be argued that there is no alternative, and that unless a child is potentially one with formally defined special needs (which, of course, some of these are and in these cases INRS is applied) there are no adequate diagnostic instruments available. The educational provision a materially or socially disadvantaged child needs, it is asserted, is a matter of judgment, and indeed trial and error, rather than the application of proven procedures. The approach, then, is essentially an updated version of the post-Plowden EPA principle. It has three components: increased staffing, improved buildings and resources, and a generalized advocacy of the broadly-based curriculum and flexible teaching strategies. But its central thrust is what the Authority terms the 'quality learning environment'.

This emphasis on milieu is in marked contrast to alternative strategies adopted elsewhere, notably as part of the national Educational Priority programme in the 1970s, in which the content and style of the curriculum experienced by such children came in for very close scrutiny. That programme also included, it should be added, the same kinds of emphasis as in PNP on parallel initiatives like increased nursery provision and improved home–school links.

It should also be added that the notion of a special 'community curriculum', as tried by Midwinter and others (Midwinter, 1972), came in for a certain amount of criticism on the grounds that it smacked of ghetto education (see Merson and Campbell, 1974) and that in any case, in Bernstein's words (1970), 'education cannot compensate for society'. In turn, the locally specific curriculum was defended on the grounds of dramatically enhanced pupil motivation and increased parental and community commitment to, and involvement in, the life of the school, which, it was asserted, were the essential prerequisites to improving these children's chances of competing on something appoaching equal terms with socially and materially more fortunate children in respect of the conventional examination hurdles.

In any case, there are different kinds of curricular compensation. Instead of, or alongside, the community curriculum some have advocated a much more direct and hard-headed approach, that of a sustained attack on basic literacy and numeracy skills, on the grounds that in the end, regardless of progressive educationists' ideals, these are what a school-leaver seeking a job is going to be judged by, and in lacking these he or she is far more disadvantaged than if other kinds of experience are omitted at the primary stage. In response, primary educationists cite evidence showing that they have never, contrary to claims by politicians and in the tabloid press, neglected basic skills and that indeed these are most effectively pursued in the context of a broad and varied curriculum.

The fact remains, however, that the lesson of other comparable initiatives is that close attention to the content of the curriculum is an essential part of any attempt to offset the adverse impact of social or material disadvantage on children's educational or occupational prospects. Perhaps a sharper debate on the PNP curriculum, especially in relation to these children, is now indicated. It is an issue we shall return to later.

Another lesson of other urban education projects concerns the deployment of extra staff. In many of the Leeds schools whose children experience particular social and material disadvantage extra staff are used in a variety of ways and schools have in addition other adults fulfilling various roles. Most schools have recognized the critical importance of time invested in home-school contacts, and some have enabled their staff to combine teaching with a liaison or visiting role. In view of the success elsewhere of teacher/social worker and similar schemes, the Authority might wish to examine a broader range of liaison roles. We encountered frustration by some teachers whose full-time class teaching commitment prevented them from establishing the kinds of links with homes and support services that they felt they and their children urgently needed. This point may relate to one made in PRINDEP Report 5 (Chapter 5), where we note a tendency for staff without classes to have problems of status and credibility with colleagues. As we said there: 'It is imperative that all staff recognize that there are several different, and equally valid, ways in which a primary teacher can work in a school, and teaching a class full-time is only one of them.'

The heads and teachers we have observed and talked with, and the many more who have returned our questionnaires, are convinced that enhanced staffing, increased capitation and refurbishment have made a difference to the way they and their children can work and what they can achieve. There is little doubt about the impact of the Authority's concern with the visual environment of children's learning: Leeds primary schools are becoming increasingly attractive and stimulating places for children to be in. Nor is there much doubt about the way extra staffing leads to extra attention for individual children, especially those with greatest need, and particularly where ways of working in schools and classrooms are freed from traditional assumptions about what a primary teacher should be doing.

The educational outcomes of such initiatives are notoriously difficult to measure objectively, especially after such a short time, but the importance of the frequently reported outcomes like reduced stress levels, a calmer and more stable working environment and problems more readily contained than hitherto, should never be underestimated.

Other Groups with Specific Needs

We have seen that the only other group mentioned by a number of respondents was children of high ability. This is not one of the LEA's official categories of need, so there is no policy at that level to analyze. However, these children exist, they are recognized by teachers, and they have needs. Moreover, their existence, and the lack of attention to them in LEA policy, raise important questions about the notion of needs which underpins PNP. These we mention in the conclusion, but for the present, the following brief points should be noted.

First, these children were mentioned only in some schools, yet they exist in every school. Second, considerable evidence has accumulated nationally over the past decade or so that many children in primary schools are underachieving, and those at the top end of the ability range most notably so. One might reasonably expect, therefore, greater attention to this problem in policy and practice, at both LEA and school levels, than our evidence suggests at present. Third, we have noted a certain degree of vagueness over how bright children are defined and identified, and how their educational needs can be diagnosed and provided for. Yet there is now a useful body of educational literature offering clear guidance on definition, identification and diagnosis, and a range of approaches and materials for acceleration and curriculum enrichment and extension. Fourth, as with every other category of need referred to in this report, one of the best forms of support the LEA has given is enhanced staffing. In several schools this enabled very able children to be given the specific attention or provision that their teachers judged them to need. At the same time such resources are not used to best effect if not all staff concerned are clear about basic indicators of high ability or the range of curricular options open to them. Schools themselves can and do provide their own programmes of professional development and support in respect of this category of need as with all others, and indeed there are certain teachers in Leeds primary schools who have done pioneering work in this field.

The Authority, however, now has to decide whether this laissez-faire approach is sufficient, or whether it sees a case for providing more substantial central support. Our evidence suggests that such support should concentrate on professional development: the issue is not so much teacher numbers as professional understanding and skill, particularly in relation to identification, needs diagnosis and appropriately matched and challenging provision.

Conclusion

We move now to some final comments. The first concerns the Authority's designated categories of primary need. There seem to be two main issues concerning special needs in PNP schools, a highly resourced, well-organized and in many ways very successful area: first, the discrepancies between PNP and non-PNP schools, and indeed between individual schools within PNP phases, which may raise questions about both the PNP phasing and resourcing criteria and the ways teachers use INRS; second, the relatively low numbers of children in both statemented and non-statemented categories.

Ethnicity is a sensitive and challenging area in which many schools are working extremely hard and effectively, often with considerable and carefully nurtured parental and community support. Occasionally, however, there seems to be a failure properly to grasp the interdependence of the two essential strands of a multi-ethnic policy: meeting the needs of children from ethnic minority groups, and providing a multicultural education for all children. The latter is more patchy than the former, and is perhaps under-resourced in relation to teacher development.

Equal opportunities and gender, though an area of importance in Authority policy, receives extremely uneven treatment, ranging from the non-existent or negligible to the ambitious and imaginative. It could well be underresourced at LEA level, though the quality of what is available is high. Again, the paramount need is for teacher development in this area. Professional understanding and commitment are the prerequisites to changed practice in the area of gender, as with multiculturalism.

Social and material disadvantage attract the largest proportion of PNP funding, but such funding is a relatively blunt instrument, and everything hangs on how schools take advantage of the massive investment in extra staffing, capitation and refurbishment which the Authority has made. The policy on social and material disadvantage, therefore, is essentially an enabling one, and it is clear that it has indeed enabled a great deal in many schools. Our evidence shows heads and staff working exceptionally hard to provide a stable, caring and stimulating environment for these children. However, there may now be a case for giving much greater attention to the content of the curriculum experienced by these children: what and how they learn are surely as important as the physical and human environment within which their learning takes place. We have also suggested that the move to more flexible use of staffing beyond the traditional class teacher role needs further exploration and encouragement.

What of the general impact of PNP on schools' capacity to define and meet these various needs? We have charted the many kinds of influence of PNP funding on LEA and school needs policies and practices, and all are important, but undoubtedly the single most potent aspect of PNP is enhanced staffing. For many schools it has been a truly liberating force, enabling them to concentrate attention on individuals and groups of children having particular needs to an extent not hitherto possible.

The impact of enhanced staffing is on two main areas of a school's work: classroom provision, and professional awareness, knowledge and skill. Improvements in provision are readily charted, but the extent to which professional awareness keeps pace with the new opportunities and practices is less easy to pin down. In this report we have shown that more work needs to be done to ensure deeper understanding of two of the more contentious and problematic areas of need — multiculturalism and gender — and that the nature of the issues makes the individual school the most appropriate context and focus for such activity. We also showed in earlier reports how some of the classroom strategies facilitated by enhanced staffing, notably TTT and other kinds of collaborative activity, place new and critical demands on teachers' professional understanding and skill, which the Authority seems not to have anticipated.

The emerging picture is of enhanced staffing as a strategy which has considerable potential, but only if backed by increased emphasis on appropriate forms of professional development. Since the Authority has also invested substantially in a PNP in-service support programme, our impression of some degree of shortfall between policy and provision on the one hand and professional awareness and development on the other may also raise questions about the targeting, focus and style of such in-service activities.

In particular, in the present context there seems to be a convincing case for concentrating much more attention, in programmes of professional development, on *identification* and *diagnosis*; that is to say, on helping teachers accurately to locate those children having particular kinds of needs and to establish as precisely as possible what their particular problems are and how they can best be dealt with. Overarching all these matters are the basic questions of what is meant by a specific need, which needs merit policy and resources, and which needs, indeed, matter most. In simple terms, the LEA's policy is one of positive discrimination. All children are held to have certain basic educational needs, but those children disadvantaged in some way are regarded as meriting extra attention and support. The corollary of this is not that other kinds of needs are deemed unimportant, but rather that schools and their staff are assumed to have the ability and resources to define and meet these as necessary. This is a familiar and widely applied approach, grounded in basic principles of social justice: those lowest on the ladder are given the most help. Expressed like that, it is hard to see how anybody can do other than support such a commitment, and we certainly do not intend to gainsay it. As put into practice in Leeds, however, it raises a number of questions which we have already outlined and discussed. There are two further points to be made.

First, are there specific needs other than those singled out in the LEA's policy which merit particular attention? Some of our teacher respondents had no doubt that there are, and our discussion of the issue of very able children summarizes their views and adds further comments. However, the problem with discussion of high ability is that it usually becomes muddied by talk of elitism and privilege. In a human sense it is a privilege to have ability. It is also the case that material wealth is often used to buy the forms of education which nurture and extend ability. But it is dangerous to confuse the two, since otherwise it can too readily be assumed that high ability is only to be found in well-off families, and this does the greatest possible disservice to children from materially less advantaged backgrounds. It is an assumption, indeed, which is widely held and which results in some teachers holding low expectations of such children, with the result that these children then underachieve.

The full range of human potential, of course, is to be found in every social context. Therefore, it has to be asked whether the Authority has given sufficiently broad attention in its policies to the *full range of ability-related needs*. Is there a case for concentrating quite specific attention on other levels of ability and attainment *in addition to* the lowest? (The italics are there to emphasize that this is not an either– or situation.)

The second point concerns the efficacy of the broadly-based curriculum allied to flexible teaching strategies within a stimulating learning environment. The Authority asserts that this has the capacity to meet the 'identified needs' of all children. We have seen how *need* can be defined in terms of the 1981 Education Act's reference to 'learning difficulties which call for special educational provision to be made'; in terms of race; in terms of gender; and in terms of social and material disadvantage. So need, for policy purposes, is defined partly in terms of level of ability and partly in terms of social justice.

Leaving aside the matter of whether there might be other kinds of pressing social need which could make a claim for inclusion in policy, a question remains about the way ability-related needs tend to be defined in terms of *levels* (the least able, the most able and so on). They can also be defined in terms of *kinds* of ability. Human potential is not monolithic, but variegated, and nearly all children have very particular talents which, if schools are able to recognize and foster them, can be extended immeasurably to provide both self-fulfilment and, frequently, marketable skills for later life.

Is the broadly-based curriculum a sufficiently sharp tool for meeting the needs of children whose potential takes such specific forms? Does it meet the needs of those with potential of a scientific, or artistic, or physical, or linguistic kind? Or with potential less readily classifiable but none the less high? Does it provide children with the sort of experience and opportunities which will allow their specific abilities to reveal themselves to the teacher? Does it provide the basis for teachers accurately to diagnose such children's specific needs? As educational provision, does it offer the scope, depth and challenge which will enable the children's particular abilities to be fully developed?

The final question this prompts, therefore, is whether a view of needs which focuses so much on children's *problems* ought to be balanced by one focusing upon children's levels and kinds of *potential*. If so, then the same process of definition, identification, diagnosis and provision is implied, but the issue of defining and meeting children's needs becomes a considerably larger one than currently conceived.

3
Curriculum Continuity: Reading Standards

Introduction

The goals of the Primary Needs Programme, in sharp contrast to central government policy since 1987, mentioned neither learning to read nor educational standards. PNP's aims had less to do with the specific content and outcomes of the primary curriculum than with its general character and context. This is not to say that content and outcomes were deemed unimportant, but rather that it was believed at that stage that an emphasis on the *quality* of classroom, school and community life would deliver these and much more besides, particularly in the inner city. A broad curriculum and an attractive learning environment would motivate and stimulate children, it was argued, and effort put into improving relationships between school, home and community would consolidate these gains.

It is always necessary to question assumptions like this, particularly when they occupy such a central place in educational policy. We began to do so towards the end of the previous chapter, and will extend the analysis during later chapters and in the second volume. Nevertheless, it has to be said that there is nothing particularly maverick about the PNP line. It has a respectable pedigree in Plowden (CACE, 1967) and the subsequent Educational Priority Area projects (Halsey, 1972), and is to some extent reinforced in more recent studies. HMI, for example (DES, 1978a), argued that progress in the 'basics' could best be achieved in the context of a broad curriculum, and Tizard *et al.* (1988) highlighted curriculum 'coverage' as one of a number of school and classroom factors which could be shown to have an impact on infants' progress in reading, writing and mathematics.

In any case the LEA's treatment of reading was not entirely oblique. Reading scores, after all, were used as the measure of schools' educational need and as a basis for determining the level of extra resources they would gain under PNP. Once they were in the programme, the combination of extra staff and access to the LEA's in-service courses enabled schools, if they so wished, to devote much more attention than hitherto to reading in general and to children experiencing reading difficulties in particular. Yet, it must be stressed, this choice was for each school to make, since the programme as a whole placed upon them no formal obligation in this regard.

For this and other reasons — some to do with our basic approach to the evaluation as outlined in Chapter 1 — it seemed inappropriate to use test scores in reading (or, for that matter, mathematics) as measures of the success of the Primary Needs Programme as a whole.

At the same time reading *is* one of the basic continuities in primary education. This was reflected in the LEA's 1988 policy document on primary education, which placed competence in reading first in a list of fourteen objectives:

> By the end of the primary school stage the Authority would wish the majority of primary school children to have learnt:
> (i) to read fluently and accurately, with understanding, feeling and discrimination.... (Leeds City Council, 1988, p. 5)

All this is the necessary background to the analysis which follows. The particular place of reading in the primary curriculum made it an obvious and sensible target for monitoring; yet the particular objectives of PNP precluded its use as a measure of the programme's success.

Our analysis examines trends in the scores obtained by Leeds children in the LEA's 7+ and 9+ reading tests over a five-year period, from 1983 to 1988 — that is, from two years before to three years after the start of PNP. The analysis, for the reasons indicated above, is presented fairly neutrally: we offer several conclusions and questions, but avoid any suggestion that PNP can or should be called to account on the basis of what our analysis shows.

Reading Standards in PNP Schools

The Tests Used

The test used at 7+ was Young's *Group Reading Test*, originally devised for an age range from 6 years 5 months to 12 years to 8 months. It was first published twenty years ago, but reissued in a new edition in 1980. The test is in two parts. Part 1 involves word–picture matching (e.g. a picture of a crab beside the words 'much', 'pass', 'duck', 'crab'; the child draws a ring round the right word). It contains fifteen items and lasts for four minutes. Part 2 is a sentence completion exercise containing thirty items (e.g. Eggs are eaten with — 'bar', 'bear', 'bacon', 'boat', 'bank', 'better'). It lasts for nine minutes.

The test's validity (measured against other reputable reading tests) is high, generally exceeding .87. It undoubtedly measures reading ability among other things. However, as well as the more familiar difficulties, this test poses an extra problem in that it includes a set of pictures which may or may not look much like the things they are supposed to represent. To succeed in the test, a child must be able to make sense of these pictures, and must also be familiar with the objects depicted (if she has never seen a crab, for example, she cannot hope to solve the item involving a picture of a crab except through guesswork, or by a process of elimination). Throughout the test, some items favour children from a particular social class or ethnic group, or have simply become outdated. For example, there must be many children in England nowadays who have never eaten bacon with eggs in their lives.

The reliability of the test is generally good, but the test manual cautions against the dangers of working with reading ages and quotients rather than with raw scores (Young, 1980). In particular, quotients on this test are less reliable for 7-year-olds than for older children. This tends to be a problem with all tests of this type: at the bottom end of the test a child needs to gain so few points to get a typical score for his age that a fairly arbitrary difference of one or two in the number of points he gains can have quite dramatic repercussions on his reading age or reading quotient. The manual of this particular test warns:

> Unreliability may lead to a false impression of progress. However, if genuine improvement is assumed only if there is a gain of six points or more, then the chance of making a mistake is only one in thirty . . . . Judging improvement by means of differences between reading ages is best avoided because of the additional complications. (Young, 1980)

The test used at 9+ was the *NFER Reading Test AD*, originally published in 1954, and restandardized in 1977. It contains thirty-five multiple choice sentence completion items to be done in fifteen minutes (after a short practice period). The intended age range of the test is 8 years to 10 years 7 months. This is a much narrower range than that of the Young *Group Reading Test*, and this may be seen as a point in its favour. It is certainly appropriate as a 9+ survey instrument. In form and content it is similar to the second part of the Young *Group Reading Test*; a typical item reads as follows: 'Jane was made responsible for answering telephone enquiries on account of her pleasant voice and good (complexion, clothing appearance, typing, manners.' [NB: the comma is missing between 'clothing' and 'appearance' in the original.]

Its reported reliability is high but, curiously, there is no reference to its validity in the manual (Watts, 1978). Of course, this does not necessarily mean that it is not valid; most of the comments made about the Young test also apply to this one.

Analysis of Test Results, 1983–88

The cut-off point selected by Leeds Educational Psychology and Family Advisory Service (EPFAS) as being of particular significance is a reading quotient of 80; below this point a child is considered to be experiencing reading difficulties severe enough to cause special concern. Consequently, for each individual school EPFAS holds a record of the number of children taking the tests each year, and the percentage scoring a reading quotient of 80 or below.

Valuable as these particular figures must be to EPFAS in its vital task of monitoring the identification and treatment of reading difficulties, they give an incomplete picture of reading standards throughout the Authority as a whole. One of the problems (though not the only one) is that all the schools are treated separately; there are no overall figures for Phase 1, Phase 2 and Phase 3 schools. If we examine the 9+ results from a single Phase 2 school taken at random from the EPFAS list of 1988, and reproduced in Table 3.1, we can see the limitations of the information they yield for our present purposes.

Table 3.1. 9+ Scores from a Single Leeds Primary School (EPFAS figures)

Year of test	Number tested	Percentage with RQ 80–
1983/84	9	0
1984/85	13	15
1985/86	10	0
1986/87	11	0
1987/88	17	6

At first glance, these figures seem to show a dramatic deterioration in reading after the advent of PNP. During the year before Phase 2 began and the first year of Phase 2, there were no children at all with reading quotients of 80 or below. After one year of PNP however, 6 per cent of the pupils were in this category. The use of percentages for such very small numbers, however, can be somewhat misleading: the 6 per cent is 6 per cent of only seventeen children, and thus represents one child only. Similarly, the 15 per cent from 1984/85 is 15 per cent of only thirteen children and therefore represents two children only. In short, Table 3.1 indicates that between 1983 and 1988 the school in question had only three children with reading quotients of 80 or below. Two of these were failing in reading before PNP and one of them since. Certainly no sensible generalizations could be made from such a finding.

It can be equally misleading to make comparisons between schools purely on the basis of percentages, partly because of the inappropriateness of percentages to represent very small numbers, and partly because the schools vary so greatly in size. To produce overall figures for Phase 1, Phase 2 and Phase 3 schools it is necessary to convert all the percentages of the EPFAS list back to numbers of children, and then to find the sum of the numbers from all the schools in each phase. The results of this exercise are set out in Tables 3.2 and 3.3.

These tables confirm that every year between 1983 and 1988 schools which are now in Phase 1 of PNP had a higher proportion of low-scoring children on both tests than schools which are now in Phase 2; and that the Phase 2 schools consistently had a higher proportion of such children than Phase 3 schools. This is no cause for surprise, since it was partly on the basis of these same scores that some schools were selected for the first two phases of PNP while other schools were not.

Table 3.2 also shows a slight rise in the proportion of children making low scores on the 7+ test after the advent of PNP in both Phase 1 and Phase 2 schools (1985–86 and 1986–87 respectively), although the same pattern does not hold for the 9+ test results summarized in Table 3.3. It should be observed that the numbers of children tested at 7+ steadily rose over the same period, although this is not true of the numbers tested at 9+.

However, the proportion of children who make very low scores for their age on a reading test is simply not adequate as the sole index of a school's success in teaching reading. For example, a school staff which devoted most of its attention to the provision of what the LEA calls 'a stimulating and challenging learning environment' for all its pupils, and which consequently allowed itself relatively little time to identify specific difficulties and give intensive individual help where it was needed, might conceivably bring

Table 3.2. *Children with RQ 80– on the 7 + Reading Test (based on EPFAS figures)*

		1983–84	1984–85	1985–86	1986–87	1987–88
Phase 1:	Children tested	3036	2806	2867	3171	3242
	Number with RQ 80–	449	476	402	508	559
	% with RQ 80–	14.8	17.0	14.0	16.0	17.2
Phase 2:	Children tested	2148	2009	2067	2199	2338
	Number with RQ 80–	108	97	104	123	153
	% with RQ 80–	5.0	4.8	5.0	5.6	6.5
Phase 3:	Children tested	2456	2248	2328	2501	2599
	Number with RQ 80–	76	43	60	69	72
	% with RQ 80–	3.1	1.9	2.6	2.8	2.8
All:	Children tested	7640	7063	7262	7871	8179
	Number with RQ 80–	633	616	566	700	784
	% with RQ 80–	8.3	8.7	7.8	8.9	9.6

Table 3.3. *Children with RQ 80– on the 9 + Reading Test (based on EPFAS figures)*

		1983–84	1984–85	1985–86	1986–87	1987–88
Phase 1:	Children tested	411	385	355	297	307
	Number with RQ 80–	43	56	37	25	32
	% with RQ 80–	10.5	14.6	10.4	8.4	10.4
Phase 2:	Children tested	1035	969	946	894	943
	Number with RQ 80–	72	56	77	60	57
	% with RQ 80–	7.0	5.8	8.1	6.7	6.0
Phase 3:	Children tested	1852	1801	1668	1556	1672
	Number with RQ 80–	95	59	66	55	56
	% with RQ 80–	5.1	3.3	4.0	3.5	3.3
Middle:	Children tested	4866	4557	4424	4131	4042
	Number with RQ 80–	639	581	630	591	502
	% with RQ 80–	13.1	12.7	14.2	14.3	12.4
All:	Children tested	8164	7711	7393	6878	6964
	Number with RQ 80-	849	752	810	731	647
	% with RQ 80-	10.4	9.8	11.0	10.6	9.3

about a measurable improvement in the overall standard of reading in the school while making only a negligible impact on those children who were stuck at the earliest stages.

It is therefore important to look at the numbers of children scoring very high on the tests (i.e. those with reading quotients of 120 and above) as well as those scoring very low; and to examine the yearly mean raw score of the schools in each phase. These analyses have involved an examination of the original lists of individual children's scores forwarded to EPFAS over the years by the teachers who marked the tests. This has been a lengthy and laborious task, and would have been impossible without the help and cooperation of EPFAS. Inevitably with the passage of time some scores have gone missing, but the analyses which are summarized here were based on all that are still available. The numbers of children involved are set out in Table 3.4. In all, just under 70,000 test scores were available, although in Phase 1 schools there were nearly twelve times as many 7+ as 9+ scores to draw from, and in PNP schools as a whole, just over four and a half times as many. This is simply because the great majority of children taking the 9+ test were either in middle schools or in primary schools which were not yet in PNP.

Table 3.4. Numbers of Children with Available Scores on the 7+ and 9+ Reading Tests

		1983–84	1984–85	1985–86	1986–87	1987–88	Total
7+:	Phase 1	2518	2806	2795	2989	3190	14298
	Phase 2	1654	1929	2015	2147	2298	10043
	Phase 3	2195	2227	2288	2538	2582	11830
	7 + Total	6367	6962	7098	7674	8070	36171
9+:	Phase 1	243	286	237	230	225	1221
	Phase 2	754	849	872	688	828	3991
	Phase 3	1459	1800	1552	1615	1658	8084
	Middle	3324	4376	4164	4064	4190	20118
	9 + Total	5780	7311	6825	6597	6901	33414

Table 3.5. High, Medium and Low-scoring Children on the 7+ Reading Test (PRINDEP analysis of all available raw data)

		1983–84	1984–85	1985–86	1986–87	1987–88
Phase 1:	% with RQ 80–	12	15	14	14	16
	% with RQ 81–119	83	80	82	82	79
	% with RQ 120 +	5	5	4	5	5
Phase 2:	% with RQ 80–	4	5	6	6	7
	% with RQ 81–119	87	86	85	85	84
	% with RQ 120 +	9	10	9	9	9
Phase 3:	% with RQ 80–	3	2	2	3	2
	% with RQ 81–119	84	84	82	84	85
	% with RQ 120 +	13	14	16	13	13

The first task was to examine the proportion of children with reading quotients of 120 or above, and it is immediately clear from Table 3.5 and Figures 3.1 to 3.4 that this has remained virtually static over the last five years; what changes there are certainly do not indicate an upward or downward trend, and can safely be attributed to random variation. Thus the slight increase in the proportion of low-scoring children since the advent of PNP does not reflect an across-the-board deterioration in reading standards at 7+ .

Figure 3.1. Percentage of Children Scoring Low at 7+

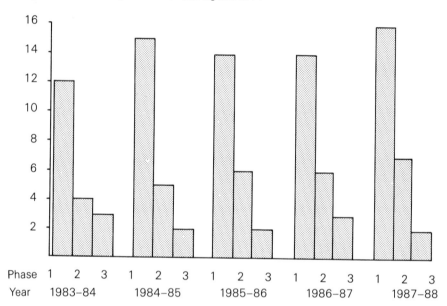

Table 3.6 and Figure 3.4 show an apparent slight rise in the proportion of high-scoring children at 9+ in PNP schools: since the advent of PNP the proportion in Phase 1 schools has risen from 5 per cent to 7 per cent and then to 9 per cent, while in Phase 2 schools there has been an increase from 7 per cent to 8 per cent. However, it is important to remember the size of the sample. We cannot sensibly claim significance for upward trends involving 5000 children while brushing aside the importance of downward trends involving 24,000; and when we include the results for the years before PNP in our analysis, the observed changes look more like random fluctuations than evidence of a genuine improvement in reading standards.

Figure 3.2. Percentage of Children Scoring High at 7+

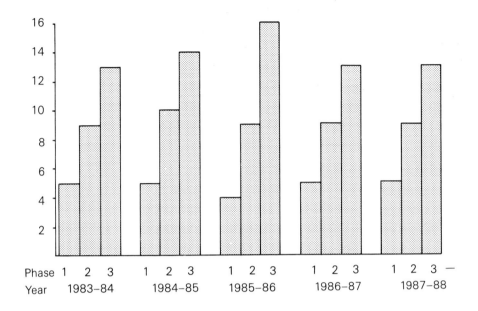

Figure 3.3. Percentage of Children Scoring low at 9+

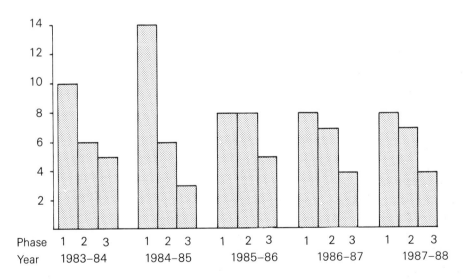

Figure 3.4. Percentage of Children Scoring High at 9+

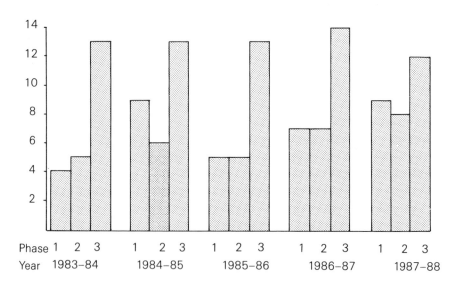

So far we have ignored what may be considered the most straightforward index of success on the tests, namely the test scores themselves. Mean raw scores from successive years will reflect any overall improvement or deterioration in reading, both within the separate phases of PNP and for the city as a whole. However, two factors must be borne in mind. First, scores from *the same test* in successive years do not relate to the same children, but to successive waves of children reaching the age range 7+ or 9+, and there may be marked differences between successive waves of children quite apart from the ways in which they have been taught reading. Second, scores from *the same group of children* at 7+ and again at 9+ are not derived from the same test. In general it would not be expected that two different tests administered two years apart would necessarily correlate very highly with each other.

Tables 3.7 and 3.8 show the mean scores on the two tests for each phase every year for the last five years. These scores are simply the means (or arithmetical averages) of the scores of all children doing the test: for example, the Phase 1 mean score of 25.9 on the 7+ test for the year 1983–84 is the average of the scores of all the 2518 children who did the test that year and whose test scores have survived.

The mean scores on both tests confirm what we have already learned: in general the children in Phase 1 and Phase 2 schools have been scoring lower than those in Phase 3 schools for many years, and PNP has not changed this state of affairs. Similarly, the scores from Phase 1 schools are (and have long been) lower than those from Phase 2 schools.

Table 3.6. High, Medium and Low-scoring Children on the 9+ Reading Test (PRINDEP analysis of all available raw data)

		1983–84	1984–85	1985–86	1986–87	1987–88
Phase 1:	% with RQ 80–	10	14	8	8	8
	% with RQ 81–119	86	78	87	85	83
	% with RQ 120 +	4	9	5	7	9
Phase 2:	% with RQ 80–	6	6	8	7	7
	% with RQ 81–119	89	88	87	86	85
	% with RQ 120 +	5	6	5	7	8
Phase 3:	% with RQ 80–	5	3	5	4	4
	% with RQ 81–119	82	84	82	82	84
	% with RQ 120 +	13	13	13	14	12
Middle	% with RQ 80–	12	12	14	13	12
	% with RQ 81–119	83	82	81	81	82
	% with RQ 120 +	6	5	5	6	6

Table 3.7. Mean Raw Scores on the 7+ Reading Test (PRINDEP analysis of all available raw data)

		1983–84	1984–85	1985–86	1986–87	1987–88
Phase 1:	Mean	25.9	24.8	25.9	25.7	25.0
	SD	10.4	10.4	10.3	10.2	10.2
Phase 2:	Mean	29.7	29.8	30.0	30.0	29.2
	SD	9.3	9.5	9.4	9.9	9.7
Phase 3:	Mean	31.6	32.1	32.6	32.2	32.1
	SD	8.9	8.7	8.5	8.9	8.7

Table 3.8. Mean Raw Scores on the 9+ Reading Test (PRINDEP analysis of all available raw data)

		1983–84	1984–85	1985–86	1986–87	1987–88
Phase 1:	Mean	22.3	21.6	21.9	22.4	22.5
	SD	7.2	7.9	7.5	7.1	7.6
Phase 2:	Mean	23.1	23.1	22.6	22.5	23.6
	SD	7.0	7.0	7.1	7.3	7.0
Phase 3:	Mean	25.2	25.2	25.0	25.6	25.4
	SD	6.5	6.1	6.5	6.2	6.2
Middle:	Mean	21.8	21.6	21.0	21.5	21.7
	SD	7.8	7.9	8.1	8.2	8.1

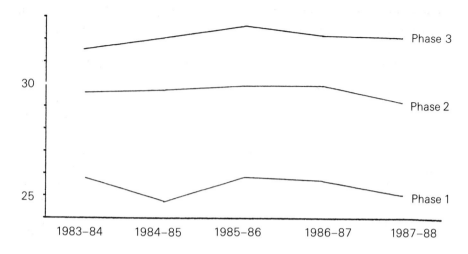

Figure 3.5. *7+ Mean Raw Scores*

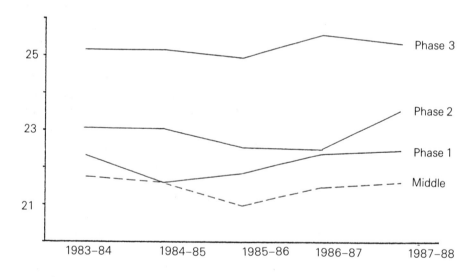

Figure 3.6. *9+ Mean Raw Scores*

At 7+ the mean scores from both Phase 1 and Phase 2 schools have fallen slightly since PNP began, while at 9+ there has been a slight rise in the mean scores. However, in each case the differences are extremely small, as can be clearly seen from the graphs in Figures 3.5 and 3.6 which are based on the data in Tables 3.7 and 3.8. If we take into account the scores which predate PNP, these changes again look less like real trends and more like random variations.

Tables 3.7 and 3.8 also include standard deviations (SDs). The standard deviation is a measure of the spread of scores about a mean. If the mean score on a particular test is about 50 per cent, this could mean that all the children scored between 45 per cent and 55 per cent (in which case the standard deviation would be very small), or it could mean that some children scored full marks while others achieved no marks at all (and here the standard deviation would be very large). In Tables 3.7 and 3.8 an increase in the standard deviation from year to year would indicate a gradual drawing apart of the most and the least successful children as the former forged ahead with their reading and the latter lagged ever further behind. A decrease would suggest that the slower readers might be receiving enough extra help to narrow the gap between themselves and the rest of the class (as well as raising the possibility that the most successful readers might be marking time rather than making further progress).

Table 3.7 shows that at 7+ the standard deviations have always been largest in those schools which are now in Phase 1 and smallest in the Phase 3 schools. This undoubtedly reflects the comparative heterogeneity of the school mix in Phase 1 schools, and the relatively high proportion of children with quite severe learning difficulties, and these are matters which are treated at some length in PRINDEP Report 7 (Chapter 2). It is noteworthy, however, that the standard deviation on this test in Phase 1 schools has grown very slightly smaller each year over the last five years, and this might suggest a narrowing of the gap between the least and the most able readers at this age. Elsewhere and at 9+ there is no very striking pattern in the fluctuation of standard deviations from one year to the next.

There remains one further analysis which may, for some readers, put the whole of the foregoing into a clearer perspective. Teachers are very familiar with the idea of converting raw scores into reading ages, and the raw scores in Tables 3.7 and 3.8 can easily be treated in this way (although it is important to bear in mind the cautionary remarks quoted earlier from the test manual). In relation to the 7+ test it is simply a matter of consulting the table of reading ages in the manual; for the 9+ test there is no such table and it is necessary to use the table of standard scores to determine the age at which a particular raw score yields a reading quotient of 100. The resulting reading ages are set out in Table 3.9. For the 7+ test they are the familiar decimal reading ages (7.5 means 7½ years, or 7 years 6 months, not 7 years 5 months). For the 9+ test, however, the values are given in years and months for the reason explained above.

Table 3.9 and the related graph in Figure 3.7 give a clear indication of how small the changes are which have taken place over a five-year period. In each of the three groups of schools taking the 7+ test, the mean reading age has never varied by more than a tenth of a year. The fluctuations which show up clearly in the earlier analyses are thus seen to be of negligible practical significance. At 9+ some of the fluctuations are a little wider, but still small.

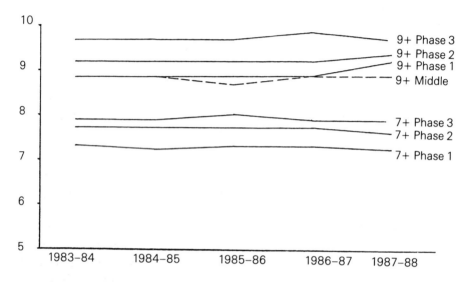

Figure 3.7. *Mean Reading Age at 7+ and 9+; PNP, Non-PNP and Middle Schools*

Table 3.9. *Mean Reading Ages on the 7+ and 9+ Reading Tests*

		1983–84	1984–85	1985–86	1986–87	1987–88
7+ :	Phase 1	7.4	7.3	7.4	7.4	7.3
	Phase 2	7.8	7.8	7.8	7.8	7.7
	Phase 3	8.0	8.0	8.1	8.0	8.0
9+ :	Phase 1	9–00	9–00	9–00	9–00	9–00
	Phase 2	9–03	9–03	9–03	9–03	9–06
	Phase 3	9–09	9–09	9–09	10–00	9–09
	Middle	9–00	9–00	8–10	9–00	9–00

Table 3.9 also reveals that reading standards in the Authority's primary schools as a whole have for many years been entirely unexceptional. It would scarcely be surprising if, when the extra resources of PNP became available, heads and their senior colleagues turned their attention first to objectives which had previously seemed unrealizable, and which have since been listed in the Authority's primary education policy statement. In short, it seems as if without in any way neglecting reading, teachers have been devoting the bulk of their effort to areas where the need was more pressing. In the words of one of the teachers quoted elsewhere (Chapter 4):

> It goes very much further than teaching them subjects.... It doesn't stop at the school gate.... I still have a commitment to wanting the children to be literate and numerate, and I could do that, but it would be to the exclusion of everything else I want to do. So there is a conflict.... It's all the time trying to strike a balance. You just hope you've got that right.

There is other evidence to support the proposition that, in general, reading has not been among the top priorities of PNP. For example, PRINDEP Report 8 (Chapter 4) gives an account of a survey of teacher attendance at courses, and shows that only half of the Phase 2 schools and fewer than half of the Phase 1 schools in the PRINDEP representative sample have participated in any reading courses since PNP began. Even this proportion is surprisingly high. In the Authority's own programme of in-service support for PNP the main emphasis has been on teaching strategies, classroom organization, curriculum leadership and so on, while reading courses (unlike courses relating to some other areas of the curriculum) have played a very small part indeed, accounting for well under 5 per cent of the total number of courses offered since PNP began.

Further evidence comes from an examination, also reported in detail in PRINDEP Report 8, of the amount of the Authority's PNP development funds devoted to the various curricular areas by both Phase 1 and Phase 2 schools. In each of the two phases the proportion of the available money used for reading schemes has been small, although it has steadily increased from year to year as other more pressing problems have been resolved. Over the first three years of Phase 1 the proportion rose from 6.6 per cent in 1985–86, through 12.5 per cent the following year, to 16.6 per cent in 1987–88. Over the first two years of Phase 2 the proportion rose from 9.7 per cent to 13.3 per cent.

There are other ways in which the Authority seeks to support teachers and influence their practice in the teaching of reading, ranging from intensive activities like the annual reading week to the day-to-day work of advisers and advisory teachers. However, in comparison with certain areas — mathematics in particular and to a lesser degree science as well — reading appears not to have been one of the Authority's priorities in recent years. It should be pointed out, however, that, unlike mathematics and science, reading has not received any additional government funding. Indeed, the whole field of language remains, since long before Bullock and Kingman, notably underfunded in relation to what is deemed to be its educational primacy.

This is significant in the present context in that the relatively high profile enjoyed recently by primary mathematics and science in Leeds has been partly a consequence of national initiatives like PrIME and the DES Education Support Grants scheme (ESG) in science. In the case of science the LEA has been able to combine national and local funds; in the case of mathematics the local investment has gained added impetus from association, if not direct funding, from PrIME, and from a national climate of the strongest possible endorsement of the subject's importance. Reading, in contrast, has experienced a curious ambivalence in its national and local profile. At both levels it is held to be of the utmost importance, yet this commitment has extended neither to specific policy initiatives nor to support grants and projects.

Conclusion

The 7+ and 9+ reading tests administered annually by Leeds LEA have been used primarily as a screening device to enable EPFAS and individual schools to identify and provide for children with reading difficulties. Since they have been administered systematically in every primary and middle school for many years, these tests also provide a unique resource for other kinds of analysis, not least in relation to the evaluation of PNP. However, we stress the dangers of using a procedure like a reading test for purposes other than those for which it was designed. We can analyze what has happened to reading scores before and during PNP, and we can speculate about what we find, but it is not really legitimate to view reading scores as more than partial or contributory indicators of the impact or efficacy of the Primary Needs Programme.

PRINDEP has studied all the available reading test results from 1983–84 onwards and has subjected the 70,000 or so individual test scores to various kinds of computer analysis. We have examined, for each PNP phase and for both the 7+ and 9+ tests, the reading quotients and raw scores at the bottom, top and middle of the range, the means or averages, the standard deviations or spread of scores, and the mean reading ages.

There are substantial differences between the means of the scores of schools in Phase 1, Phase 2 and what is now Phase 3, but since these same scores were used as one of the two criteria for selecting PNP schools in the first place, this is hardly surprising. There are annual fluctuations in the high and low scores for each PNP phase, but no more than can be explained in terms of expected random variation; and the mean reading ages for each phase, and for the city as a whole, have remained remarkably steady for the whole of the five-year period.

Such results point inescapably to two overall conclusions. First, as measured by the 7+ and 9+ tests, PNP has had no dramatic positive or negative effect on reading standards in the city's primary schools. Second, whatever else primary schools in Leeds have been doing over the past few years, they have continued to devote attention to the teaching of reading, and in this respect PRINDEP's findings for Leeds mirror those of HMI for the country as a whole.

The period since 1985 has been one of change and development for Leeds primary schools, sometimes on a large scale and often in new and challenging directions. Change of this kind, whatever its long-term benefits, invariably also carries the risk of short-term destabilization. The staff of Phase 1 schools bore the brunt of this. They had to cope with the day-to-day consequences of a major and radical policy initiative which changed its emphasis during its first year. Many of them experienced serious confusion about its very nature and unease about the way it was introduced and disseminated. The introduction of Phase 1 also coincided with major industrial action by the teacher associations. The disruptive impact of building and minor works programmes has also been most severe in Phase 1. In short, though there are few teachers who would characterize the national educational climate of the last few years as anything less than precarious, for Phase 1 teachers this precariousness has had an added local dimension.

It could be argued that to maintain consistency in basic educational activities against this sort of background can be counted as no mean achievement. That kind of judgment, however, we leave to others, since it could be argued equally that change is a basic and necessary condition of education which schools should expect to cope with as part of their daily work. It could also be argued that as far as reading test scores are concerned there is no cause for complacency either. In any event, PRINDEP's analysis raises a number of questions.

The fact that reading scores have been stable does not necessarily mean that they have been as high as they could have been or that all children have been reaching their potential. It is very easy, but not really legitimate, to translate current attainment levels into future expectations and norms, and to be content if the next generation does no worse than the last. That kind of thinking carries an obvious and suspect circularity. Anyone reading this report is bound to ask: could the situation be improved? Should it be?

The question has added point in the context of the analysis contained in PRINDEP Report 7 (Chapter 2), where we raised important issues about how the needs of particular children are defined and met at LEA and school level in Leeds and about the kinds of educational expectations which are held of them. Since there is a well-established relationship between what we expect of a child in school and what that child achieves, we should be doubly wary about treating test scores in any way as indicators of potential. They tell us what the child has achieved already; nothing more.

The discrepancy between the initial highlighting of reading, through its use as a major criterion for selecting PNP schools, and its subsequently reduced emphasis in the Primary Needs Programme itself, might seem to an outsider to be distinctly odd, even though to insiders the reason is clear enough. PNP was not a remedial reading package but a comprehensive programme aimed at enhancing the quality of primary education across the board, and reading seemed as good a basis as any for allocating PNP resources. Even so, the discrepancy does provoke two interesting questions. First, what would have happened to reading attainment if the reading criterion had been followed through into specific reading provision in the schools thereby selected? Second, applying this to the curriculum as a whole, what are the relative merits of specific targeting of particular curriculum areas as opposed to a generalized investment, PNP-style, in curriculum breadth and classroom quality? Most readers will be aware of HMI's 1978 survey conclusion that progress in the basics is best achieved in the context of a broad curriculum. However, it does not follow that a broad curriculum of itself delivers such progress. On the contrary, HMI showed that progress requires both breadth *and* depth, together with the kinds of professional expertise and support which will secure them.

The importance of this issue is underlined by our reference above to the advantage the Authority has gained from national support for primary mathematics and science. In these cases, at least, the Authority has been able to pursue both curriculum breadth and depth in its own professional development activities. Can such a combination be pursued only with that kind of support? If so, is there a case for seeking it for other curriculum areas (such as reading) or for looking again at the distribution of existing funds? In any event, regardless of the availability of external funding, does a project like PrIME offer a model for professional support and curriculum development which the Authority might usefully extend to areas other than mathematics?

Our figures show standard deviations to be largest in Phase 1 schools.

This could indicate a wider gap in such schools between the ablest and least able readers, and/or a higher proportion of children scoring at the extremes. In many such schools the gap is indeed wide and there is a high proportion of less able readers. The transfer to some of these schools of numbers of children with moderate learning difficulties will tend to accentuate this. Consequently the challenge to Phase 1 schools in terms of teacher skill must be greater than in many schools in later PNP phases. Is the level and kind of support for these teachers what it should be?

Relatedly, and referring back to Chapter 6, if the teaching of reading is of itself a complex and challenging professional task, and if on top of that the professional needs of teachers in respect of reading are so variable, to what extent can a still fairly modest and generalized programme of centralized INSET courses on reading meet such diverse challenges and needs?

Few would dispute the status of reading as a basic skill. It is in fact an array of skills, many of them not tapped by the kinds of screening tests used by this and other LEAs. Given the general emphasis in PNP on breadth and richness in children's educational experiences, and the allocation of enhanced staffing and material resources to achieve this, might it not be reasonable to expect children to make considerable progress as a result of PNP, not so much in fundamental reading skills as in their general attitudes to reading? Schools are investing a good deal of time and effort to provide an environment where children and parents are encouraged to enjoy books, and the extent of their success in this cannot be measured in raw scores and reading ages.

The government's National Curriculum testing programme is bound to raise the further question of whether the Authority should continue its own independent testing of reading. Children coming into reception classes in September 1989 will be tested in 1991, and although theirs will be an 'unreported' or trial run, the tests taken by the 1990 cohort in 1992 will probably not be. What, then, happens to the Leeds 7+ and 9+ tests, given the arrival of the SEAC testing programme and the fact that the SEAC Standard Assessment Tasks in reading could well cover a wider range of skills than do the Young's and NFER tests used in Leeds? What happens to the Authority's policy on the teaching of reading meanwhile?

These are all questions which PRINDEP can raise but others will have to answer. For the time being the undeniably useful exercise of testing reading attainment and diagnosing reading difficulties at 7+ and 9+ will continue. As we move into the preparation of the project's final report, we shall supplement the kind of analysis offered here by looking more closely at differences between schools as well as between PNP phases and considering how such differences might be explained.

4
The Curriculum: Policy and Management

Introduction

We noted at the beginning of the previous chapter that the Primary Needs Programme was less concerned with the specific content of the curriculum than with its general character and context. Thus, one of the main aims of PNP was 'to develop a broadly-based curriculum within an environment rich in stimulus and challenge . . . '. Thus, too, the recurrence of certain key terms and phrases in LEA documents and in-service courses, indicating the kinds of practice teachers and heads were expected to strive for: 'flexible teaching strategies', 'quality learning environment', 'first-hand experience', 'thematic approach' and so on. These constituted an imprecise but nevertheless powerful shorthand, whose progressive antecedents are unmistakable. The language is familiarly and comfortably that of mainstream primary education. Alongside it, however, appeared newer messages concerning, for example, parental involvement, equal opportunities, multiculturalism, early years provision and the teaching of science and mathematics. Many of these echoed concerns expressed by HMI and DES during the late 1970s and early 1980s.

The two views of curriculum stand in marked contrast to each other and effectively illustrate the gulf between recent professional and political ideologies in primary education. One espouses a timeless, culturally disengaged universality — the classic child-centred position; the other requires instrumental relevance to what are perceived as society's most immediate needs (Ashton, 1981; Alexander, 1988).

It was also clear that the LEA recognized that to appeal to individual teachers in isolation was not enough. The curriculum and curriculum change required deliberate acts of collective management, and an agenda emerged which indicated the responsibilities of heads, deputies and senior staff in this regard, emphasized the key role of the PNP coordinator (explored in detail in Chapter 5), and, drawing on our own material (see Chapter 7), began to explore the potential of professional collaboration in the classroom. Again, in many respects this agenda borrowed from the official one emanating from Elizabeth House and Westminster, particularly the HMI primary surveys and the 1986 Select Committee Report on primary education (DES, 1978a, 1982; House of Commons, 1986).

Curriculum is a broad and complicated field, and there are those who might suggest that the LEA's published concept of curriculum was at the same time incomplete and somewhat vague. However, though we raise this possibility in the final part of the present chapter, it is not at this stage our main concern. Instead, given that the LEA opted for a strategy in which messages on curriculum delivered authoritatively from above were prominent, it seemed necessary that our first task in opening up the agreed theme of curriculum should be to examine the impact of such messages at school level.

To this end, we pursued four lines of enquiry. First, in 1987, we conducted an interview programme with heads and teachers in the thirty Fieldwork B (representative sample) schools. This explored respondents' knowledge and understanding of the LEA's policy and messages on curriculum and the ways these were being implemented in classrooms. The interviews also covered respondents' awareness of their own schools' curriculum policy, and finally explored the strategies being used to review and co-ordinate curriculum throughout the school. Second, a programme of follow-up interviews in 1988 focused more precisely on the management of curriculum development at school level, concentrating on the allocation of posts of curriculum responsibility, the particular areas of curriculum being reviewed or developed, and the strategies being used. Third, a linked observation programme in some sixteen of the sample schools studied the purposes, content, format and dynamics of staff curriculum meetings. We did this because both the LEA and many of the heads asserted that whole-staff discussion was the key to successful curriculum development at school level. Finally, we gathered and analyzed two related sets of data on support for curriculum development provided by the LEA: schools' use of the extra capitation allocated under PNP, and teachers' attendance at curriculum-related in-service courses.

The study is in three parts. Part 1 considers issues arising from the 1987 and 1988 interviews: how successfully the LEA messages on curriculum were disseminated and how they were received and interpreted by heads and teachers. Part 2 looks at the management of curriculum development and offers perspectives on activities taking place during 1987 and 1988. Part 3 identifies and discusses three critical issues which emerged from the fieldwork: curriculum management in the school; relationships between schools and the LEA; and the reality of the 'broadly-based curriculum'.

It should be noted that the schools referred to as 'non-PNP' had that status during the two years in question. They became third phase PNP schools in September 1988.

Part 1: The LEA Message: Attitudes and Understandings

Although heads and teachers had rather different perspectives to offer on LEA messages about curriculum in 1987, three general issues emerged from the discussions which were common to both groups. First, almost universally, heads and teachers acknowledged that they were aware of the existence of an LEA policy on curriculum. Moreover, when outlining LEA policy, many respondents' choice of wording indicated just how forcefully they felt it was being delivered:

> The LEA is pushing . . . .
> There is pressure . . . .
> They are interested in . . . .
> The LEA preach . . . .
> Messages are coming through strongly . . . .
> Mr X really prefers . . . .
> This Authority wants us to . . . .
> We must try to . . . .
> The LEA's wishes . . . .
> The advisers say we have to . . . .

Second, when asked how they had come to hear about LEA policy on curriculum, virtually all respondents said it was from courses, the advisory team or from their colleagues. Often the PNP Coordinator was singled out as the transmitter of PNP messages. The few heads who suggested they might have encountered the policy in writing were, by and large, the ones who also indicated that they did not know or agree with it. Some respondents specifically volunteered that it was an oral message:

> It's not written down, it comes from courses and from colleagues. (Head of a Phase 1 school)

> There's nothing in school except the coordinator's job description. (Head of a Phase 2 school)

> I have never seen the policy in writing. (Coordinator in a Phase 1 school)

Third, in response to the question, 'How do you think the policy was arrived at?' the vast majority of respondents said categorically that it was the philosophy and direct influence of the Director of Primary Education himself, or the primary advisory team. A few indicated that this 'philosophy' was one that reflected a long-standing tradition of primary practice:

> All the elements of good primary practice, which have been around for years, have been crystallized into the PNP programme. (Scale II teacher in a Phase 1 school)

> It's just what everyone has been doing all along. (Scale I teacher in a Phase 2 school)

Others suggested it incorporated the recommendations from national bodies: HMI, DES, the Cockcroft and Bullock Reports were mentioned. However, a small number of respondents stated that they had no idea where the policy had come from.

Several conclusions may be inferred from these responses. By the summer of 1987, the notion of a PNP message about the curriculum had become firmly embedded in the professional consciousness of Leeds primary teachers and heads. Disregarding respondents' opinions as to the acceptability or value of this message, it undoubtedly had a powerful presence and was felt to exert some considerable pressure. As one teacher remarked:

> There is a great deal written and spoken about curriculum issues today. It comes from a great many sources: the LEA and their advisers, the government, the media, academics, the unions. Each brings with it its own pressure which schools are finding harder and harder to ignore. I would suggest that in Leeds, PNP is fairly difficult to ignore. (Scale III teacher in a Phase 1 school)

Moreover, it should be remembered that the PNP message had been delivered almost entirely through *oral* channels of communication: via extensive in-service activity by the advisers and subsequent feedback from colleagues and also via school-based advisory contact. It is likely that this very strategy has been a major factor in the success of the dissemination process. A direct parallel, at school level, would be those heads who recognize that any attempt to influence practice solely by means of a written policy document rarely meets with success. Even so, as we show elsewhere, oral messages can be selectively listened to and variously interpreted. Feedback by colleagues may not always ensure accurate reportage, and above all it requires that the relayer has both the opportunity and aptitude to transmit the message convincingly. All or any of these points should be taken into account when considering, in our next two sections, the reception of the PNP messages on curriculum by heads and by teachers.

Headteachers and the PNP Message

When the headteachers from the PRINDEP sample were asked, 'Do you know the main principles concerning the primary curriculum as a whole which are contained in the LEA's PNP policy?', many of their responses employed the well-known PNP phrases, or personalized versions of them:

Broadly-based . . . .
It should be broad . . . .
As wide a curriculum as possible . . . .

Relevant . . . .
Practical . . . .
Creative . . . .
Offer enriching experiences . . . .

A variety of teaching styles . . . .
Teach flexibly . . . .
Have flexible teaching approaches . . . .

First-hand experience . . . .
Offer lots of different experiences . . . .
We must interest the children, getting them to learn by discovery . . . .
Use the local environment . . . .

Children to work to their own ability . . . .
Every child is special . . . .
Treat every child as an individual . . . .

There were notable differences between phases of school in the use of the terms 'broad' and 'broadly-based', the characteristic of the curriculum that the LEA articulates in its aims for PNP. Most Phase 1 heads repeated this phrase; it was used less by Phase 2 heads and by only one non-PNP head.

Disregarding phase of school, the replies to this question fell largely into four types:

1. those heads who chose to reiterate the standard PNP phrases on curriculum, and to state that they concurred with LEA policy;
2. those heads who expressed themselves in such a way as to suggest

they were uncertain about curriculum policy in Leeds;
3. those heads who said that they knew PNP policy, but chose to express some divergence from it, demurring in one or more of the following ways:
    — that they did not attach much importance to what it said;
    — that they did not find it very useful;
    — that they did not agree with its style of delivery;
4. those heads who stated that they did not know what the PNP policy on curriculum was.

The group who said they did not know PNP policy did not include any Phase 1 heads or any Phase 2 heads who had their complement of PNP staffing, but all other viewpoints were expressed by heads from each phase of the programme. It was difficult to avoid the conclusion that several of the heads' responses were influenced by a disappointment with their schools' current position in relation to PNP staffing and/or additional capitation. In other words, a question about PNP curriculum policy also — and perhaps inevitably — revealed respondents' attitudes towards the makers and principal proponents of that policy.

Taking this dimension into account, the varying responses of heads to LEA messages about curriculum might be classified as *concurring*, *uncertain* and *demurring*. This categorization is intended to convey broad trends: it is not meant to depict, characterize or caricature individuals. Nevertheless, further trends became apparent in subsequent fieldwork: very often the headteachers who had responded with each of these three broadly different attitudes towards LEA messages had other aspects of curriculum management in common.

Type One: Concurring Responses

Typical responses in the concurring category were:

> The LEA policy is to have a broad curriculum with more first-hand experience for children and a variety of teaching styles according to what's being taught and children's needs . . . . (Head of a Phase 1 school)

> We should aim at a broad curriculum — children should be given practical and first-hand experience, using the local environment. Children must work to their own ability . . . . (Head of a Phase 2 school)

The main principles embodied in LEA thinking on curriculum are that it should be broadly based, practical and creative. These are the principles that I believe should guide any curriculum initiative.... (Head of a Phase 1 school)

The curriculum should be broadly based, and include problem-solving, communication skills, and personal development. It should all be enriched by the quality learning environment and first-hand experience.... (Head of a non-PNP school)

Very often heads in this category went on to acknowledge how fundamental these principles were to their own school and way of working:

PNP constitutes the whole philosophy of this school.... (Head of a Phase 2 school)

I am in total agreement (with LEA's policy on curriculum). I cannot imagine how a school runs without these principles.... (Head of a Phase 1 school)

Further questioning revealed that a number of these heads felt they had a supportive relationship with their schools' adviser and also recognized and had utilized the advisory team as a professional development resource for school-based INSET activity. Significantly, the in-service attendance for their schools was usually above average, taking into account the phase and staffing level of the school. In other words, familiarity was ensured by their schools' frequent first-hand contact with LEA messages at both central and school level.

Type Two: Uncertain Responses

There was, in contrast to heads who concurred with PNP curriculum policy, a category of heads who appeared to be unclear about the curriculum principles which the LEA was advocating:

It's constantly changing — at the moment I think it seems to be about staff development, internal and external, curriculum change, teach flexibly in groups.... (Head of a Phase 1 school)

The main principles seem to be about presenting opportunities for children to reach their full potential, treating them as individuals and meeting individual needs. They also speak about children with special needs and the importance of meeting these.... (Head of a Phase 2 school)

Responses like these were classified as 'uncertain' because they did not address the characteristics of the PNP curriculum, despite the Authority's very public statements on this issue. Only a very small number of heads were in this category. It was found that heads who gave imprecise responses to this question generally lacked clarity about their own schools' curriculum aims and development strategies. Not surprisingly, teacher INSET attendances were usually below average (for phase and staffing levels) in these schools. Very often these heads felt they had relatively little contact with their adviser, and some commented that they did not receive, or know how to request, the kinds of curriculum support they wished for.

Type Three: Demurring Responses

The third group of respondents were those heads who in some way chose to distance themselves from PNP curriculum policy, and/or its policy-makers. Some heads in this category implied that they did not take much notice of LEA policy:

> We pay little attention to these things on a day-to-day basis, but as we do try to cater for individual children's needs, we must pay some attention indirectly . . . . (Head of a Phase 2 school)

> I only take what I think is correct . . . . (Head of a Phase 1 school)

> I have always done my own thing here . . . . (Head of a Phase 2 school)

Some indicated that they did not find it very useful and sometimes additionally commented on their discomfort with its style of delivery:

> I know we were on that wavelength before PNP . . . . (Head of a Phase 1 school)

> Leeds is behind us [the old West Riding], and PNP is an attempt to catch up . . . . (Head of a non-PNP school)

> [PNP curriculum policy] has been at the centre of primary education for years. They seem to treat us all with contempt, offering us something we've had for years and getting upset when we do not respond as positively or enthusiastically as they wish . . . . (Head of a Phase 2 school)

> Of course I am in total sympathy with what the Authority is trying to do for the curriculum of its primary schools, but I am not always

so sure I agree with the way they've gone about it. Good practice didn't need bringing to this school. It was already here and needs to be nurtured and appreciated . . . . (Head of a Phase 2 school)

Finally, there was a very small number of heads who claimed that they did not know LEA policy on curriculum.

As head, I'm aware of all current curriculum initiatives e.g. Curriculum 5–16, Cockcroft. I'm not sure what is contained in the Authority's PNP policy, although I imagine they're in line with current national thoughts . . . . (Head of a Phase 2 school)

As we're not PNP I don't know — I know the principles that govern this school, I'm not sure if they match up . . . . I just don't attach much importance because this is a good school, in a good catchment area, our pupils read by the time they leave us and the parents and feeder school are happy . . . . (Head of a non-PNP school)

These answers were classified as an extreme form of demurring because, as the last example shows, the respondents often went on to reveal they were not so much unintentionally ignorant of LEA messages on curriculum as selectively ignoring them. However, as already stated, this response came only from a very small number of non-PNP heads, and from those in the programme who, in the summer of 1987, had not yet received their PNP development funding or additional complement of staffing. It is at least possible that professing ignorance of LEA curriculum policy was the reaction of those who themselves felt selectively ignored and overlooked by PNP.

Overall, then, the group of heads classified as 'demurring' expressed, in various ways, some distance between themselves and the Authority's PNP message. The motivation for their divergence from PNP policy — and sometimes the policy-makers — seems variable. Given that no head suggested direct or complete opposition to the PNP message itself, the source of their discontent seemed to lie elsewhere. Two very different kinds of demurring head became apparent.

For some heads it would appear that the very idea of higher authority suggesting a version of good practice for their school was considered unnecessary, intrusive and inappropriate. Their hostility arose from a sense of encroachment. It would seem also that the implications of the PNP message, with its commitment to change and to more rigorous — and delegated — curriculum development, clashed with some heads' own particular management style — or lack of it. This group's demurring appears to be related to a view of headship which highly values autonomy and stability, and for this reason it could be labelled 'traditionalist'. Like the group who were less than clear about PNP curriculum policy, some of these heads also were imprecise about strategies for developing curriculum within the school, or alternatively retained tight control over the procedures they did employ. Their schools tended to have below average INSET attendance. A number of these heads also indicated that they did not often receive, or particularly encourage, advisory contact on curriculum issues at school level.

Other heads who expressed some divergence from the Authority, however, chose to emphasize their disappointment with the content of the PNP message itself: it was simply not informative, innovative or subtle enough. Generally these were heads (from every phase of the programme) who were seriously attempting to advance practice and encourage curriculum responsibility in their schools, and because of this commitment to contemporary approaches to school management, their demurring could be labelled 'modernist'. They welcomed the additional resources — in-service, staffing and financial — that the PNP programme did (or would) provide, but considered that the curriculum messages, albeit entirely laudable, were somewhat underpowered. Despite having above average INSET attendance, these heads often felt a lack of advisory contact with their schools. They valued and encouraged professional dialogue among their staff and regretted that such open interchange about curriculum issues was not occurring enough between schools and the Authority. Several indicated that, in an authority where remediating practice has been felt to be a very necessary first consideration, the professional development needs of its more able heads, in relation to curriculum and curriculum management, may have temporarily had to take second place.

After outlining their understanding of, and attitude towards, LEA policy on curriculum as a whole, the heads were then asked what they thought it meant in terms of school and classroom practice. Not surprisingly, this open question triggered a variety of answers, but it was clear that responding to PNP messages, by and large, provoked consideration of a number of fundamental curriculum issues and this sample of heads discussed the implications of these messages by referring to one or more of the following: the *design* of the curriculum; the *delivery* of the curriculum; *differentiation* within the curriculum.

Design of the PNP Curriculum

Some heads chose to pinpoint those subject areas which they felt needed to be present in order to meet the criteria of a 'broadly-based' curriculum.

> More science, with practical work and art and craft . . . . (Head of a Phase 1 school)

> The importance of creative subjects like art and drama, and the integration of maths with science and CDT . . . . (Head of a Phase 2 school)

> The LEA has drawn our attention to science and gender . . . . (Head of a Phase 1 school)

Others answered by giving consideration to the *overall* design or substance of the PNP curriculum, and gave their interpretation of the meaning of 'broadly-based'. On occasion, these had notably differing emphases:

> Broadly-based means maths and language as priorities and other subjects in order of importance . . . . (Head of a Phase 2 school)

> A broad curriculum [means] one area of the curriculum is not more important than another . . . all areas of the curriculum should be represented in every classroom . . . . (Head of a Phase 1 school)

> It means getting away from the 3Rs, as practical as possible and first-hand experience . . . . (Head of a Phase 2 school)

> A mixture of traditional and enjoyment activities, a mixture of spontaneous and planned activities . . . . (Head of a Phase 1 school)

Possibly these heads were not saying anything fundamentally different from each other: the commitment to include, and yet go beyond, the 'basics' is apparent in all cases. However, such responses could also intimate that consensus on the meaning of the 'broadly-based curriculum' cannot be assumed, and a serious attempt to define its implications is an important exercise at school level. Pages 123–6 contain extracts from extended discussions held with heads and teachers in 1988 and these clearly show that any attempt to define the 'broadly-based curriculum' may involve staff in considering and reconciling a number of other fundamental curriculum issues — balance, progression, range and depth of subject understanding.

Delivery of the PNP Curriculum

When asked about their understanding of PNP curriculum messages in relation to school and classroom practice, some heads chose to refer to teaching approaches. In other words, to them, the Authority's message spoke forcefully about how, as much as what, to teach. Here consensus was much more evident: 'grouping children' and 'flexible teaching styles' were most frequently mentioned. A few heads went on to acknowledge that curriculum delivery and the notion of 'flexibility' were highly complex issues, not easily prescribed or dictated.

Differentiation within the PNP Curriculum

Several heads, when describing their interpretation of LEA messages, referred to the principle of differentiation within the PNP curriculum. They spoke in such terms as: 'taking into account each child as an individual', 'providing for all needs', 'assessing each child on an individual basis, and catering for them according to ability'. These are all incontestable educational principles and, as Chapter 2 showed, differentiation has been prominent in all PNP policy and rhetoric. However, it was generally those heads who were classified as 'uncertain' about PNP policy who responded solely in these terms.

Finally, there was a small group of heads whose answers implied that the onus for implementing and interpreting PNP curriculum policy lay not with them but with their teachers.

> Classroom practice is up to the class teacher . . . . (Head of a non-PNP school)

> How the principles are applied is up to the individual teacher . . . . (Head of a Phase 2 school)

Other heads, who equally acknowledged teachers' own responsibility towards implementing PNP policy, were acutely aware of how important but complex an area influencing practice is:

> We always talk about matching work to the individual needs and abilities of children. For me, that doesn't stop when you're an adult. You can't just tell teachers what the policy is on good practice, or the curriculum or whatever, and then send them off to do it. So, I'm talking about individual teachers' abilities and understandings being catered for as well, and for that to happen we — heads, advisers and teachers — all need to make sure certain principles are really understood. (Head of a Phase 1 school)

Such insights open up the area of structuring, guiding and supporting the work of the classroom practitioner. As the next section will show, there has been a substantial investment by the advisory service to offer such structure and support in matters of classroom practice and curriculum delivery.

Teachers and the PNP Message

In the summer term of 1987 teachers from the PRINDEP sample of schools were interviewed about their understanding of PNP policy on curriculum. Their responses, like those of the headteachers, focused on curriculum *design, delivery and differentiation*. Very few teachers used the term 'broadly-based curriculum'. As classroom practitioners, their emphasis was much more heavily placed on *delivery*, that is, how their pupils' learning experiences should be organized. This is perhaps to be expected as the Authority had given clear advice and guidance on classroom management in its courses to class teachers and probationers during 1987. Teachers' replies to the question, 'Do you know the main principles concerning the primary curriculum as a whole which are contained in the LEA's PNP policy?' showed considerable consensus on what the LEA expected: integration of subject areas, experiential learning and grouping. Typical responses in each of these areas were:

Topic-based learning as much as possible . . . .
Cross-curricular approach . . . .
Thematic approach . . . .
Integrate all the topics and include everything in what we do . . . .
All subjects covered . . . .
Mr X believes in the linked-up curriculum . . . .
Moving away from the 3Rs, the whole curriculum approached through topic . . . .
Don't divide into subjects, the work should be organized on a topic base . . . .

Practical . . . .
First-hand experience . . . .
Children to talk more . . . .
Take children on visits . . . .
Learning from practical experience . . . .
Learning from personal experience . . . .
Learning by discovery . . . .
Children be asked to think more and carry out practical activities . . . .
Not watch TV . . . .

Use the TV and try to broaden [children's] outlook . . . .

Group teaching . . . .
Group work . . . .
Grouping by ability . . . .
Children to work in groups doing different things . . . .
The LEA want different activities going on in each group . . . .
Not class teaching . . . .
The advisers are interested in seeing more group work in classrooms . . . .
Group work is the favoured way of teaching . . . .
Children in small groups on different activities . . . .

A few teachers referred to curriculum differentiation and design:

We should deal with individual needs . . . .
Meeting the needs of individual children . . . .
We must present more than the basics — also subjects like science and art . . . .
The LEA is pushing basics, especially reading — but also science and maths are to the fore.

Some also stressed classroom arrangements:

The classroom should be organized in bays . . . .
Arranging the classroom differently to seat groups of children . . . .

or mentioned the whole area of collaboration:

Team teaching . . . .
Being part of a team . . . .
Have a cooperative approach . . . .

It was obvious from these interviews that many of the teachers were in accord with what the LEA was advising them to do:

It is the best approach to teaching . . . .
The group system is the most sensible . . . .
The natural way of working . . . .
That's how my class works. Personally I feel I couldn't class teach . . . .
The only way that children learn . . . .
It's part and parcel of my everyday practice . . . .

However, the interviews also revealed that such clear prescriptions could produce tensions and dilemmas as teachers attempted to absorb and adapt the PNP message to their existing practice.

Some found the school contexts in which they were working made implementation difficult. As an example, a probationer identified the constraints of her school and pupils:

> I cannot carry out these principles — children cannot cope with choice or a work programme, I'd have to be on their backs all the time. And I can't do exclusively topic-based either. The way this school works does not match up with a total cross-curricular approach. It may be possible in a school where the children are more subdued. (Probationer in a Phase 1 school)

Instead of referring just to their own difficulties (and perhaps, in the former case, inexperience), some teachers tended to contest the value of prescription. For example, a more experienced teacher indicated that the suggested method of classroom organization caused a lowering of standards:

> It makes life more difficult. The theory is that everything should be related to everyday life, more emphasis on children finding things out rather than approaching the teacher, groups doing lots of different things at the same time. This is great in theory but hard in practice, e.g. in maths — I've found the non-intensive groups' work is not of the same quality . . . . (Scale II teacher in a Phase 2 school)

This teacher's intuitive critique of the practice that she believed she was expected to implement coincides with the findings of ILEA's recent research into effective junior schools. Two of the conclusions of that study are:

> Where the tendency was for the teacher regularly to organize classroom work such that three or more curriculum areas were running concurrently, then pupils' progress was marred . . . .
> When pupils were given a large measure of responsibility for managing a programme of work over a whole day or over lengthy periods of time, the effect was found to be negative in a number of areas . . . . (Mortimore *et al.*, 1988, p. 253)

This research dealt only with teachers working solo in the classroom. In contrast, TTT (or collaborative teaching), perhaps PNP's most significant development in the whole area of curriculum delivery at classroom level, may have a considerable impact on the effectiveness of teaching a range of curriculum activities simultaneously. Since the publication of its report on TTT (Chapter 7), PRINDEP has undertaken further fieldwork on professional collaboration which includes sustained and systematic classroom observation. This will be discussed in later reports.

In contrast, another teacher, who used single subject area teaching for much of her working week justified her choice by a quite different interpretation of LEA messages. Her response also shows some awareness of the problematic nature of mixed curriculum teaching:

> When the Authority talk about integration, I don't think they are interested in children doing different things in a classroom at the same time, so much as children doing things that are relevant and meaningful. I've tried to make that happen, and I think I've been successful. I can get better discussion going and better language from the children if I deal with one subject at a time. (Scale III teacher in a Phase 1 school)

Other teachers made a more generalized point about following what they saw as LEA prescriptions:

> I do strive to do what they say, but the children are most important, and I have to choose ideas that work for me. There is pressure, not from the head, but from the LEA to evaluate and change classroom practice. It's a matter of personal conscience to strive towards the ideas put forward and take them on board — with experience and experimenting you know what ideas to throw out. (Scale II teacher in a Phase 2 school)

> I try very hard to carry out the LEA's wishes, but I worry how to decide which ideas are good or bad. (Scale II teacher in a non-PNP school)

Such comments intimate that delivering curriculum to children is a highly complex, and perhaps very personalized activity. Adapting teaching style and curriculum content needs support and discussion at least as much as an approved version to imitate. Some teachers were in no doubt where that support was best offered. Their responses specifically indicated how important a role they felt the headteacher had in ensuring LEA policy was carried out: '[The LEA's curriculum policy] is very important, but difficult to implement without the head's support' (Scale II teacher in a Phase 1 school).

In summary, it is very clear that the issues of classroom management and curriculum delivery have been dramatically opened up by INSET in 1987. A small number of teachers reiterated the viewpoint expressed by certain heads in 1987 and 1988: discussions should continue, and the forum for such dialogue should now be in the schools. As a Phase 1 head put it, during PRINDEP's 1988 fieldwork: 'A teaching force needs to understand what an Authority is saying, and I'd say there is not that at the moment; there is only one that *thinks* it knows. Classroom organization is still the foremost issue for schools to address.' Addressing this issue might involve schools reflecting on the proportions of time that teachers in action actually spend on the various activities which comprise their broadly-based curriculum. Preliminary analysis of data gathered during PRINDEP's intensive study of classrooms in the summer term of 1988 suggests that in many classrooms with mixed curriculum teaching more time and a qualitatively different kind of instruction are given to pupils engaged in the 'basics' — maths and language — than those undertaking any other curriculum areas. Thus pupils who were involved in such activities as art, construction play, even science, were *monitored* by their teachers but were given less opportunity to engage in exteneded discussion about the prescribed task. This raises the question of how, or indeed whether, teacher time can be shared more equally among all the curriculum activities on offer to children. The issue might also need careful consideration in relation to the demands of the National Curriculum, when teachers have to integrate a third 'basic' — science — into their classroom organization.

The first part of this report has examined teachers' and heads' perceptions of LEA curriculum messages and concludes with extracts from extended discussion on the same theme held in the summer term of 1988. One final question remains: will these versions of the 'broadly-based curriculum', and the language currently used in the Authority to describe and promote it, remain unaffected by the arrival of the National Curriculum in Leeds primary schools in September 1989?

Eight Versions of the Broadly-based Curriculum

By 'broadly-based curriculum' I would assume the Authority means that we're offering children a range of activities: they are not having purely reading, maths and writing activities within a day. There is an understanding that if we can offer other areas of curriculum as well, and if we can take those three areas and build them into something that has relevance to children, then in fact, the learning that will take place across the curriculum is going to be more easily assimilated by children: they are going to want to learn. If it's a narrow curriculum, then children will not have acquired the skills and concepts that they need for later life. In this school we use that phrase 'broadly-based curriculum' too — we mean offering maths, music, art, about the children's own environment and how to care for it, science, technology. We mean range. (Headteacher in a Phase 1 school)

I think 'broadly-based' means to be able to offer to children as wide a curriculum as possible. Obviously you have to look at this within the confines of staffing, expertise, and resources: all these are important considerations. The aim here in this school is towards being as broad as possible. This means covering curriculum areas formerly mentioned as subject areas, e.g. maths and language development, and looking at these to see where there are opportunities to have work developing out of a set curriculum area leading into other curriculum areas. I think that's important, that we see the links that there are with other curriculum areas. I think we, as teachers, need to develop this understanding so that children too can understand that, say, mathematics is not to be seen as completely in isolation. Yet at the same time, we have to develop a depth of subject understanding for children. It's very important, and sometimes quite problematic, to consider the relationship between how the broad curriculum should be delivered and how the various parts are fostered. (Headteacher in a Phase 1 school)

Our core curriculum, and its record system, is in maths and language, with science to come and it was devised as a staff. It's objectives-based, which could be criticized as narrow, but if you work thematically, that's how you get a broadly-based curriculum. This objectives-based core curriculum is our framework, it stops us missing bits out which we could easily do . . . . To the Authority, 'broadly-based' means including all areas of the curriculum they mean the same as me: curriculum thematically approached. But core curriculum isn't the same. There we're talking about breadth within the core curriculum areas, but the Authority meant getting away from just the 3Rs, and [from the situation] where, for example, some schools did no science, or just did some willy-nilly, with the attitude: 'If we feel like doing floating and sinking, we'll do it.' Not many schools have got to grips with producing a core curriculum, including science, which has a thematic approach and progression through the years. All those aspects are my personal view of broadly-based. (Headteacher in a Phase 2 school)

'Broadly-based curriculum' means all things to all folk. There is a

core philosophy in primary education which believes children should have access to a whole range of things. I do worry that we trip ourselves up with all these terms. A good teacher knows she wants to bring up a rounded child, who is self-motivated, disciplined, involved in his own learning, who has access to a whole range of first-hand experiences, who is taught the skills of numeracy and literacy. We're not allowed to say 'back to basics', but I care very much about standards and I want to hear words like standards and quality. It's not the done thing, since the sixties, to say your role as a teacher is to teach a child to read. I can't be doing with interviewees who come here and say they want to 'care'. Our children need to be able to adequately apply for jobs, have the same expectations as those from [the affluent suburbs], so I need teachers who have the skills and know exactly how to teach these children reading and number. When I'm talking about the broadly-based curriculum, I'm talking about standards, skills and magic — a whole range of things from scientific logical thinking to stories from the Bible and the Koran, the basics and also respect and discipline. (Headteacher in a Phase 1 school)

The 'broadly-based curriculum' means covering all areas of the curriculum, so as to include things like RE, PE, geography, history: it's about scope. That phrase doesn't tell me how to cover these areas. (MPG teacher in a Phase 2 school)

I think 'broadly-based curriculum' means we're not only concerned with the 3Rs. It's especially the case in a school of this type where the children have had very little experience, and some none, in all sorts of areas — drama, play, library, music, theatre visits. All of this is part of their curriculum and should be what their education is to be about, not just to be numerate and literate, although those are key components. I wouldn't start listing subjects in isolation — that we're going to do number, drama, language, science, art, history. I see it goes beyond that. I wouldn't like to isolate subjects; they all overlap so much, and I don't see subjects in isolation, hopefully . . . . I think of my role as more of a teacher/social worker. It goes very much futher than teaching them subjects. It doesn't stop at the school gate; I've got a bigger commitment to the children, to parents. I still have a commitment to wanting the children to be literate and numerate, and I could do that, but it would be to the exclusion of everything else I want to do. So there is a conflict. If the children had had the experiences, they could do a lot more in school. It's all the time trying to strike a balance. You just hope you've got that right. (MPG teacher in a Phase 1 school)

'Broadly-based curriculum' has never really been explained to me. I presume it means a curriculum that involves the child physically in his environment and what he's learning. So, it isn't a passive learning — like looking at a book or listening to a teacher — it's going out, being in it, being involved in it. And it's bringing in a whole range of educational aims, not a distinct reading, distinct number, distinct science, but blending them together in a continuing spiral with no beginning and no end, all interrelated. When we have a topic, the number cards and the practical activities are related. We relate everything to a topic, but at the same time we're not 100 per cent rigid on that. I can't relate, say, handwriting skills to a thematic approach but they can still be made exciting and nice. In the first three months, I can't relate Breakthrough to the topic because of my system, with all the relevant games and checklists and sequence of learning. That's my priority, to get them to read: it's what I believe is most important. With someone else it would be number or tactile experience or logical thinking. (MPG teacher in a Phase 1 school)

For me I'm very concerned to get the reading, the maths and the number recording done, but there's a lot more: there's the science, the music, the drama and of course, you can get marvellous language and writing if you do music to a great degree. But, in this school, I feel accountable to parents in relation to maths and reading. By saying 'the broadly-based curriculum', the LEA exerts a counter pressure for me to do the rest [of the curriculum]; and my headteacher, as well as the Authority, insists on quality, high expectations and progression through the years — so all that's part of broadly-based . . . . And for me, it also includes the hidden curriculum: the need for teachers to be aware of sexism and stereotyping. It's really much much more than just headings [for different areas of the curriculum]. (MPG plus Allowance B teacher in a Phase 2 school)

Part 2: Curriculum Management in Schools — Practices and Priorities

There are a number of factors which need to be kept in mind when deciding on the staffing establishment of a Primary School . . . .
. . . the need to enhance the staffing establishments of primary schools to allow:

— opportunity for movement of other staff to exercise leadership responsibility and to observe and advise colleagues
— curriculum and staff development, in-service training and joint curriculum planning.

The Authority's Primary Needs Programme, established in 1985, recognises these needs . . . . (Leeds City Council, 1988, pp.6–8)

Part 1 of this report looked at the range of attitudes towards and understandings of LEA curriculum policy; Part 2 now focuses on curriculum management issues at whole-school level.

PNP's aim 'to develop a broadly-based curriculum' has always implied that schools within the programme will take the opportunity to expand their curriculum development activities. In other words, the programme is intended to affect the whole-school management of the broadly-based curriculum as a means of ensuring its effective delivery in the classroom. With this in mind, PRINDEP has gathered detailed information on a range of curriculum management issues over the last two years, in order to monitor the impact of PNP upon curriculum review and development activities. The major focus has been practice in the representative sample of schools. Data relating to all the Authority's primary schools have also been referred to where relevant. This section of the report offers interim perspectives on trends and variations in four major areas of managing curriculum development:

the allocation of posts of responsibility;
strategies for curriculum development;
curriculum areas under review;
schools' use of INSET and PNP development fund.

Differences in curriculum activity are inevitable given the very nature of a representative sample. Like the overall composition of the Authority's primary schools which it was designed to reflect, the PRINDEP sample contains schools that range in size from over 500 pupils (and some forty staff) to those that have fewer than sixty pupils (and around four staff). This in turn means that there are wide variations in the role, status, remuneration (and very existence) of senior staff. Pupil–teacher ratios vary in the sample —

from around fifteen pupils per teacher in some Phase 1 schools to over twenty-six in certain non-PNP schools. On top of that there are differences in the composition of schools' staff — in the proportion of male and female teachers and in their age, experience, expertise and length of service at the school. The resourcing of each school is not in any way uniform. Finally, the sample is a selection of infant, junior, junior and infant, and primary schools located in inner-city, suburban and outlying semi-rural communities. Quite clearly, managing the development of curriculum in these vastly different establishments is going to be a very different exercise for their heads (and senior staff). Nevertheless, comparative study is useful: whatever the size, pupil–teacher ratio or location of their school, these heads are, by and large, receiving and responding to the same national and local imperatives on curriculum and curriculum management. No sample is likely to reflect *all* development activities in primary schools throughout the Authority. Notwithstanding this, it is quite possible to detect distinctive and consistent patterns of activity which should still give considerable insight into trends within the Authority as a whole.

Allocation of Posts of Responsibility

> With the exception of teachers in their probationary year, each primary teacher should take responsibility for advising the rest of the staff on a major aspect of curriculum and associated matters. Such responsibility should be clearly defined and understood by individual teachers and by the whole staff. (Leeds City Council, 1988, p. 7)

Two kinds of expansion in curriculum responsibility may be expected, given the additional staff which PNP schools have received and the recommendations of the Authority outlined above. The numbers of teachers with 'clearly defined responsibility' *and* the number of areas covered might increase.

Overall numbers of postholders and areas covered have risen steadily each year since 1985, and this increase is not confined to schools in Phase 1 and Phase 2, although some of the additional areas for responsibility are clearly PNP-related. In the PRINDEP sample a post of SEN was officially held in every Phase 1 school, in all but one of the Phase 2 schools and in three-quarters of the non-PNP schools. This represents an increase of 20 per cent since 1986, though half of those taking responsibility for SEN in non-PNP schools were headteachers. However, home–school links and multi-cultural education (two issues also central to PNP) exist as areas of responsibility almost exclusively in the Phase 1 schools, and indeed in less than half of these. Other expansions reflect more general trends in the primary curriculum. For example, responsibility for computers has more than doubled since 1985 to 70 per cent of the sample, and the increase has occurred in all phases. A slight rise in the number of responsibility posts for environmental studies is also apparent. The numbers of posts of responsibility for major areas such as maths, language, science, art and craft, and PE have remained fairly stable over this period in each phase, but they are not by any means present in every school.

Excluding probationers and supply staff, more than a quarter of all main professional grade (MPG) teachers in the sample had no designated responsibility. There are no doubt some logistical problems in providing sufficient areas of curriculum, or even curriculum-associated, responsibility in very large schools, and conversely having sufficient teachers for all major areas of the curriculum in some of the smaller schools. However, the shortfall between areas covered and the number of teachers currently without responsibility is very evident. For example, a third of all the schools in the sample were without an art and craft or music coordinator; nearly two-thirds without anyone coordinating environmental studies or RE; nine-tenths without anyone officially responsible for the area of CDT, multicultural education or drama.

The sample shows considerable variability in the proportion of total staff with designated responsibilities: some schools had all eligible staff undertaking one or more areas of curriculum responsibility. This tended to be the case more often in non-PNP than in PNP schools. One in four schools had more than 25 per cent of their eligible staff without designated responsibility; the majority had two or three staff with no curriculum (or associated) development role.

These variations in allocating posts of responsibility were not significantly related to either PNP phase, size of school, or pupil–teacher ratio: above all they seemed to reflect particular management decisions and attitudes on the part of the head, and sometimes staff themselves. Schools whose heads had expressed ignorance of or distance from PNP (and were labelled 'traditionalist' in Part 1 of this report) consistently had proportionately fewer MPG staff with curriculum responsibility.

In 1988 there was some evidence of schools responding to the notion that all staff should have a curriculum leadership role. Several heads spoke about their intention to reallocate responsibility posts to include every teacher — salary restructuring as well as LEA messages were influencing this. Other heads indicated that it was proving problematic to ask staff to take on curriculum responsibility without financial reward. Another factor here has been the ongoing process of renegotiation of job specifications between the Authority and teacher associations.

Of course, numbers of staff with responsibility is a very different issue from how these staff operate when they actually undertake curriculum responsibility — no doubt *who* coordinates an area crucially affects *how* it is coordinated. PRINDEP's analysis has included a breakdown of the status and gender of postholders for the seven most frequently coordinated curriculum areas in the representative sample. Again these findings relate to the representative sample: at this stage of the evaluation PRINDEP is not presenting a city-wide picture. The limited number of schools has facilitated very close scrutiny of postholder allocation since 1985, and the findings should have relevance to the Authority as a whole.

A general overview on the issue of gender and curriculum responsibility is worth itemizing first: the sample has some 300 teachers, of whom, in all, 12 per cent are men. This percentage is slightly below the national figure and that of Leeds Authority, both of which stand at about 16 per cent according to current DES statistics. Figures available for the primary sector within the Authority as a whole show men hold 38 per cent of headships, 41 per cent of deputy-headships, 25 per cent of posts with additonal allowances and 10 per cent of MPG posts. Though again slightly below the city-wide picture, the sample shows a very similar range of percentages: exactly a third of the heads were men, and men held 38 per cent of the deputy-headships, 20 per cent of the additional allowance posts and 5 per cent of MPG posts with curriculum responsibility. In the sample all MPG teachers without curriculum (or associated) responsibility were women. Twice as many men worked in Phase 1 schools as in schools in the other two phases. More than half of the Phase 2 and non-PNP schools were all-female establishments, compared to only two schools in Phase 1.

The general picture on the issue of status and curriculum responsibility is also worth noting: there were four times as many MPG plus Allowance B (MPG + B) posts in the sample's Phase 1 schools as in its Phase 2 and non-PNP schools: no doubt because the Phase 1 schools were generally larger. At the time this fieldwork and analysis were undertaken Allowance A posts had not been negotiated or distributed. Three-quarters of non-PNP heads had a curriculum responsibility, compared to a third of heads in Phase 1 and half in Phase 2. Only three deputy-heads in the sample took no responsibility for a curriculum area.

From this general overview, the seven curriculum areas can be looked at in turn. The gender and status of postholders for each are summarized graphically in Figure 4.1.

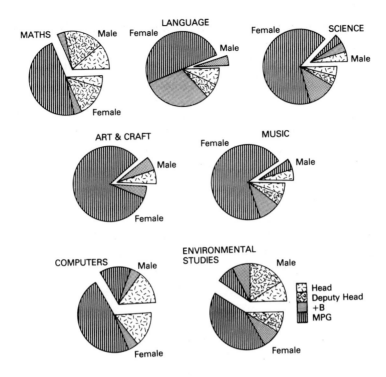

Figure 4.1. *Status and Gender of Postholders in Seven Curriculum Areas*

Maths

Twenty-eight of the thirty schools had a maths coordinator; the two schools that did not were in the Group 2 or Group 1 category. More than half of all maths postholders were of higher status than MPG.

All male maths postholders were of higher status than MPG. Female MPG staff held half of the sample's maths coordinator roles, but in only three of the seventeen schools which had any male staff at all were women rather than men responsible for maths.

In schools of Group size 3 or 4, men who took on the maths coordinator role tended to have higher status than their female counterparts. In schools of Group size 5 and above, the post was generally held by both men and women of higher status than MPG.

All maths coordinators were above Scale I prior to the introduction of MPG.

Ten maths coordinators combined the post with other areas of responsibility: computers and science were most frequently mentioned.

Language

Twenty-five of the thirty schools had a language coordinator, and there was only one male with responsibility for language in the sample.

Half of the female coordinators had MPG + B status, but unlike maths, language was very infrequently coordinated by deputy-heads or heads. Only two female deputies, in small schools, had responsibility for language, and there was only one head in the sample temporarily coordinating language.

All language coordinators were above Scale I prior to the introduction of MPG.

Seven language coordinators combined the post with other areas of responsibility: SEN was most frequently mentioned.

Comparison of the personnel who coordinated maths and language, the two so-called 'basics' of the primary curriculum, shows distinct parallels and also quite marked differences. Both subject areas had exactly the same number and proportion of higher status and MPG teachers acting as coordinators. But whereas language was virtually exclusively a female role, maths was definitely not. Men made up 12 per cent of the sample but they held 33 per cent of all maths posts, and consistently did so at a higher remuneration. A third of the sample's deputies coordinated maths. Occasionally, deputies may take on this responsibility in the absence of other willing or suitable staff. Nevertheless, the association of maths with a senior management position is likely to signify a great deal about the status of the area — to staff and children alike. The pre-eminence of maths will, in fact, be shown to recur in other aspects of curriculum development.

Science

Twenty-four of the thirty schools had a post of responsibility for science. Science coordinators were predominantly female, and MPG grade. Unlike maths or language, where the number of teachers of higher status than MPG equalled those coordinating the area on MPG grade, science had relatively few high status coordinators. The total number of MPG + B and deputies responsible for science was rather less than half those on MPG. The sample had just one deputy working as science coordinator. Half of the MPG post-holders were previously on Scale I. Science coordinators with MPG + B status occurred mainly in larger schools, where there was a higher number of allowances available.

Only three of the twenty-four science coordinator posts were held by men.

Seven science coordinators combined the post with other areas of responsibility: environmental studies and computers were the most frequently mentioned.

As science is set to become the third 'basic' in the primary curriculum, comparison with maths and language is timely. Using the criterion of postholder status, science was not afforded such high standing in this sample of schools. Although it ranked higher than areas like music and art and craft, it was still coordinated predominantly by women teachers of comparatively lower status. The coordinators of each of these subject areas *tend* to play a servicing role — organizing resources, offering informal advice, perhaps taking children for specialist teaching — rather than lead extended whole-school curriculum development. This is not to downgrade the valuable work often being undertaken by science coordinators, and indeed a very small number of schools have given their science coordinators' work considerable emphasis. But the general impression remains: in the spring of 1988 these teachers seemed to be operating in a professional climate that had not fully acknowledged the centrality of their curriculum area.

Computers

Computers is the area which had most expanded its number of postholders since 1987. Twenty-one schools mentioned a teacher with responsibility for computers in 1988, as opposed to fourteen the year before. However, the expansion was mostly accounted for by coordinators of maths and, to a lesser extent, science officially adding computers to their responsibilities. In all, eighteen of the twenty-one computer posts were currently combined with other areas.

Three postholders were previously Scale I. MPG + B and deputy-heads with responsibility for computers constituted nearly 40 per cent of the sample, in science about 20 per cent. Unlike all other areas of the curriculum, no headteacher had responsibility for computers.

A third of computer coordinators were male, and this area had the highest number of male MPG. In two-thirds of the schools which had male staff, men held responsibility for computers. Of the nine schools that had no designated member of staff for computers, seven were all-female establishments.

Music

Twenty schools currently had a member of staff with responsibility for music. In the sample, music was the only subject area to have, overall, fewer post-holders in 1988 than in 1987.

Music was a subject area coordinated predominantly by women (90 per cent), and by those on MPG (76 per cent). Nine of the twenty music post-holders were previously on Scale I. Three were part-time.

Seven of the music coordinators combined the post with responsibility for another area of the curriculum. There was a wide range of combinations — SEN, CDT, art and craft, maths, drama and language were all mentioned. These combination posts were usually held by ex-Scale II teachers and above.

Art and Craft

Art and craft coordinators were mentioned in nineteen of the thirty schools. Like music, it was an area coordinated predominantly by women (89 per cent), and by those on MPG grade (84 per cent). Four art and craft post-holders were previously on Scale I, and five combined the post with another area. Often display was mentioned as part of the responsibility, perhaps again reflecting the servicing role of postholders in this area.

Environmental Studies

Although only twelve, mostly larger, schools in the sample had an environmental studies postholder, this represented the second most expanding curriculum area, with three schools adding it to their list of responsibilities in 1988.

Nearly half of these postholders were men. Deputy-heads and MPG + B accounted for nearly half those undertaking this area of responsibility.

Five schools had this subject area as a combined role; science and PE were mentioned most often as the other responsibilities. This may suggest that environmental studies is seen as predominantly a kind of outdoor science activity, and the geographical or historical dimension is given less prominence.

The Overall Picture

Analysis of subject area coordinators gives some insight into whole-school development of the 'broadly-based curriculum'. It would be entirely erroneous to assume that subject areas held largely by lower status teachers are less efficiently or competently coordinated. Indeed, the very notion of status may seem inappropriate to the kinds of professional relationships proclaimed in many primary staffrooms. However, as later sections of this report will show, schools in the sample consistently gave priority to developing curriculum areas coordinated by high status teachers, and these areas also tended to have a high proportion of male teachers holding responsibility. Moreover, a number of these higher status teachers, particularly deputies, appeared to be accumulating extra areas of responsibility in key subjects like computers and environmental studies. The consequence of this is that arts subjects were receiving comparatively less attention. If teachers with responsibility for these areas lack the opportunity to exercise a proper leadership role, the possible outcome is a curtailing of serious discussion about the place of the arts in the primary curriculum. Indeed, a general restriction on leadership opportunities for teachers wishing to share officially their particular arts expertise may even affect career prospects.

In management terms the 'broadly-based curriculum' appears to have a definite hierarchy: the profession's rhetoric may currently proclaim all subjects to be of equal importance, but it would seem that in relation to allocation of curriculum responsibility some are rather more equal than others.

A final point on curriculum leadership must be that *where* teachers exercise curriculum responsibility also crucially affects *how* they can operate: PNP has had considerable impact on the role of the curriculum coordinator. From discussions held with senior staff in the representative sample during the spring term of 1988, and from intensive observational fieldwork undertaken in the summer of the same year, it is clear that PNP staffing has offered some curriculum coordinators enormous opportunities to develop their advisory and specialist role. However, as PNP increasingly allows more curriculum coordinators the opportunity to teach their subject area to a wider range of children, the issue of gender/subject area stereotyping within the profession itself may also need closer attention by schools.

Strategies for Curriculum Development

The Primary head teacher is responsible for the ethos of the school and should exercise that responsibility in order to create agreed policies in curriculum, organization and management. A major aspect of the head's role is to coordinate vision and thinking and to use the talents of members of staff. (Leeds City Council, 1988, p. 7)

Although the curriculum coordinator is now well established, both locally and nationally, as central to the effective development and delivery of curriculum in schools, it is, of course, the head who ultimately determines that coordinator's effectiveness. With this in mind, during the spring term of 1988 heads in each of the sample schools were asked to outline strategies currently being used in curriculum development and review. Some seventeen types of activity were regularly mentioned, all of which involved whole-staff discussion. These fell into the following rough categories and sequence:

Familiarization with staff's professional needs and interests
e.g. appraisal interview
     use of GRIDS

Delegation of responsibility
e.g. postholder designated to write draft guidelines or requisition
     resources
     instituting coordinating team or working party

Extension of expertise
e.g. course attendance
     advisory contact
     presentations by outside expert
     visits to other schools

Staff discussion
e.g. staff meetings
     workshops
     training days
     informal discussion
     structured small group discussion
     production of guidelines

Classroom implementation
e.g. TTT (collaborative teaching)
     year group planning
     reorganization or introduction of resources

Most heads suggested a relatively small number of these strategies as their current curriculum development procedure, and on one level this is not surprising: they were employing a particular approach for a particular stage in their review. Equally, each school is a unique institution, operating with particular priorities and constraints. Some heads stressed the obstacles which were currently prohibiting the kinds of development work that they really wished for: a high percentage of temporary staff; the resignation of a key postholder; the non-arrival of relevant resources ordered through PNP development funding; their own temporary headship; the expending of Directed Time; staff's general attitude to change. Only very occasionally was it difficult to avoid the conclusion that these responses were rationalizations for non-activity rather than the real cause.

Three general points on significant trends can be made in the light of these discussions. First, there were some noticeable differences in the range of curriculum development procedures described by PNP and non-PNP heads. More than half of non-PNP heads suggested informal discussion as a viable, even major, strategy for curriculum development in their school, compared to only two in each of the other phases. These were non-PNP schools of equivalent size to some within the programme that were indicating very much more structured approaches to curriculum development. On the whole, non PNP-heads tended to emphasize the writing of curriculum documents rather more than heads in the other two phases. No non-PNP head mentioned working parties, year group planning or organized small group discussion, but half of the sample's PNP heads indicated that these were an intrinsic part of their curriculum review procedure. All this suggests that the lack of extra staff in non-PNP schools could often seriously handicap structured professional dialogue on curriculum issues. In turn, having less scope for such dialogue may account for the tendency in non-PNP schools to stress the importance of documents as a means of defining practice. Non-PNP schools referred rather more frequently to their use of outside expertise (such as advisers and advisory teachers, higher education lecturers or publishers' representatives) as the main strategy in their development work. Perhaps this confirms the lack of opportunity to exploit and develop professional expertise from amidst their own ranks. As non-PNP schools were also not eligible to attend the course on curriculum leadership in 1987, it is at least possible that some of these schools were unaware of the kinds of responsibilities being advocated by the LEA for curriculum coordinators.

Second, although some heads pointed out that different curriculum areas might demand a different kind of development procedure, it was also noticeable that there was a wide range of interpretations given to the actual notion of curriculum development. This varied from the very ad hoc and informal to the comprehensively designed review, and such variation occurred within every phase of the programme. Thus it was suggested that an area was being developed when a postholder was offering advice on request to colleagues, or when resources had been prominently displayed, or when course notes were passed around after INSET attendance. Sometimes these low-key procedures ran concurrently with each other, or with more structured curriculum development activity in other areas. Sometimes they were described as a non-threatening way to begin to raise staff's curriculum awareness. In complete contrast, other heads outlined a management strategy which involved placing emphasis on a single area of the curriculum and utilized most of the items from the categorization listed on page 136. Often these were operated in a carefully thought out sequence of activities which began with the garnering of opinion from staff on the area of priority, and then moved to a finely balanced schedule of presentations of expertise, focused staff discussion, implementation in the classroom and evaluation. Above all, this overview was carefully tailored by a sensitivity to the current professional needs of staff; and the preplanned schedule was always closely monitored, though not necessarily led, by the heads themselves.

Finally, as was pointed out in Part 1 of this report, the marked variations in heads' accounts of their current curriculum development activities often coincided with particular styles of headship and attitudes to PNP. It was not always a school's inclusion in the programme which determined the range of strategies used. Thus in 1988 the schools whose heads had been categorized as 'traditionalist' or 'uncertain' about PNP curriculum policy were undertaking less development work, using fewer strategies, than those whose heads had offered views classified as 'concurring' with or 'demurring' at PNP curriculum policy from a 'modernist' standpoint. These schools were, by and large, continuing to engage in more extensive reviews by means of a wider range of development strategies.

After this consideration of general trends and variations in curriculum development, it is worth itemizing one of the most frequently mentioned components: whole-staff discussion on curriculum issues. Virtually all heads referred to the value and place of staff discussion in any development activity. There were marked differences in the frequency of curriculum meetings within the sample: from twice weekly to once a term to 'when it seems necessary'. Most schools stated they had a weekly or fortnightly meeting where curriculum matters were discussed, although this appeared not to be always the case in practice: when PRINDEP asked to observe a curriculum meeting in each of the thirty schools, sixteen schools invited our neutral and non-participant observers to attend, three others held meetings which we could not attend, and eleven held no meetings at all that term.

It is possible to identify several common factors in all the meetings that were considered to be successful and valuable by participants.

The meeting had a clear place and purpose within an overall design for curriculum review.

A specific focus for discussion had been prepared, and the format of the meeting itself had a clear structure.

There was full support from the head for the meeting though it was not necessarily led by him/her.

Staff involvement and opinion were *genuinely* encouraged, and the content was relevant to all participants, usually practical in orientation, and it had evident and fairly immediate applications for the classroom.

A number of the meetings attended did not adhere to these four principles. The effectiveness and outcomes of some meetings were clearly undermined by the head's lack of interest or even lack of seriousness; other meetings found teachers passive and without a voice, receiving rather than determining intended school procedures. Some meetings spent considerable time on issues that did not have relevance to the majority of the participants; others were concluded indecisively with no sense of future direction. On the other hand, a number of the meetings attended were a lively exchange of ideas; some had a clear and succinct presentation of expertise by a member of staff or outside speaker. Above all, successful meetings demonstrated how certain heads and curriculum coordinators had considerable skill in leading discussion and decision-making. As the rhetoric of PNP so strongly emphasizes the importance of whole-staff discussion and decision-making, it may be that some heads and curriculum leaders need assistance in further developing these specialized skills.

Areas of Curriculum under Review

During the spring term of 1988 each head in the sample was also asked to specify which curriculum areas or curriculum-related issues were currently the focus of whole-school development activity. The following is a complete list of responses:

All areas	Equal opportunities	None
Art and craft	Handwriting	Phonics
Breakthrough	Health education	PE
Calculator	Home-school links	Reading
Child abuse	Humanities	Record keeping
Classroom organization	INRS (special needs)	RE
Computers	Language	Science
Discipline	Maths	Technology (CDT)
Dance/drama	Multicultural Education	Themes
Environmental studies	Music	Topic work

However, as the previous section indicated, not all subjects and issues are given the same amount of attention by schools just as not all schools give attention to the same areas.

Some issues, particularly those of a pastoral kind, such as child abuse and discipline, tended to be the focus for a single staff meeting. In fact, a meeting to discuss child abuse was made mandatory by the Authority. Equally some of the arts subjects were the focus of a staff's attention for a brief period only; whereas other curriculum areas — most obviously maths — were looked at in some depth and for a considerable time.

For the sample as a whole Table 4.1 shows how frequently ten major curriculum areas were mentioned by schools as being under review. Table 4.2 shows a breakdown by phase of how many schools were reviewing the three 'basics' subject areas of maths, language and science during 1986/87 and 1987/88. A slight increase in schools reviewing maths is noticeable for this year. In 1988 computers and record keeping were also looked at by four schools, music in three and then all other areas were being reviewed by only one or two schools.

Table 4.1.   Subject Areas Reviewed in the PRINDEP Sample

	1986/87 n = 30	1987/88 n = 30
Art and craft	1	1
Computers	4	4
CDT	0	1
Drama	0	1
Environmental studies	2	1
Language	11	10
Maths	12	15
Music	2	3
PE	1	2
RE	1	1
Science	6	6

Table 4.2.   Subject Areas Reviewed in Each Phase

	Phase 1 n = 10		Phase 2 n = 10		Non-PNP n = 10	
	1986/87	1987/88	1986/87	1987/88	1986/87	1987/88
Maths	6	7	4	5	2	3
Language	4	3	4	4	3	3
Science	2	1	3	3	1	2

It is clear that maths followed by language are by far the most frequently reviewed subjects in this sample of schools. However, it is only when comparing the kinds of review procedures undertaken in the schools that the real differences are apparent.

Maths

Of the fifteen schools undertaking a maths review, ten had advisory support — the maths adviser to talk to staff and sometimes parents; the maths advisory team to work alongside teachers. The PrIME team also was evident at four schools. Eight of the schools were involved in a whole-staff evaluation of their current maths scheme. Training days and workshops on calculators and other equipment, parental involvement in making and using maths games and an appraisal of record keeping were all mentioned by three or four schools. When schools referred to INSET as part of their maths review procedure, it usually involved attendance at a series of courses. In all, maths curriculum review was multifaceted and long-term, with plenty of INSET resources available at school and central levels. There was considerable consistency among the schools as to the range of strategies and the kinds of support used.

Language

The picture in the area of language is much less consistent. Of the ten schools looking at language, four mentioned they were concentrating on reading schemes or reading materials, two that their focus was specifically oral language, and four that they were reviewing all aspects of language. Only one school was at the time making its language review work a priority. The rest of the schools were either running it parallel (or in second or third place) to development activities in other areas, or it was described as the next major area under review, with preparations such as ordering books, introducing parts of a reading scheme for later whole-staff evaluation, instituting a working party, a language coordinator drawing up draft proposals. Outside speakers and advisory contact or support were mentioned by only one school, staff from two schools had undertaken visits to other schools to see reading materials in operation and two schools had sent staff to visit the John Taylor Teachers' Centre. Although, as the next section will show, a number of schools in the sample did attend INSET courses on language and reading, no head referred to INSET activity as part of their review procedure. Indeed, one curriculum leader with responsibility for language regretted that there were 'no decent courses on reading' for some of her colleagues to go on.

Comparisons between the two major areas are inevitable. It would seem that schools have been left very much more to their own devices in the area of language, whereas there was Authority-wide backup for schools undertaking maths development work. This is a direct result of 'Maths Year'. It is not surprising, therefore, that three schools in the sample abandoned development work on language and took up maths instead. Nevertheless, there was ample evidence that schools and their language coordinators were still conscientiously continuing development work by undertaking collaborative teaching, organizing resources, improving reading records and so on.

Science

The review activities in relation to science were different again. Only one of the six schools undertaking any whole-school science development activities used a full sequence of procedures as outlined in the previous section. Three schools mentioned the visits of the ESG Science team, but this generally did not accompany any great emphasis on reviewing science subsequently. Two heads specifically mentioned lack of support in science; for example, 'We do not know what to do next. No one on the staff is knowledgeable enough. The staff as a whole feel they need help from someone with science expertise, but we do not know where to get help . . . ' (Head of a non-PNP school).

One school had a part-time MPG teacher working alongside her colleagues in the classroom, and another mentioned that guidelines were in the process of being written by a member of staff. Again, as indicated in the section on postholders, a considerable gap between science and the other two core curriculum areas was apparent.

INSET and the PNP Development Fund

> The good school is constantly evaluating its work. There is a real concern for professional development, keeping up to date by reading and attending courses. (Leeds City Council, 1988, p. 9)

The last part of this report on the impact of PNP upon schools' curriculum offers an overview of two of the Authority's most direct sources of influence: the courses offered at central in-service and the successful bids for resources which schools within the programme have made with the extra capitation provided by the PNP development fund. Together these present a clear picture of the combined views of schools and the Authority on what provision is necessary for the 'broadly-based curriculum'. PNP development fund spending could be described as a school-initiated and Authority-approved selection of appropriate resources, whereas INSET attendance gives a picture of teachers, as consumers, selecting from Authority-initiated professional development resources.

INSET Activity

Analysis of the Primary Centre's records of course participants shows that there were over 4500 teacher attendances at the Authority's INSET programme between January 1986 and July 1988. An enormous range of courses was on offer in that time, and a fuller account of them will be given in later PRINDEP reports. For present purposes the INSET attendance of the representative sample is the main reference. However, an Authority-wide analysis shows that Phase 1 schools accounted for just over 2000 of the attendances, Phase 2 around 1500 and non-PNP slightly under 1000. A marked difference in professional development opportunities available to — and taken up by — PNP schools is very evident from these figures. A more dramatic illustration is a comparison between two Group 4 schools within the representative sample itself: one inner-city Phase 1 school had recorded sixty attendances between 1986 and 1988, while an outlying non-PNP school of equivalent group size had just two recorded attendances for the same period. These examples represent the highest and lowest attendances in the sample: the average figure, for both the sample and the city as a whole, is nearly thirty teacher attendances for a Phase 1 school, twenty-four for Phase 2 and ten for those not in the programme.

Overall such figures confirm that there has been rather less opportunity for certain schools to undertake INSET activity. Lack of extra staff, ineligibility (through not being part of the PNP programme) and the outlying locations of their schools were all mentioned by heads as factors prohibiting their staffs' INSET attendance. However, because the sample also showed such marked variation in attendances *within* phases, there are other factors to be taken into account. As was indicated in Part 1 of the report, it was schools with heads expressing 'traditionalist' or 'uncertain' views on PNP which consistently had the lowest INSET attendance. In other words, heads — and teachers — themselves have also had responsibility for determining their school's professional development opportunities since the inception of PNP.

Besides looking at how often schools made use of INSET provision, PRINDEP monitored the range of courses actually on offer since 1986. Table

Table 4.3. *INSET Attendance in the PRINDEP Sample (January 1986–July 1988)*

	Phase 1 (n = 10)	Phase 2 (n = 10)	Phase 3 (n = 10)
Maths	10	9	9
Science	4	5	1
Language	4	5	3
Reading	3	6	3
Art and craft	3	3	4
PE	4	1	4
Drama	4	2	1
Multicultural education	6	7	6
Curriculum leadership	7	9	0
Teaching strategies	9	9	3
LISSEN	6	7	1
Gender	5	3	1

4.3 shows the number of representative sample schools in each phase which have sent staff to courses on record at the Primary Schools' Centre. The table uses a selection of major curriculum or curriculum-related areas and does not include any INSET undertaken at the John Taylor Teachers' Centre.

The table not only shows considerable differences in attendance for subject areas — with maths once more having the highest profile — but the discrepancy in the frequency of attendance between non-PNP and PNP schools is again illustrated. Non-PNP schools were not eligible for the curriculum leadership courses, and also record very low attendance on courses dealing with teaching strategies and classroom management. As the findings of this report indicate, these two areas are viewed by teachers and heads as relaying the quintessential philosophy of PNP on the effective delivery of the curriculum at both whole-school and classroom levels. This might be a further consideration with regard to some non-PNP heads' professed unawareness of LEA policy on curriculum. It is worth noting that these particular courses are now repeated in the 1988–89 INSET programme. How far the Authority will be able to provide the now Phase 3 schools with the same INSET opportunities afforded to those in the earlier stages of the programme is a future evaluation issue.

PNP Development Fund

Available data show that nearly £350,000 worth of extra materials were received by PNP schools between 1985 and 1988 to augment their provision of the broadly-based curriculum. This sum has included some £14,000 on classroom furniture and furnishings and £25,000 on audiovisual aids. Then there are such items as materials to support provision for early years (£36,000); special needs (£9500); multicultural education (£4000); home-school links (£3600) and around £1600 specifically requested for resourcing staff libraries. All this is evidence of schools' very varied use of an additional financial resource directly arising from PNP. However, for the purpose of this report PRINDEP's analysis of successful bids made by PNP schools since 1985 has concentrated on expenditure specifically earmarked for ten main curriculum areas: art and craft, CDT, computers, drama, humanities, language, maths, music, PE and science. A complete account of PNP development fund expenditure will be given in a later publication.

Figure 4.2 shows the total number of successful bids for resources in each of these ten areas since 1985, while the annual expenditure is summarized in Figure 4.3. It is evident that since PNP's inception, maths and language have been very much the main areas of expenditure. In each of these areas over £70,000 has been granted in response to more than 200 bids from schools. Over the three-year period resources for maths have taken precedence over all other items; although in 1987–88 language resources became the top area of expenditure for the first time, as Phase 1 schools' bids for language materials outnumbered those for maths. In each year, except 1985, reading schemes have constituted half of the total outlay on language — the PNP development fund has allowed over 100 schools to spend nearly £36,000 on renewing and replenishing this particular resource.

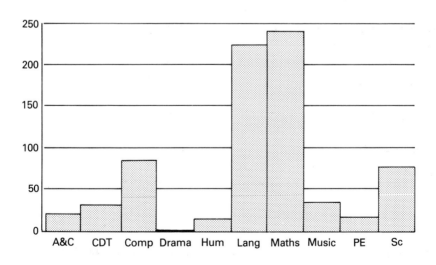

Figure 4.2. PNP development fund: Total number of successful bids in ten curricular areas

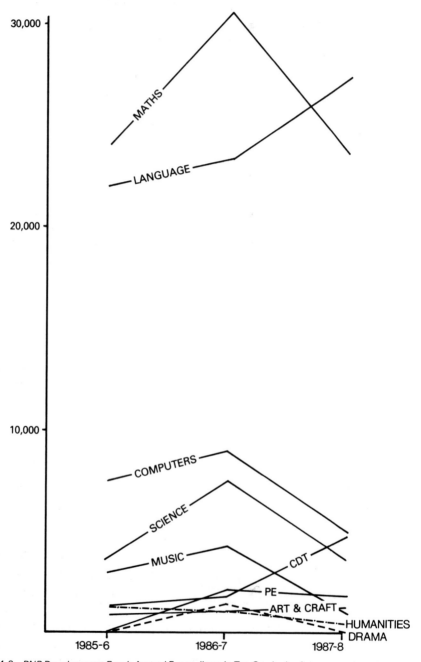

Figure 4.3. PNP Development Fund: Annual Expenditure in Ten Curricular Areas

The outlay on all other curriculum areas fell well below these two so-called primary 'basics'. Resources for the areas of computers (£21,500 to eighty-seven schools) then science (£14,800 to eighty schools) were the most requested items after maths and language, although schools had already received additional capitation under the ESG Science scheme. Computer-related resources were requested by half of all Phase 1 schools and a third of those in Phase 2 on entry to the programme, but both the numbers of bids and total outlay dropped annually since then. The areas of the curriculum for which schools least requested extra funding were art and craft, drama and environmental studies/humanities and PE. Each of these had under £4000 total outlay since PNP began. The areas of CDT and music each received in total some £8000, although CDT expenditure increased each year, while the number of bids for music resources dropped by more than half since 1986. Such fluctuations probably represent the 'one-off' acquisition of equipment and resources which do not need frequently augmenting or replacing. The growing expenditure on CDT may signify that schools were responding to national trends, albeit slowly and with some financial caution. The figures could also indicate that resourcing classrooms for the area of technology, as prescribed in the National Curriculum, requires rather more financial attention than it is currently receiving.

Overall though, when schools exercised choice in the matter of provision for 'the broadly-based curriculum', they remained committed to their responsibilities in the areas of numeracy and literacy above all else. It is worth noting that schools' commitment to language and reading continued despite having a comparatively low profile in the Authority's INSET programme over the same period.

Summary

Before we move to some of the larger issues which are signalled by the analysis in Parts 1 and 2, it is probably helpful briefly to summarize the main areas discussed so far.

Part 1 started with a theme explored in earlier reports, that of principles, policies or *messages* of a broad educational kind which emanate from the Authority in the context of PNP and are expected to be translated into school and classroom practice. The present analysis underlined the problems noted in Report 6 (Chapter 6) concerning the transmission and reception of such messages: initial ambiguity, variation in interpretation, distortion, selective reception, selective use and so on. A wide range of versions of the 'broadly-based curriculum' emerged, though most of them revolved round one or more of the themes of curriculum *design*, *delivery* and *differentiation* and, not surprisingly, class teachers' versions of 'broadly-based' were more concerned with minute-to-minute classroom challenges and dilemmas than were heads'.

The present report goes further on this issue, however. Part 1 categorized the ways heads, as key agents in the process of communicating and implementing policy, reacted to the curriculum message and influenced its onward transmission. The report's distinction, in its discussion of heads' versions and views of LEA curriculum policy, between 'concurring', 'uncertain', 'traditionalist demurring' and 'modernist demurring' responses is no mere academic flight of fancy: the attitudes represented by these labels have clear practical consequences and seem to be related in a fundamental way to heads' leadership styles and management strategies on the one hand, and to their attitudes towards the Authority on the other. Heads, if they so choose, can operate very much as filters or gatekeepers in relation to class teachers' awareness of issues and developments outside the school; because of this, their attitudes to the LEA can be of critical significance for teachers and hence for classroom practice and children's learning.

In Leeds this tendency has been modified or challenged by the Authority's conception of PNP coordinators. In some schools, therefore, the gatekeeper function may have been dissipated, and in some such cases heads may be happy that staffing now allows this degree of delegation. Elsewhere little may have changed, or roles and relationships may be in a state of transition, so the issue remains an important one.

Part 2 looked at four aspects of curriculum management in PNP schools. The first was the growth area (in Leeds as nationally) of curriculum-related posts of responsibility, and here the report moved from the logistics of numbers and kinds of posts to the status and gender of postholders and the very different levels of human resourcing which the various curriculum areas received during the period in question.

Part 2 next outlined the range of strategies for curriculum review and development adopted in the sample schools, and recorded a clear difference between PNP and what were then non-PNP schools in this respect, with PNP schools opting for more formalized and diverse strategies in comparison with non-PNP schools' use of the more traditional combination of informal encounters and written documents. Such differences were shown to be partly related to levels of staffing and partly, once again, to the attitudes and leadership styles of heads. If, as was suggested, the scale and significance of individual teachers' curriculum responsibilities can be represented on a basic continuum from *servicing* to *leading*, the PNP/non-PNP difference can be summarized as a greater incidence of developed curriculum leadership roles in the well-resourced PNP schools as compared with more limited curriculum servicing in the non-PNP schools. A particularly common strategy, that of curriculum meetings, was discussed in more detail, and certain factors in the success of such meetings were identified.

The report then moved to a closer look at the various curriculum areas under review in the sample schools during 1987 and 1988, showing the wide variation in the depth and kind of attention each received, ranging from the detailed and sustained to the superficial and brief. This reflected, naturally, broader educational priorities. But the analysis also revealed marked discrepancies in the treatment of the two areas traditionally given parity as 'basics' — language and mathematics — which, when taken together with the subsequent analysis of INSET support and certain issues raised in Chapter 3, should perhaps prompt further debate.

Finally, Part 2 analyzed the levels of support given to various aspects of the curriculum as reflected in INSET course attendance and schools' use of PNP development funds. Here again the portrayal of variation and discrepancy within and between schools was consolidated.

We move now to a consideration of three particular issues which have been generated by the analysis so far.

Part 3: Issues and Implications

Parts 1 and 2 have raised a large number of issues. Many are self-evident and can be responded to in context without further highlighting but there are three areas which seem to merit additional comment. They are: (1) curriculum management within the school; (2) the relationships between schools, and particularly their heads, and the LEA; (3) the reality of the 'broadly-based curriculum'. These are the subject of Part 3.

Curriculum Management in the School

Levels and Kinds of Curriculum Development

The wide range of curriculum areas subject to review and development during the two-year period testifies, on the face of it, to curriculum breadth and diversity. But equally varied is the scale and kind of activity denoted by 'review' and 'development'. This raises three important questions. First, given what is now known about the strengths and weaknesses in the primary curriculum nationally, have schools always got their development priorities right? A good example here, but by no means the only one, is the case of science — frequently noted as primary schools' Achilles heel, and now one of the National Curriculum's core subjects. However, the question needs to be asked about every other aspect of the curriculum as well.

Second, bearing in mind the *servicing-leading* continuum for teachers' curriculum responsibilities, is there a level of curriculum development activity which is so low (and in some cases it was very low indeed) as to be likely to have little impact on the quality of provision? Should there be a minimum level of investment of time, expertise and resources to give review and development in a particular curriculum area the best chance of success? This question is particularly important in the light of continuing national evidence about the lack of continuity and progression in curriculum areas other than the so-called 'basics' of language and mathematics (DES, 1989a). Achieving continuity and progression demands whole-school development strategies to ensure that the child receives one continuous and evolving set of curriculum experiences rather than a disjointed sequence. The occasional meeting seems unlikely to take a school far in this direction. Yet the curriculum areas most likely to receive the minimalist servicing approach to curriculum development tended to be precisely those which were criticized by HMI nationally for lack of continuity and progression. It might be argued, therefore, that there is a cycle here which needs to be broken; and that part of the answer to the earlier question on curriculum development priorities may now be clear.

Third, which of the various strategies for review and development recorded in this report are most likely to generate long-term curriculum improvement? There is now strong evidence nationally to suggest that the combination of occasional, unstructured informal discussions and written documents is less effective than more structured and sustained procedures. Since the former was more prevalent in the non-PNP schools, one obvious obstacle to a more thoroughgoing approach is staffing (see below), but since some schools without enhanced staffing do manage to adopt more extended procedures, this cannot be the whole story: choice of some kind is always possible, even in the most constrained setting.

Staffing and the Range of Curriculum Development Strategies

The variation in strategies noted above raises important questions about staffing, an issue which features prominently both here and in previous reports. There seems little doubt that enhanced staffing under PNP has made an important contribution to many schools' ability to undertake more ambitious and comprehensive curriculum development programmes. To take advantage of the increased opportunities for curriculum development requires that schools are aware of the many ways in which it can be approached. An extensive vocabulary or repertoire of such strategies has evolved both nationally and in the context of PNP. Armed with this, a school can choose the best strategy or combination of strategies for its particular circumstances.

In this context the analysis contained in PRINDEP Report 5 is significant (see Chapter 5, pp. 169–71). There we show how PNP coordinators were operating, variously, as curriculum managers, curriculum specialists, curriculum enhancers and curriculum facilitators. When considered in conjunction with the 1986 Select Committee's analysis of curriculum coordinators' roles, and evidence from other research projects, PRINDEP's data from Leeds schools tend increasingly to confirm the potentially powerful role in curriculum development of *teachers working alongside each other in the classroom*, whether in one of the various forms of TTT described in Chapter 7, or in other collaborative roles. This is because, as it is now almost a cliché to maintain, staff development is the essential precondition of curriculum development.

Thus having extra staff facilitates the kinds of professional collaboration which whole-school curriculum development requires. But there are other preconditions, notable among which is the leadership given in such matters by the head. Again, our data in this and earlier reports point increasingly to the validity of the factors in effective schooling identified in other projects, notably the ILEA study by Mortimore *et al.* (1988): positive leadership by the head; clearly defined and significant roles for senior staff; involvement of all staff in decision-making and development activity; support by the head for staff having curriculum and managerial roles so as to give them the best chance of achieving credibility and success.

Curriculum Meetings

Such factors come together in one of the most frequently mentioned strategies, that of curriculum meetings. PRINDEP staff systematically monitored a number of such meetings, and this report has listed the four main prerequisites to their success which emerged. We shall report more extensively on the dynamics and outcomes of curriculum meetings at a later stage, but two points can be stressed which underline the focus here on heads' leadership and teachers' involvement. The first is that though informality is a powerful part of primary culture, and people have an understandable preference for relaxed and chatty encounters, progress in a demanding field like curriculum development requires something more systematic and rigorous. Meetings need *purpose, preparation, structure* and *follow-up*. The second is that for staff to contribute to such meetings in any meaningful way they should want and be encouraged to do so: therefore, however well structured a meeting, it will have little success unless the professional climate of the school is genuinely conducive to openness and collaboration, and this takes us back, in part, to the importance of relationships at the informal level. Formal procedures and informal relationships are not mutually exclusive: on the contrary, both are essential aspects of school development.

Curriculum Responsibility, Status and Gender

The final point in this section is rather different but, we suggest, of profound importance. Part 2's discussion of the allocation of posts of responsibility noted a clear and repeated relationship between *curriculum area, staff status* and *staff gender*. Thus, for example, mathematics was often led by male senior staff but art almost exclusively by female main professional grade teachers.

The gender imbalance in primary teaching is well known, as is the way it is inverted the higher up a school one goes. Overall, men are a small minority of the primary teaching force. At class teacher level, particularly where younger children are concerned, they are even more thinly represented; but at deputy and headship levels their representation is disproportionately high. Because of this, and whatever individual readers might feel about the equal opportunities aspects of this situation, it might be argued that PRINDEP's findings about the curriculum/status/gender relationship were inevitable.

We suggest, however, that there are important reasons why this situation cannot be ignored. The first two are *professional*. One is that the pattern might seem to many staff to carry a clear career message to those disposed to hear it: namely, that among the various factors in promotion one is gender and another is the area of the curriculum in which a teacher happens to have specialist expertise. Regardless of whether such assumptions have any justification, if they are subscribed to with any conviction, they will hardly be helpful to the cause of the broadly-based curriculum. We stress '*if*' here: this is an area for necessary speculation. Indeed, it should be noted that in Leeds the proportion of female primary heads is above the national average. Current DES statistics indicate that, nationally, 51 per cent of primary heads are male; the figure for Leeds is currently 38 per cent. The other problem, of subject expertise and promotion, may be aggravated by the fact that while teachers enter primary education with a wide range of subject backgrounds as a basis for curriculum consultancy, there are far greater opportunities for retraining and/or advanced professional study in some subjects, for those who wish to change direction, than in others.

The second professional reason has to do with the relationship between *seniority* and the scope of curriculum development. A main professional grade full-time class teacher with school-wide curriculum responsibility on top of his/her teaching role may have rather less scope for the various kinds of curriculum development role outlined in Part 2 and in Chapters 5 and 7 than some senior colleagues. The latter may well have the time, resources and the professional standing among fellow-teachers to achieve success on the various fronts — preparing documents, organizing meetings, TTT and so on. The outcome of this discrepancy is not inevitable: as was argued earlier, seniority is no guarantee of quality, and there are many junior staff ably fulfilling cross-school curriculum roles. But the task of teachers in the latter situation would seem to be particularly taxing.

The other aspect to this problem is *educational*, and it too has two dimensions. Children's learning, as is well known, does not start and end with formally designated curriculum activities. Children also learn a great deal from the way teachers treat their pupils and colleagues and the way in turn they are treated. Teachers can be important role models. In the present context the association of certain subjects with men and others with women may unintentionally convey and reinforce messages that are too familiar in British society to need spelling out here; similarly, the association of particular subjects with status. When status and gender are combined, the message may become even more irresistible. This issue is an important extension of the discussion of policy and provision in the Authority and its primary schools in relation to gender which is contained in Chapter 2.

The second educational consideration in this context is the fundamental matter of quality of classroom provision. We repeat that there is no suggestion whatsoever that seniority, let alone gender, is causally associated with better provision. The real point here is rather different: within any one classroom the quality of provision is to a large extent dependent upon the individual teacher; but achieving consistent quality in a given curriculum area *throughout the school*, being a managerial challenge, is easier to achieve with the time, resources, experience, support and credibility which tend to be concomitants of seniority than without them.

Schools and the LEA

Heads' Attitudes to the LEA

Antagonism to 'the office' is part of the professional culture or folklore of teaching, just as within school staffrooms 'the boss' can be the object of comment ranging from the mildly uncharitable to the scurrilous. This is a fact of life in any hierarchy, and buck-passing, scapegoating or frustration-venting will occur whether justified or not. This is particularly the case when individuals and groups are made insecure by decisions implying or requiring change to their established habits of practice and thought.

In view of the extent of change heralded by PNP, it was inevitable that PRINDEP would uncover some degree of dissent and even hostility in relation to the Authority and its representatives. This meant that the project would need to weigh very carefully the comments it received and seek to distinguish between the almost casual or kneejerk response and the observation or reservation having substance and perhaps justification. This is one reason why in-depth interviews are a prominent feature in PRINDEP's evaluation methodology. We use questionnaires — and keep in touch with every PNP school by this means — but interviews enable us to penetrate beyond the immediate response to deeper levels of thinking. The relationship established since 1986 with the sample schools is particularly valuable in this respect, and we continue to be very grateful for their cooperation. However, face-to-face encounters in the school setting now extend well beyond this sample and at the time of writing PRINDEP has undertaken fieldwork of one kind or another in some eighty-five schools.

This is a necessary preamble to the point that the attitudes of heads described in Part 1 of this report deserve to be taken seriously. The 'concurring' and 'uncertain' responses are perhaps less problematic than those in the 'demurring' category. Some of these, characterized as 'traditionalist', reacted to the LEA's prescriptions as an encroachment on their autonomy; others, the 'modernists', saw themselves as if anything well ahead of the Authority's thinking on the content and management of the curriculum and frustrated at what they saw as a mismatch between their own espousal of open professional dialogue on such matters in the school and the apparent resistance to such dialogue at the level of the Authority; dialogue which, because of their professional experience and expertise and their position as the people who actually have to try to turn educational policy into classroom reality, they were uniquely qualified to engage in. To these heads it was they themselves, rather than the Authority or PNP, who were the real innovators, and they sometimes felt patronized by what they saw as an assumption that this could not be so.

Beyond such responses lie both commonality and diversity. What heads have in common is that they are all doing a complex and extremely demanding job for which they need all the support, both moral and practical, that they can get — from staff, from parents, from advisers and officers, and from politicians. Where they differ is in the kind and severity of the challenges they face, the experience and expertise they bring to bear, and most fundamentally in the values, beliefs and understandings which inform and shape their work.

Heads' Needs: Support and Involvement

The propositions above raise several issues and questions. First, though the Authority has evolved a major and variegated approach to in-service support and professional development, does enough of this focus upon the needs of *heads*, particularly in this context in relation to their curriculum development roles and responsibilities? PRINDEP is aware that the Authority has recently begun to develop more courses for heads and it may well be that these meet some or all of the needs identified. The question is posed not because it presumes anything about the content of these courses but simply because it has arisen from PRINDEP's recent fieldwork and is clearly of importance. Second, managing the curriculum demands two distinct but interlocking kinds of expertise: mastery of the curriculum area in question and of its translation into appropriately structured and sequenced learning activities; and skill in the interpersonal and managerial process of promoting review, development and improved practice. Have both kinds of expertise been adequately fostered (a) by heads in their schools, and (b) by the Authority through its in-service programmes and advisory support activity? (A similar proviso to that in the previous paragraph has to be made here. The revised curriculum leadership courses could well deal with the second half of this question, but this does not eliminate the need to ask it.) Third, how far is the Authority's support able to discriminate between the very different curriculum-related needs which individual heads and schools have, which may range from virtual remediation on the one hand to the facilitation and celebration of immense professional talent on the other? Fourth, how can the Authority alleviate and counter some heads' sense that in the formulation of policies on primary education in general, and on primary curriculum and teaching strategies in particular, their professional insight and skill have been undervalued, bypassed or ignored? Fifth, and relatedly, what then *should* the role of heads be in the development of LEA curriculum policies in a period of rapid educational and social change?

In considering these questions it is worth bearing in mind the earlier point about the function of heads as filters or gatekeepers to external policies and developments. If heads have been involved in the formulation of policies which affect them, they are much more likely to be committed to their successful implementation. The same principle applies at school level of course: if teachers have been involved in formulating policies which affect them, they too are more likely to want to see them through. Indeed, the principle is explicitly conveyed by the Authority on courses and in documents like the 1988 policy statement on primary education: 'Teaching staff are not afraid to learn from each other and to use their expertise for the good of the school and see themselves as having a part to play in the shaping of school philosophy and the ways of implementing it', (Leeds City Council, 1988, p. 9). For 'teaching staff', perhaps, one should read 'teachers, heads and advisers'.

Supporting Curriculum Development through INSET

Finally, in relation to INSET support for curriculum development, the total INSET picture is one of extensive and diverse provision, ranging from centralized courses (see Chapter 6) to the school-devolved GRIST experiment, the day-to-day work in schools of advisers and advisory teachers, and the professional development initiatives of heads, PNP coordinators, curriculum postholders and other staff. In the earlier stages of PNP the advisory team was operating considerably under its present strength of fourteen. PRINDEP's analysis of INSET attendances from the sample schools (in Part 2 above) touches on just one aspect of all this activity. Nevertheless it is an important one, not just for the opportunities it offers to teachers but also for what it signals to them about the Authority's priorities. However, we recognize that in Leeds the balance of courses is always a compromise among national priorities, local priorities and teachers' preferences as indicated in an annual survey conducted by the LEA.

Two further questions are prompted, therefore. First, notwithstanding the last point above, is the balance between the various aspects of the curriculum always right in the LEA's centralized courses? Second, how can an already much-expanded range of INSET provision continue to keep in step with professional need? In the present context two possible growth areas can be highlighted. One is the need of class teachers for support in the areas we have identified of curriculum *design, differentiation* and *delivery*. The concern with differentiation supports a point made in Chapter 2 about the importance of support for teachers in their vital task of identifying and meeting specific children's needs — the skill of matching. The other potential growth area is support for curriculum management and development. As is emphasized above, this kind of professional role, whether performed by the head, the PNP coordinator, a curriculum postholder or any other member of staff, has a *curriculum* and a *managerial/interpersonal* component. If the evidence suggests a relative neglect of the latter, how can this be redressed? How, in supporting staff having curriculum management responsibilities, can their differing levels and kinds of responsibility best be catered for, bearing in mind that the schoolwide, cross-curricular management role of the head, for example, is rather different from that of the science postholder with a full-time teaching commitment?

In considering how they might support staff with curriculum development responsibilities, schools and the Authority might care to note the earlier point about the need for a *vocabulary* of curriculum management skills and procedures. This argument parallels current thinking about teaching strategies in the classroom: teachers, it is now widely accepted, need a repertoire of teaching strategies from which they can choose those which are most appropriate to their particular classroom situation and which sit most readily with their unique professional persona, rather than having to conform to somebody else's version of the 'one right way'. The same point could be made about styles of curriculum management: a standard management package is simply not adequate for such diverse circumstances and personalities as are to be found in Leeds primary schools. There are alternatives, and a fair number have emerged from recent research, including PRINDEP's own studies.

All these points are made (in October 1988) without prejudice to the 1988–89 in-service programme. Most of this programme has not yet taken place, and it may well be revised in the light of the 1988 Education Reform Act.

The Reality of the Broadly-based Curriculum

Alternative Curriculum Realities

Curriculum development is undertaken for explicit purposes which have to do with improving the quality of educational provision available to children in schools. If successful, it has *intended* consequences: a greater measure of continuity between teachers and classes, for example, or a more adventurous use in thematic work of the local environment, or a uniform system of record keeping, or more successful kinds of TTT. But curriculum development also has *unintended* consequences. Being unintended, they are less likely to be noticed, beause they will not be looked for. One prominent example to emerge from PRINDEP's present study is the kinds of messages which may be conveyed to children by the repeated association of certain subjects with staff gender or status. Another is the issue of professional cooperation and collaboration — a powerful contribution to children's social learning which we noted in the context of TTT (see Chapter 7). This distinction between intended and unintended consequences of particular curriculum development strategies is an extension of the contrast between the formal and hidden curriculum with which all teachers are familiar.

The point is made here because in asking the question, 'What is the reality of the broadly-based curriculum?' two arguments have to be acknowledged. One is that there is not one curriculum reality, but many, depending on where in the educational hierarchy one is situated: curriculum looks and feels different to an adviser, a head, a teacher, and a child. The other is that in the final analysis it is the last — the child's version and experience of the curriculum — which matters most.

'Broadly-based' in Practice

How heads and teachers understand the Authority's PNP principle of the 'broadly-based curriculum' was the starting point for PRINDEP's fieldwork within its curriculum theme. The examples given on pages 123 to 126 repay close study and it is hoped that schools will find them useful for staffroom discussion purposes. However, although this report has shown that this phrase is interpreted in almost as many ways as there are teachers, no less important than such variations are the professional and educational attitudes with which they are associated.

Beyond the LEA definition and the heads' and teachers' redefinitions are school and classroom practices, and it is at this level that the real meaning of the phrase becomes apparent. At that level, as this report shows, a consistent pattern emerges. It is that as far as curriculum development activity is concerned, certain areas of the curriculum receive a far greater investment of money, human resources, time, expertise and commitment than do others. The discrepancies are very marked and they are mutually reinforcing: curriculum areas which have less time and money invested in them are also the responsibility of less experienced staff, are also supported by less in-service activity and so on.

The justification for such discrepancies is familiar enough: they are in line with popularly assumed educational values concerning what kinds of learning are most and least important to primary children. However, our analysis here and in Chapter 3 suggests a lack of parity even between the 'basics' of maths and language. Such degrees of discrepancy may well call into question the viability, if not the sincerity, of the commitment to a 'broadly-based curriculum' since one of the almost inevitable consequences is that there will be comparable discrepancies in the *quality of provision in the classroom*.

This problem raises the question of the real force of 'broadly-based'. At one level breadth has been achieved: children are experiencing a wide range of aspects of the curriculum as a result of sustained effort by heads, teachers and the Authority's advisory staff, with a greater degree of consistency than in pre-PNP days. The messages about the content and environment of learning are getting through and generous extra staffing and funding are enabling them to be translated into development programmes and classroom action. But because these resources appear to be used somewhat unevenly, and with a consistent pattern of unevenness, there is a real possibility that while overall a greater breadth may be achieved, some of those curriculum areas lower down in schools' scales of priorities may be so superficially treated as to make the claim to breadth a somewhat hollow one.

Broadening the Concept of Breadth

In their report, *The Curriculum from 5 to 16*, (DES, 1985) HMI developed their own principle of curriculum breadth in a way which bears importantly on this problem. They argued for two senses of breadth: first, a wide range of curriculum areas; and second, a wide range of educational experience *within* each area. Further, they urged that 'care is needed that breadth is not pursued at the expense of depth since this may lead to superficial work' — a tendency they noted particularly in art, craft, history, geography and topic work. It might be suggested that the chances of achieving breadth in this more comprehensive sense for some of the curriculum areas near the bottom of the curriculum development ladder portrayed earlier are somewhat slender.

A further gloss on curriculum breadth is offered at the beginning of the 1988 Education Act, where the phrase 'broadly-based' actually appears, but bearing a particular definition which is rather different from that offered by many PRINDEP respondents. Here, a 'broadly based curriculum':

(a) promotes the spiritual, moral, cultural, mental and physical development of pupils at the school and of society; and
(b) prepares such pupils for the opportunities, responsibilities and experiences of adult life. (Education Reform Act, Section 1 (2))

The Act goes on to require schools to provide a *basic* curriculum of religious education together with the three core subjects and six other foundation subjects of the National Curriculum, and to indicate the main components of each such subject in terms of 'knowledge, skills and understanding . . . matters, skills and processes . . . arrangements for assessing pupils.' It should be noted that the 'basic curriculum' of RE plus the National Curriculum is but a part of the 'broadly-based curriculum' as defined in the 1988 Act.

Schools and LEAs are well aware of their obligation during the next few years to ensure that they meet these requirements. In view of this, it might be sensible to review two major issues covered by this report. The first is the matter of strategies for curriculum review, management and development, at both school and Authority levels. How far will they be able to deliver what is required? Which particular strategies, or combinations of strategies, are most likely to secure change in both school policy and classroom practice? The second need, it might be suggested, is for the primary community in Leeds to look again at the concept of 'broadly-based'. There is no doubt that it has served a useful purpose since 1985 in directing attention to the importance of diversity, stimulation and challenge in children's learning. At the same time PRINDEP's evidence indicates that as a concept it is somewhat vague, and as practice it may sometimes satisfy only limited criteria of breadth. Although any such words carry similar risks, and they are after all only words, it might be helpful to develop the concept of breadth with greater reference to the other principles with which it is frequently associated: 'depth', 'balance', 'relevance', 'differentiation', 'progression', 'continuity'.

If a curriculum can meet all these criteria, it will certainly be broad in the best sense. But equally, a curriculum will have no chance at all of meeting such criteria unless *each* of its constituent parts (not just those one or two parts deemed the most important) is supported by an adequate level of curriculum development.

5
Change from Within: The Coordinator

Introduction

In Part 2 of the previous chapter we considered some of the strategies for managing and developing the curriculum which were adopted in the context of the Primary Needs Programme. Most are familiar, and many did not owe their existence to PNP as such, but PNP contributed the extra time and material resources to make them more effective. More distinctive is the managerial role we examine in the present chapter: that of the Primary Needs Coordinator. It was one of the LEA's key stratagems in its bid to revitalize the city's primary schools, both a symbol and an instrument of change. It was the most tangible indicator to a school's staff that PNP had arrived. Extra capitation could be absorbed without comment — there could never be enough of it; staff could go on LEA courses, but then they always had; but a PNP coordinator really was something new.

The LEA's job specification, quoted below, indicates the novelty of the new role and hence the anxieties which, initially at least, many felt about it. Who were these people bearing this unfamiliar label? What exactly would they coordinate? Did their elaborate job description herald something novel and exciting, or did it boil down to no more than a high status remedial teacher or ancillary? Were they going to support existing staff in their endeavours, or were they really there as agents of the LEA? Spies, perhaps, charged with seeking out and reporting ideological lapses? Or even a new breed of super-teacher planted strategically to succeed where others had failed? (None of these characterizations, extreme though they may sound, is fictitious.)

Coordinators had to respond to these kinds of anxiety as part of their task of making the specified role a practical reality. This chapter charts some of the possibilities and problems, solutions and prerequisites. It also places the Leeds role in the context of the wider national trend towards styles of primary school management which give teachers cross-school roles in addition to their traditional one of taking a class. Such roles are certainly not new, but they have become much less peripheral in recent years, mainly as a result of consistent pressure from HMI, with the 1986 Select Committee Report providing one of the most succinct yet comprehensive justifications (House of Commons, 1986, paras 9.1–9.30). Research studies by Rodger (1983), Campbell (1985) and the Birmingham-based Primary Schools Research and Development Group (Taylor, 1986) explore how the idea works in practice and the present chapter can be seen as an extension of this line of enquiry.

However, the established professional culture of primary schools, pivoting as it has done for over a century on the roles of class teacher and head, is a powerful and resilient one, and this can make the full institution-alization of a new role cutting across these existing professional boundaries difficult (Alexander, 1984a, Ch. 8). The Leeds experience bears this out, and indeed our later fieldwork on PNP coordinators (discussed in Volume 2) showed the traditional culture reasserting itself, sometimes even to the point where the coordinator role effectively disappeared.

The study draws on the following data: questionnaires completed by PNP Phase 1 coordinators in 1986 and 1987; questionnaires completed by Phase 1 heads in 1987; interviews with heads and coordinators in the thirty Fieldwork B (representative sample) schools in 1987; and observation of coordinators at work in the same year.

The study opens with the coordinator's original job specification. This provides the point of reference for the outline of the various roles we found coordinators to be undertaking and our analysis of factors influencing their ability to operate effectively. We then deal briefly with the LEA's later modifications to the role, before offering a discussion of wider implications.

What Coordinators Do

The June 1985 job description reads as follows:

> There will be in each school a senior member of staff responsible to the Head Teacher for coordinating the Primary Needs Programme.

> The job description will include:

> (a) Cooperating with colleagues and the various support agencies working within the school and with linked schools in order to:

> — develop within the school a curriculum which is broadly-

based within an environment rich in stimulus and challenge;
— help teachers see the value of first-hand experience and environment as a resource for learning;
— help teachers develop flexible teaching strategies;
— help colleagues develop evaluation skills and to match work at an appropriate level;
— develop productive links with parents and the community.

(b) Assisting colleagues within the school and in linked schools [in] the production of written guidelines/agreed procedures concerned with special educational needs.

(c) Advising colleagues concerning pupils with special educational needs, keeping an up-to-date knowledge of appropriate teaching and learning strategies — having a knowledge of appropriate support agencies whose expertise can be used — attending appropriate courses and making contributions to school-based in-service training.

(d) Assisting in the establishment within schools of a resource base for special educational needs which would include responsibility for buying in appropriate materials and setting up the system for maintaining and using such resources.

(e) Working *alongside* teachers within the school in order to:
— monitor the effectiveness of the guidance given [and] resources provided;
— help diagnose specific and general learning difficulties and devise appropriate strategies to deal with them;
— provide specific, practical help for individuals and small groups within the context of general classroom provision;
— set up a coordinated and effective system for monitoring and recording the progress of pupils with special educational needs.

(f) Liaise with teachers in linked schools in order to interpret pupil progress at the point of transfer and to give clear guidance concerning future teaching strategies for individual pupils. (Leeds City Council, 1985c)

An initial point here is the striking difference between the detail of the SEN role outlined in sections (b) to (f) and the broad generality of section (a). This section indicates the coordinator's involvement in curriculum development, staff development and home-school links, and is often now referred to by schools as 'the primary needs' part of the role. The contrast between the two sections of the same job description might have some bearing on the tensions which a number of coordinators have expressed between 'primary needs' and special needs, more particularly as the original job description of April 1985 placed the details of the SEN role first.

A second point is that the role outlined in this job description is very extensive. It is now clearly stated by the advisory service that this list is to be used selectively and indeed it is unlikely that any one coordinator could, or should, take sole responsibility for so many initiatives. Undoubtedly schools will have different priorities in developing the teaching skills and curriculum expertise of teachers and responding to the learning requirements of pupils. Section (a) of the job description, particularly, appears to offer considerable flexibility and scope for tailoring the coordinator's role to a wide range of specific circumstances.

Our data indicate that during the period in question most coordinators did undertake a number of different roles and combine several aspects of the job specification. These fell into five main categories, each of which we now discuss: special educational needs, curriculum development, staff development, home-school links and whole-class responsibility.

Special Educational Needs

In the questionnaire returns of both 1986 and 1987 nearly three-quarters of the coordinators stated that they were involved with SEN provision. In both years it was the most frequent response to the question asking which aspect of their role they considered to be successful. About half of all respondents nominated SEN. Their success was described with two different emphases. First, many coordinators indicated that since their arrival the needs of the children with learning difficulties were more accurately identified, more appropriate learning tasks were being prescribed and more individualized attention was being given. Heads confirmed this view. Second, a few coordinators chose to emphasize that they had succeeded in developing greater staff awareness of the most appropriate strategies for teaching these children. Typical responses were: 'awareness of SN and how to organize it is under way . . .'; 'staff's recognition of the need for adequate strategies in SEN teaching . . .'.

A significant difference between the 1986 and 1987 surveys was that in 1987 SEN ranked as the highest response in the section of the questionnaire where coordinators were invited to mention any challenging or difficult aspects of their work. Nearly half of all replies indicated that SEN provision was problematic. The same question in the 1986 questionnaire had rather less than one-eighth of the respondents referring to SEN. In 1987 there were two main obstacles to success: insufficient time to deal with children who had special educational needs (a problem that was sometimes exacerbated by timetabling disruption), and differences of opinion among staff about the style of SEN provision. It is worth examining each of these problems in some detail.

The difficulty of fitting in SEN provision was a recurring problem in the 1987 questionnaire returns and in the interviews. Coordinators were finding that undertaking detailed diagnosis, maintaining the Authority's Individual Needs Recording System (INRS) and producing individual work programmes placed heavy demands on their work schedule, especially when they had other 'PNP' responsibilities in school. They stated that staff absence and covering for in-service also disrupted the timetabling of their work. Some typical comments were:

> developing an established practice for SN is difficult without adequate time and resources and with commitments elsewhere . . . .

> covering for absences and courses prevents continuity so vital for SN children . . . .

> insufficient time to devote to those requiring individual tuition on a regular basis . . . .

> finding enough time to put appropriate inputs into primary needs and special needs aspects of the curriculum . . . .

By and large heads supported this view, and typical problems mentioned by them were:

> allocating proportion of time spent on special needs rather than primary needs . . . .

> identifying children with special needs but being unable to support them adequately . . . .

> staff are so busy on special needs, they've been unable to carry out other work . . . .

Only a few coordinators (and usually those in larger schools with a high number of PNP appointments) defined their role solely in terms of SEN. Many others combined the role with other components of the job description and a few also supported on a part-time basis the work of the school's SEN coordinator already in post, perhaps taking responsibility for children on Stage 1 of INRS (Leeds Individual Needs Recording System) or the children with learning difficulties in a particular age group.

In general terms these problems of time and timetabling may represent a deeper issue concerning the degree of emphasis on special needs within PNP. This has plagued the programme since its inception. The following comments from our interviews give a stark indication of the initial confusion:

> When PNP began I received two messages about its purpose: that it was for children with special needs but there again it wasn't for special needs, but for the general enhancement of the curriculum. (Headteacher in a Phase 1 school)

> When I first heard about PNP I thought it was a special needs initiative. Even at early meetings there were variations in emphasis according to who was talking. (Headteacher in a Phase 1 school)

> The information I received with the application form and the style of interviews led me to believe I would be dealing with special needs. This emphasis changed between my appointment in May and my taking up the post in September. (Coordinator in a Phase 1 school)

However, by now the message has been clearly stated that special needs are not by any means the sum of PNP. Some schools which initially employed their PNP staff in a full-time remedial capacity were advised that this was an inappropriate use. Nevertheless, various factors may contribute to the continued sense of tension between 'primary needs' and special needs, at least in Phase 1 schools, and particularly in those with a low number of extra appointments.

A number of coordinators and heads have suggested that the implications of the LISSEN training, coupled with the detail of the current job description, could require virtually full-time commitment. If we use Warnock's axiom that 20 per cent of every school's pupils have 'special needs', then simultaneously undertaking a number of other responsibilities in school may put some coordinators under considerable pressure. Moreover, several coordinators have expressed a dilemma over whether to adopt the 'primary needs' or special needs approach when dealing with children with learning difficulties. They sense an uncomfortable discrepancy between the philosophy of the 'broadly-based curriculum', with first-hand experience and outside visits, and the precision teaching strategies associated with SEN provision, especially when they have limited time to work with these children. Finally, some Phase 1 coordinators, attracted to the role by the original publicity and job description, claim SEN specialist expertise which they would like to use more fully; whereas others characterize themselves as skilled generalist primary practitioners.

Even two years after the reorientation of the Primary Needs Programme, and the attempted clarification of the status of special needs within it, this issue of time clearly indicates that there is still a problematic legacy. In practice it has not always been easy to make the SEN role just one element of a much wider brief. This may be especially so in Phase 1 schools which were selected for PNP by a set of criteria which included educational need.

The second point to emerge from the questionnaire returns related to the most appropriate strategies for SEN provision. A number of coordinators said they still found resistance to their 'working alongside' in the classroom and many of these also commented that colleagues were unwilling to share responsibility for the children with special needs. Typical comments were:

> staff are not taking their share of SN work, i.e. following up programmes . . . .

> I have least success in making staff feel more enthusiastic and competent at meeting the needs of the less able within their own class . . . .

> class teachers do not want to be responsible for slow learners or to have advice. They all want slow learners out of the classroom. There is no school policy on special needs . . . .

> The staff don't see it as their job to cope with these problem children . . . .

The same points were made during interviews, and heads also have acknowledged this problem: 'two or three teachers believe there should be remedial classes . . .'; 'some staff think SN should be provided for by PNP appointments . . .'.

It seems that many class teachers are unaware of, ignore or even oppose the integrationist philosophy which has underpinned SEN provision since the Warnock Report and the 1981 Act. On the other hand, these teachers may also say with some justification that SEN provision, without adequate support, is a time-consuming addition to their busy class workload. Determining the most appropriate strategies for SEN provision often focuses on the issue of where these children should be taught. It is frequently discussed in terms of a dilemma: to withdraw or not to withdraw. Some coordinators spoke of the difficulty of breaking down the 'remedial' tradition within their schools. Others were very sympathetic to the arguments for sometimes removing small groups from the classroom for special tuition, but felt this was 'disapproved of'. This may be an excessively literal interpretation of the advisory service's recommendations that children with special needs should be provided with help within the context of general classroom provision. In fact it would seem that withdrawal, if debated as an issue solely about the physical location of the children being taught, may be an unfortunate focus for the disagreement and confusion. The more fundamental issue is the kinds of understanding that exist, at whole-school level, about the integrationist approach that underpins the current philosophy of special needs provision. When joint responsibility is fully accepted, the precise location of SEN teaching may be a much more pragmatic decision. This has been clearly stated by the advisory service. For example, a handout distributed at an in-service session in 1987, intended for newly appointed coordinators and entitled 'Primary Needs Programme — The Context', contains the following section:

7. Providing Specific and Practical Help for Children with SEN (1981 Act)

* This to be within CONTEXT of general classroom provision; this means
— support for the normal teacher within the teaching base,
— withdrawal *where this is felt to be appropriate BUT ALWAYS in close consultation*
* *Aim is to help every teacher become a teacher of SEN*

A similar statement was made in handouts during the promotion of Phase 2 of PNP in 1986. Notwithstanding this clarification, there may have been insufficient support, information or direction from the advisory service to help many of the non-PNP staff in schools understand what it is that 'good' special needs practice involves. This is in contrast with the extensive in-service work through which the LEA is transmitting its messages about good *primary* practice to all levels of teachers in the Authority.

However, as already stated, some coordinators and heads emphasized that they have successfully implemented collaboration between the SEN specialist and class teachers. A few schools also pointed out that their coordinator's work in the particular area of special needs had served to raise staff awareness about the most appropriate teaching strategies, resources and record keeping procedures for all pupils in the school.

The other components of the coordinator's work in school, often combined with special needs, are frequently referred to as 'the primary needs part of my role'. This umbrella term usually relates to work in the areas of curriculum development, staff development and home-school links.

The questionnaire returns and interviews reflect the way that the more generalized directives of the Authority's job description have given schools a good deal of flexibility in determining the contribution of the coordinator to staff and curriculum development. Yet there is evidence that on occasion a degree of tension and confusion also exists as coordinators, heads and existing staff attempt to formulate a viable PNP role within the school.

Curriculum Development

The Authority's job description indicates that coordinators are to 'cooperate with colleagues . . . in order to . . . develop within school a curriculum which is broadly based within an environment rich in challenge and stimulus.' It is clear from the survey data and from interviews that coordinators' involvement in curriculum development takes different forms. Four different emphases have provisionally been identified: a coordinator may contribute to curriculum development as a curriculum manager; a curriculum specialist; a curriculum enhancer; or a curriculum facilitator. It is likely that most coordinators work in more than one of these ways.

Curriculum Manager. Some coordinators depict their role as a curriculum policy-maker, having influence in determining overall goals and strategies for the school. Typical responses to the question about coordinators' main roles were: 'involvement in all policy decisions concerning curriculum and teaching . . . '; 'obtaining an overview of the school, the school being my total unit . . . '. Nearly a quarter of the questionnaire returns indicated that coordinators were involved in decision-making at a senior management level.

Curriculum Specialist. Just under a third of coordinators said that they were undertaking responsibility for a specific area of the curriculum; that is, they were involved in introducing or upgrading a particular subject area throughout the school.

In both 1986 and 1987 the most frequently mentioned curriculum areas for which coordinators were taking responsibility were science, music, maths and language. In 1987 multicultural education also ranked high. This response came often, but not exclusively, from multi-ethnic coordinators. Such variation in areas of responsibility indicates that schools are making independent decisions about their particular curriculum needs, and coordinators are plugging a gap, or that they are exploiting the specialist skills and interests which a coordinator might happen to offer.

Sometimes coordinators indicated that they were sharing curriculum responsibility with a member of staff already in post. Curriculum responsibility emerged as a role that presented particular difficulties as well as offering the opportunity for success. Some coordinators wrote that they had success in achieving 'continuity' or 'a whole-school approach' in a particular curriculum area, while others mentioned that this was a particular problem. Some typical responses to questions about challenges and obstacles to success were: 'taking curriculum development from theory to practice . . . '; 'my own lack of training in the area of curriculum development . . . '; 'establishing a base to work from and building up adequate resources . . . [my curriculum area] does not yet happen in all classrooms'.

Whether coordinators face different problems, or in fact have particular advantages as curriculum leaders compared to their class teaching postholder colleagues, cannot be determined from the data currently available. One factor will no doubt be the curriculum area for which they take responsibility: a coordinator undertaking development work in the new and value-laden area of multicultural education may have less success than one who is dealing with the so-called 'basics' of the primary curriculum: language, maths or even, in the current climate, science.

Curriculum Enhancer. Over a quarter of coordinators described their role in a more generalist way: it involved 'enhancing' or 'extending' the curricular experiences of children in certain classes or year groups. Their work focused on particular groups of children and perhaps on demonstrating the value of 'cross-curricular links' rather than on a particular curriculum area and its development and delivery throughout the school. Several coordinators indicated how *the year group* had become an important organizational device for improving curriculum and teaching, and some referred to their role as 'year group leader'. This role involved: 'getting teachers to cooperate in producing materials and sharing ideas . . . '; 'getting year groups to work together on projects . . . '. Some heads too mentioned that they were using their coordinators to develop topic work on a year group basis.

Other coordinators merely referred to their role as support teacher or to 'team teaching' in certain classes, leaving unstated the precise nature of their contribution. Some responses implied an equal status among the collaborating teachers. In interview it was apparent that a number of coordinators had an informal and adaptable style of support that was responsive to the particular learning requirements of each classroom: 'I see my role as support teacher as depending on staff's and children's needs' (Coordinator in a Phase 1 school).

Those coordinators who spoke of their role as year group leader, or curriculum enhancers in terms of providing children with first-hand experience or visits and the like, very often indicated that this way of contributing to curriculum development was very effective. Perhaps the direct focus on children rather than their teachers to some extent accounts for this sense of success. Many coordinators still commented that some of their colleagues were not comfortable with what PRINDEP has termed Teachers Teaching Together (TTT) (see Chapter 7).

Curriculum Facilitator. Nearly a quarter of coordinators stated that they also had a facilitating role in curriculum development: releasing colleagues to pursue some aspect of work related to their particular curriculum responsibilities. Many of these coordinators, and also many heads, said that they saw the release of postholders as an intrinsic part of the role, and both specified that this was a distinct benefit of PNP. A few coordinators indicated that they felt their releasing role highlighted the need for their school to consider more carefully the role of the postholder and the most appropriate strategies for curriculum development. There were comments on 'staff's lack of curriculum experience' and on 'the need for rethinking posts of responsibility'. These would suggest that the issue of release is a useful indicator of the general thinking on curriculum development within the school.

Coordinators themselves seem to be in no doubt about the overall impact of PNP on the curriculum offered to children in their school: many responded to the question about the main benefits of PNP by referring to the 'broader' curriculum now available. Much the same terminology was found in the heads' questionnaire returns. It is interesting to speculate whether the expanding role of the postholder, which is undoubtedly one of the outcomes of PNP, will also encourage schools to discuss their curriculum goals and achievements in terms of the other characteristics of curriculum currently being advanced by HMI and DES: balance, relevance, differentiation, progression and continuity. In other words, will PNP serve to encourage a much more fundamental reappraisal of the curriculum as a whole than is implied by the term 'breadth'?

Staff Development

The Authority's job description indicates that coordinators are likely to be involved in staff development. Their role may be to 'help teachers see the value of first-hand experience and environment as a resource for learning';

'help teachers develop flexible teaching strategies' and 'help colleagues develop evaluation skills and to match work at an appropriate level'. There is, of course, an inextricable and inevitable link between curriculum development and staff development. This being so, each of the contributions to curriculum development outlined above is likely to augment the professional expertise of the staff involved.

However, it is also clear that many coordinators and their headteachers see the role as one that directly seeks to assist colleagues change or improve their class management strategies, at the same time providing advice on appropriate curriculum content. Several heads spoke of their coordinator as a model or 'living example' of good practice. The 'broadly-based' curriculum, so strongly advocated by the Authority, requires some teachers to adopt less formal teaching methods than previously. TTT is probably the key strategem used by coordinators to help teachers adopt the so-called flexible teaching strategies through which this version of curriculum is delivered.

In 1986 'changing teaching styles' was the most frequest response to the question about what coordinators counted as their greatest challenges or difficulties. By 1987 things had improved: coordinators tended to indicate that individual teachers were resisting the PNP message, but many also confirmed that staff were trying new teaching approaches because of collaborative teaching arrangements. Several heads commented on the increase in 'group teaching' (i.e. grouping children instead of teaching them as a whole class) which had come about since the coordinator's arrival.

However, in interviews some coordinators were beginning to express frustration at the difficulties of achieving a long-term influence on teaching style in a support teaching role. They reported, for example, that some teachers reverted to their previous methods during the time that the coordinator was providing support elsewhere. A small number felt that there might be more potential in reversing the relationship so that the coordinator was the incumbent/class teacher and displayed expertise to the 'client' teacher who would then observe and learn class management skills in the support role. This viewpoint might verify the effectiveness of institutionalizing the coordinator in a 'master teacher' role, such as year group leader. Elsewhere (see Chapter 7) we have indicated that teaching alongside colleagues in a staff development capacity is a far more complex matter than many coordinators, and perhaps even policy-makers, originally believed.

TTT is not the only kind of involvement which coordinators may have in staff development. Some have referred to formalized managerial responsibilities, such as those of a staff tutor. Others indicate that they have a consultative role in policy decisions about staff development strategies or responsibility for the deployment of PNP staff.

A further contribution to staff development, mentioned in the 1986 and 1987 questionnaire returns, has been the use of coordinators as cover to enable colleagues to attend in-service courses. The ability of staff to attend in-service ranked very high in coordinators' and heads' responses to the question about the main benefits of PNP. However, some coordinators also felt that being used as cover was a distinct disadvantage for their work and indeed a few even suggested that it was a negative or corrosive influence on their status. Others stressed that they felt it was 'fair' that non-PNP staff should have the same opportunities to attend in-service as they had in the first year of PNP, and were happy to facilitate this.

Home-School Links

The last subsection of part (a) in the Authority's job description refers to the coordinator's contribution to 'developing productive links with parents and the community'. In both the 1986 and 1987 surveys', 'working with parents' ranked third in coordinators' responses to the question about their successes. A small number of coordinators and heads indicated that maintaining parental interest beyond the initial stages was proving difficult, but many others spoke positively about the continuing involvement of parents in their children's learning. A variety of successful initiatives was mentioned: parents' rooms, shared and paired reading, maths and reading workshops, activity mornings. Other coordinators referred to their involvement in the Authority's Portage scheme.

Apart from those schools with extra staff such as Portage-trained NNEBs or Home-School Liaison Assistants, the emphasis on this role was usually dependent on an individual school's (or one influential member's) belief in the educational importance of such initiatives. Several heads, and coordinators, explained that their school had not so far had sufficient time, space or human resources to undertake systematic work in this area.

As PRINDEP Report 3, *Home–School Links: First Findings*, has shown, the arrival of PNP did not automatically alter or increase parental involvement in many Phase 1 and 2 schools. Perhaps this issue reflects professional attitudes as much as school and staff resources.

Whole-Class Responsibility

Another role mentioned by a small number of coordinators was that of class teaching. They indicated that they undertook responsibility for a particular class for substantial periods of the week, perhaps sharing it with another senior member of staff. Some recently appointed coordinators have also stated that they were assigned to a class teaching role initially. In interviews during the summer term of 1987 several established coordinators said they were negotiating with their headteacher about taking on class teaching responsibilities in the next school year. This prospect was sometimes welcomed, but others felt it to be a clear indication that their innovatory and development role was being terminated. 'Taking a class would be a backward step for me. I won't be able to fulfil my coordinator's role, and many gains of PNP will be lost. On a personal level I need more than just responsibility for a class' (Coordinator in a Phase 1 school).

This itemization of five different areas of responsibility and activity demonstrates the enormous variation in the way the coordinator's role has been realized in schools. This is to a certain extent inevitable: the size and location of a school are two obvious factors affecting the coordinator's work, and PNP schools range from small semi-rural to large inner-city. It is also clear that, whatever the school, there is a constant merging of the different components of the job description: staff and curriculum development become indistinguishable; much of the work in curriculum extension and curriculum responsibility utilizes the same strategy of TTT and is usually underpinned by the same commitment to an integrated curriculum; SEN provision may involve the coordinator in working with parents.

It is also very evident from this survey of coordinator roles that PNP schools feel they can make considerable advances in providing for the educational needs of their pupils and the professional requirements of their staff in the wake of their PNP coordinator's arrival. It is hardly surprising that those heads with a low number of PNP appointments sometimes say they feel outfaced by the enormous range of initiatives suggested by the coordinator's job description, and regret the selectiveness enforced by their staffing resources.

What Affects the Coordinator's Role?

Not all coordinators or their schools have found it an easy task to implement the new role. Coordinators' work and successes are determined not only by the particular circumstances of the school they are assigned to but also by the colleagues and headteacher they have to work with and by their own professional personality, tactics and perception of the role. It is therefore important to examine the various factors within a school which influence a coordinator's ability to work effectively.

In the 1986 and 1987 questionnaire returns coordinators themselves cited three main factors in their success: headteacher's support; staff attitude; their own personality and expertise. It is both logical and likely that all three must also be implicated in any lack of success. Each of them is undoubtedly a major contributor to the realization of the coordinator's role and so merits separate attention and analysis.

The Influence of the Head

The headteacher is without doubt a crucial influence upon the coordinator's ability to operate effectively. In both years of the questionnaire returns coordinators have identified their headteacher as the second main contributory factor to their success, after their other colleagues. A significant difference between 1986 and 1987 is that in the question about the main obstacles to success 'headteacher' has dropped from the highest response to hardly being mentioned at all.

The kind of support that heads offer is not generally itemized in the questionnaires, but some respondents, not surprisingly, indicated that it was a head's own understanding of PNP and his or her effective communication of its implications to staff which made all the difference. In interviews coordinators were most positive about their role in schools where heads delegated responsibility to them but also provided authoritative backing, where specific goals and/or job specifications had been negotiated *with* the coordinator and where a consistent policy of whole-school discussion and decision-making was attempted.

The task for the head of incorporating the coordinator into a school's pre-existing professional structure was, and is, considerable. Accommodating the needs and attitudes of existing staff to those of the incoming coordinator cannot always be easy. Moreover, many Phase 1 coordinators arrived at a time when industrial action was prohibiting the kinds of staff discussion which PNP actually requires and should promote. One Phase 1 head reflected: 'Heads had to undergo a battery of training at the same time as coping with more staff and a new role in school.' However, in interviews heads varied considerably in their views about the role and significance of the coordinator in their school.

> I object to the name coordinator; it smacks of management. I see the coordinator as giving support so teachers can pursue ideas already in school, not imposed from outside. (Headteacher in a Phase 2 school)

> I want the coordinator to be a catalyst.... Teachers in this school
> have been set in their ways. (Headteacher in a Phase 2 school)

The coordinator, as the two comments above illustrate, can be seen by the head as predominantly a facilitator or as an initiator of staff and curriculum development, two functions that may result in marked differences of status and influence. Such polarity of opinion about the role no doubt reflects heads' management styles, their view of the teachers already in school, their eagerness for change and development and sometimes the perceived effectiveness of the deputy-head and other senior staff in school.

The inclusion of coordinators in senior management decision-making was a recurrent issue, particularly as some schools have commented on the overlap, or even rivalry, which exists between the coordinator's role and that of the deputy-head. Presumably this problem derives from the fact that as PNP has expanded to include (or actually stand for) 'all things good in primary practice', then responsibility for 'coordinating PNP' may have become a task which is increasingly beyond a single appointee. Deputy-heads and coordinators can both feel marginalized if they are predominantly concerned with classroom provision and not consulted or involved in whole-school initiatives. One school resolved the problem by appointing its own deputy-head to take on the coordinator's duties also. The heads, coordinators and deputy-heads of several schools spoke about the effectiveness of a three-way senior management team in which each brought important perspectives to the collective task of identifying needs, establishing goals and selecting appropriate strategies.

The Sttitude of Other Staff

Coordinators pointed to their colleagues as a key to their own success even more frequently than they mentioned their headteachers. They described colleagues' supportive attitudes in terms like 'cooperation', 'sharing aims' and 'having the same commitment and enthusiasm'. Yet they also acknowledged that there are certain teachers who still have difficulty with the new style of professional relationships in classroom and staffroom which a coordinator personifies. Some heads also commented that a few of their staff were unwilling to accept the validity of a teacher who does not 'own' a class.

> floaters cause grumbles....

> a few staff believe all teachers should have a class, so that class
> numbers can be reduced....

some staff are reluctant to accept new members of staff, new ideas and new methods of working . . . .

Many Phase 1 coordinators mentioned that, by the end of the second year of PNP (1987), they felt totally integrated and accepted into the school. This is in marked contrast to 1986, when many heads and coordinators had reported that staff — class teachers, postholders and senior members — felt threatened by the new role, and sometimes reacted with hostility. The message is plainly 'we are all PNP now'. In-service courses for non-PNP staff are said to have assisted here. Coordinators belong to the school and are not the advisers' task force or agents as many initially feared (and indeed as some coordinators' behaviour may also have implied). The possible distinction between being accepted as a good colleague and being allowed to operate effectively in an innovative quasi-management role is a matter for further exploration.

The Persona and Style of the Coordinator

All coordinators with whom we discussed their tactics spoke of the need to go slowly initially and be seen to be busy, hardworking and willing to undertake menial classroom tasks. This is recommended by the advisory staff at in-service courses for coordinators. The implication is clearly that coordinators must expect to earn their status through classroom credibility, rather than have it automatically accorded by virtue of their label. Most were deliberately using this low-key beginning to form their own views about the needs of the school, an activity requiring some discretion. Staff expressed most resentment when their coordinators came across as too critical and opinionated: 'She makes you feel everything in the school is wrong and she's going to put it right' (Scale II teacher in a Phase 2 school). Some also incurred bad feeling when they appeared too removed from the business of teaching children: 'He hasn't got a class to think about and he can spend his time ringing up or sorting out equipment . . . . It's annoying sometimes being told he's doing this and that and you've got a class to deal with' (Scale II teacher in a Phase 1 school).

Several headteachers, in the questionnaires of 1986 and in interview, suggested that internal appointments of coordinators averted these problems of negotiating entry and establishing credibility. However, some of the internally appointed or promoted coordinators indicated that they felt *less* able to develop their role precisely because they were already on the staff, and had occupied a clear (and more lowly) position in the school's pre-existing power structure. An alternative solution to this problem of initial credibility has been to give newly appointed coordinators a class teaching role at first.

Clearly at issue, for all coordinators, is a delicate balance of self-assertion and compromise, being both leader and colleague, always underpinned by a particular perception of what the coordinator's role entails. In the interviews it was very apparent that there were sometimes marked differences among coordinators in their thinking about the nature of their role. All had expected to have an impact on the practices of the school, but by the end of the second year of PNP their attitude varied from buoyant optimism to despondency, and this was almost entirely related to the degree of influence they felt they wielded.

Coordinators' influence is undoubtedly related to the roles they are allowed and expect to undertake. Whatever the particular component of the job description they contribute to — SEN, curriculum / staff development or home–school links — it is possible to define that contribution in terms of one or more of three general functions:

whole-school manager, i.e. being involved in school policy and decision-making;

enactor, i.e. participant in PNP initiatives, perhaps drawing on their specialist expertise and usually involving collaboration with other staff;

facilitator, i.e. covering for other staff to enable them to be directly involved in PNP initiatives.

Morale is likely to be low where a coordinator feels that he or she is predominantly a facilitator or is engaged in collaborations that are unsuccessful, unwanted or unrewarding, and is without a compensatory consultative or management role. In some interviews coordinators felt they had been rendered ineffective in, or reached the limits of, their innovatory role. A very small number even suggested they should be moved on, preferring the role to be a temporary change-agent rather than a permanent and integrated addition to a school. Most acknowledged that the role was one that offered a very different kind of job satisfaction from class teaching and that it required considerable interpersonal skills. Some mentioned that the role was particularly taxing because it was highly visible and at all times carried the expectation of excellence.

In all cases the role had been moulded by the particular circumstances and personalities of the school; coordinators were servicing the identified needs of the school rather than adhering strictly to a role that was defined at central administration level. This adaptation or integration is perhaps evidenced by the marked variations in coordinators' in-service activities during 1987.

Several Phase 1 coordinators in our interviews referred to their lack of ongoing in-service with regret:

> There has been a big dose of LISSEN but no continuing support for other aspects of the job.

> Since the first year of PNP, support for coordinators has been thin on the ground . . . . It has left me and many other coordinators feeling very isolated.

Virtually all the coordinators interviewed spoke highly of the in-service received so far, but a few suggested they would like additional training to help them devise and enact suitable strategies for effecting change. A few heads also commented that their coordinators would have valued extra in-service training: they mentioned general areas like 'management', 'monitoring' and 'evaluation'. When it was available, informal support from the advisory team was gratefully acknowledged.

However, a number indicated that by 'support' they also meant a clarification of their status within the school and the Authority. Some experienced a central ambiguity in that integration could mean either an increasingly influential contribution to the school's development or the effective termination of their particular innovatory role, with a sense of an increasing number of facilitating tasks. One head stated after outlining his curriculum and staff development plans for the year 1987–88: 'we may not need a coordinator any more', and one scale postholder, perhaps crystallizing the dilemma currently facing coordinators and schools, asked: 'is the coordinator here to do a specific job or to make the running of the school easier?'

The Coordinator's Role in 1987

The survey data and interview material which formed the basis of this report show that the coordinator's role is an extraordinarily varied one. Each school has evolved its unique interpretation of the Authority's job description: factors such as school size, location, the number and status of PNP appointments, the personalities and priorities within the school, the head's style of management and the coordinator's own professional expertise and personality all contribute to and influence the particular version adopted. Moreover, as the role is essentially a responsive one, it is constantly developing and changing: year 2 has been very different from year 1 for all of the coordinators we spoke to, and no doubt future years will see more change and development still.

Under the general guidelines offered by the Authority, heads have been given considerable freedom and flexibility to deploy their coordinators as they wish. However, this flexibility may also foster a degree of ambiguity about the role, and ambiguity in turn may lead to tension and dissatisfaction. That ambiguity can still shroud the role is apparent from comments in the 1987 questionnaire returns of both coordinators and heads. Some coordinators indicated the problem with such comments as:

> There is disagreement between me and my head about my role . . . .

> I would like more autonomy in deciding my role . . . .

Typical comments from heads about this issue were:

> Defining the role of PNP staff is problematic . . . .

> Establishing a definite role for PNP staff presents difficulties . . . .

> Uncertainty about coordinators' roles and responsibilities: some frequently refer to differences between what they are actually doing and what they understood they would be doing when they were first appointed . . . .

Perhaps the positive aspect of this lack of definition is the sense that each school, having been offered a mechanism for change and improvement, is itself responsible for making it work. Difficulties are no doubt an indication of the need for some closer analysis and more open discusssion of both organizational and managerial procedures and professional relationships within the school. This is perhaps the most radical implication of the coordinator's arrival in Leeds schools.

Guidelines for Headteachers in the Use of PNP Staff

In October 1987 headteachers were sent copies of a document entitled 'Guidelines for Headteachers in the Use of PNP Staff', with the request that 'all staff are aware of the contents of these guidelines'. The covering letter also stated: 'A second copy is enclosed for your PNP coordinator.' This document offers further clarification of the coordinator's role, and sheds some light on several of the ambiguities that were emerging during PRINDEP's fieldwork in the summer term of 1987. The sections which deal with PNP staff in general and coordinators in particular are as follows:

GENERAL
All teachers appointed under PNP are directly responsible to the Head Teacher of the school they are assigned to, and are an integral part of the school's teaching team.

COORDINATORS
The PNP Coordinator has a crucial role to play, in conjunction with other senior colleagues, in assisting the Head and Deputy in the development of a quality learning environment in the school.

The Coordinator should be part of the senior management team of the school, and have particular responsibilities for the coordination and development of the Primary Needs Programme.

A copy of the Coordinator's Job Description is attached. It should be a matter for negotiation within each PNP school which items on this list form priorities for individual Coordinators.

In order to carry out these functions effectively a Coordinator might expect with other colleagues to play a full part in the teaching programme of the school which may include:
(a) a substantial responsibility for a particular class;
(b) working alongside colleagues;
(c) helping to provide non-contact time.

In addition Coordinators should expect to receive reasonable release from teaching programmes for preparation, discussion with colleagues, course attendance, etc.

[Information about the use of other PNP staff is included here]

COVER
As a major objective of PNP is concerned with staff development, it is expected that teachers in PNP schools (including those appointed under PNP) will provide teaching cover for colleagues in order to enable them to participate in the in-service courses, which are both school based and external.

The additional staffing provided by PNP gives the flexibility for teachers at certain times to be released from some of their teaching commitments in order to be involved in the development aspect of the school's work.

All teachers, including those appointed under PNP, are expected to cover for absent colleagues, when this is necessary, and in accordance with the Authority's policy.

There are several significant implications for the coordinator's role in these Guidelines.

1 The coordinator is a fully integrated member of staff, does not have a separate identity and is not accountable elsewhere. The guidelines state that 'all teachers appointed under PNP are directly responsible to the headteacher of the school they are assigned to and are an integral part of the school's teaching team'. Those coordinators who wished to be temporary consultants (a use which the Authority once itself considered and publicized in April 1985) are, so to speak, firmly put in their place.

2 The coordinator is placed alongside other senior colleagues, and is 'part of the senior management team' who 'assists the head and deputy-head in the development of a quality learning environment'. The role has 'particular responsibilities for the coordination and development of the Primary Needs Programme'. The reference to the coordinator's *assistance* of the deputy-head may provide some clarification of this potentially rather ambiguous relationship, and may be a response to role anxieties expressed by deputy-heads in some schools since PNP's inception.

3 The coordinator can expect to undertake a number of facilitating tasks, e.g. 'helping to provide non-contact time' and, by implication in the final section, covering for colleagues who are absent on courses or through illness.

4 The coordinator may also undertake 'substantial responsibility for a particular class'.

5 The freedom for individual schools to be selective about their priorities for development is confirmed, as is the appropriateness of negotiation about what these should be.

A version of the Authority's job description for coordinators was circulated with the guidelines. The preface to the list of responsibilities now reads, 'The job description may include . . .', whereas in the previous version it stated, 'The job description will include . . .'. There has been no alteration to the wording of the list of responsibilities.

Conclusions, Issues and Implications

We now move beyond our account of PRINDEP's investigation of how the PNP coordinator idea is working in practice to a consideration of some of the wider issues and implications. First, however, let us pull together the main strands of the discussion so far.

It has been clear from the outset that the Primary Needs Programme, notwithstanding its explicit focus on the needs and educational experiences of children, has also been about the needs and capacities of those children's teachers. For this reason the Authority has concentrated resources and commitment on various kinds of professional support — increased in-service provision, an expanded primary advisory team, and, of course, extra staff in schools.

It has also long been clear that the impact of PNP in a particular school depends on a variety of factors, some of them unique to that school. One of these factors is the extent to which PNP is recognized as not only offering educational and professional opportunities, but also posing challenges of a *managerial* kind. For PNP requires schools to sort out their educational priorities; to work out how these can best be met; to clarify and modify staff roles; to engage at every level, from classroom to staffroom and head's office, in professional activity of a collective and collaborative kind. It necessitates, in short, that staff work together rather than in isolation. It was inevitable, therefore, that *staff roles* and the *management context of schools* would be one of the six themes to emerge from PRINDEP's preliminary studies and that we should need to focus in particular on the staff role which is perhaps most distinctive to PNP — that of the coordinator.

We looked first at the Authority's view of the coordinator's role, and at the way this has changed as the nature and purpose of PNP as a whole have evolved. We then examined and classified the various ways that PNP coordinators have been operating since the start of PNP in 1985. Next we sought to establish the kinds of circumstances in schools which most tangibly affect the way the coordinator works and the degree of success he or she achieves. Finally, we brought the issue up to date by setting our analysis in the context of the 1987 Authority guidelines on the use of PNP staff.

The early ambiguities and confusions about the nature of PNP, though apparently resolved at Authority level, continued (and continue) to resonate within some schools. The problem of special needs/primary needs has been central, and it was probably inevitable that pronouncements from the LEA about the revised 'good general practice' view of PNP would have only gradual impact, however eloquently expressed. SEN had too high a profile at the early stages to allow such revision to have immediate effect, and it was a profile reinforced by early recruitment policies and procedures, by job specifications, by in-service courses, and by schools' own understandable concern about the implications of the 1981 Education Act and the 1983 DES Circular 1/83 on statementing.

But there are other reasons for the persistence of this problem, and this report has highlighted some of them. Many of us feel more comfortable with precision than with ambiguity: SEN is now a clearly stated professional issue, with equally clear associated strategies (like LISSEN and INRS), while 'good practice', 'the quality learning environment', 'flexible teaching strategies' and 'the broadly-based curriculum' are considerably more elusive. Where SEN strategies offered teachers support with something they were obliged by law to do, the 'good practice' view of PNP opened up uncertainty, challenged teachers' existing classroom routines, implied perhaps that in their basic class teacher role they could do a lot better. Where the former provided solutions, the latter offered exhortations.

So, although at an official level the matter is now resolved, at school level it may not be. It is clear that for some PNP coordinators the SEN/PNP tension has been a continuing one, not least when they have been expected to combine, within considerable constraints of time, an SEN role with a cross-school brief for curriculum and staff development, or when, in undertaking the former, they have had to contend with the persistence into the post-Warnock era of the pre-Warnock view that special needs is solely about withdrawing 'remedial' groups (or what one or two schools initially termed 'the PNP children').

Despite all this, we have seen how an impressive diversity of ways of enacting the PNP coordinator role has emerged in what is still (in terms of educational innovations) a very short time. Coordinators are working in various ways, and in various combinations, on:

> special needs,
> curriculum development,
> staff development,
> home–school links,
> whole-class responsibility.

We have gathered data, by a combination of questionnaire, observation and interview, which have enabled us to open up each of these. We have been able to offer a preliminary classification and discussion, for example, of ways that coordinators approach curriculum development as:

> curriculum managers,
> curriculum specialists,
> curriculum enhancers,
> curriculum facilitators.

Awareness of this range of coordinators' roles should provide useful perspectives for schools and staff at different stages of involvement in PNP. Established coordinators may wish to look afresh at what they do, while those new to PNP or about to become involved can use the analysis to consider a number of possibilities. Such a list, being about what actually is happening in schools, should be a useful complement to the Authority's guidelines and job description which are more in the nature of a selection of broad possibilities.

However, it is equally important (perhaps more so) for schools to consider the factors which influence what coordinators can do and how well they can do it. We discuss these under the three headings of:

the influence of the head;
the attitude of other staff;
the persona and style of the coordinator.

In doing so, we offer perspectives which may be familiar to anyone with experience and common sense. On the other hand — as the whole of human history all too sadly demonstrates — people can be remarkably resistant to what experience and common sense teach them, and for this reason the lessons are always worth repeating and pondering.

Thus it could have been predicted that unless heads understood what PNP was about, coordinators (and other staff) would have problems; likewise if heads failed adequately to prepare the ground for the coordinator's arrival. We have also seen, of course, that this was not always, or necessarily, the fault of schools: the early messages about PNP were not as clear or as consistent as they could have been, and in any case the programme was introduced at great speed.

Less obvious perhaps are issues to do with gradual shifts away from traditional patterns of senior management in primary schools. The arrival of coordinators may overlap and perhaps conflict with the established roles of the deputy, members of staff with specific curriculum responsibilities, and perhaps even the head: unless, that is, such existing roles are reappraised as carefully as is the new one. Where the coordinator's role is fairly tightly defined, such as 'curriculum specialist', rationalization of the full range of staff responsibilities should be straightforward enough, and the coordinator will become in effect another postholder. Where the coordinator has a more general and wide-ranging function, perhaps as 'curriculum enhancer' or (as encouraged by the LEA) as exemplar of 'good practice' across the school, two kinds of intrusion may be risked, or feared. One is at the classroom level, where the associated strategy of 'working alongside' may generate suspicion that the coordinator is undertaking surveillance on behalf of the head or even the Authority. Or, more simply, it may be seen as an invasion of the time-honoured privacy and autonomy of the class teacher (see Chapter 7 for a more detailed account of reactions to collaborative teaching). The other area of territorial threat concerns the head alone. The function of defining and promoting 'good practice' across the school, after all, has traditionally been the head's, and indeed the basic route to primary headship has until relatively recently been largely on the basis of a person's track record as a sound classroom practitioner. The more the PNP coordinator's role is defined in terms of demonstrating and promoting 'good primary practice', therefore, the more a head may have to sort out the extent of his or her own role in this regard.

One inevitable consequence of all this must be that the issue of a school's 'philosophy' in respect of curriculum and classroom practice will increasingly become a collective staff concern rather than the head's personal territory. At the organizational level schools may increasingly find themselves needing to evolve team approaches to senior management. The general lesson here is that coordinator roles can never be defined in isolation: they have a knock-on effect for those of other staff, especially those with management responsibilities, and all such roles must be discussed and defined in conjunction.

Another difficulty which may prove quite persistent is the way some coordinators had problems of credibility when they did not have their own classes. This may linger because it has firm historical roots in over a century of elementary and primary education. Yet the addition to schools of numbers of staff in excess of the numbers of registration groups (as recommended by the 1986 Commons Select Committee Report) makes it imperative that all staff recognize that there are several different, and equally valid, ways in which a primary teacher can work in a school, and teaching a class full-time is only one of them.

Then there were the lessons to be learned from the ways the coordinators themselves acted, independently of the roles they were expected to undertake. Again, the advice given — go slowly, show willingness to get your hands dirty, respect existing practice, avoid the arrogance of the 'new broom', be prepared to compromise but stick to your principles — is familiar enough, yet since so many coordinators seem to have learned the hard way, it is worth repeating. Another way of putting this is that coordinators, like heads and deputies, need leadership skills and perhaps leadership training. This raises the question of how adequate the preparation and in-service support provided by the Authority was (and is) in this regard: certainly coordinators themselves, particularly in Phase 1, felt the lack of such preparation and support. But providing leadership training presupposes that in all schools coordinators are perceived as exercising leadership: in this there may be a tension between the Authority's and some heads' expectations: the coordinator viewed as member of senior management team on the one hand, and as mere facilitator, aide, cover or supernumerary on the other.

All these issues merit discussion at both school and LEA levels. They also relate significantly to wider debates at the national level which we now briefly mention. 'Coordinator' is a term which now has fairly common currency in at least two arenas. The first is special needs: since the 1981 Education Act the title 'coordinator' has replaced that of 'remedial teacher' in many schools, as the role has expanded to one of consultant and collaborator in the total education of children with special needs. This is not merely a change of label, for the special needs sector has made considerable advances in evolving detailed strategies for both class and support teachers, for grouping children, for 'room management' and so on which offer important lessons for all teachers, not just those with special needs responsibilities. The other usage of 'coordinator' is that offered by the Commons Select Committee in its 1986 report on primary education. There the issue is a curricular one: that of more effectively harnessing teachers' individual specialist strengths in order to secure a rational, coherent framework for each aspect of the curriculum, having progression and continuity within and between school years, and achieving better match at the classroom level between children's abilities and the learning tasks provided for them, particularly where more able children are concerned. The label 'coordinator' is the Select Committee's preference from those currently being used, such as consultant, specialist, semi-specialist, adviser. Their recommendations on this matter of curriculum leadership are a culmination of concern and discussion which go back to the 1978 HMI primary survey (and in fact to paragraph 937 of Plowden, though few people choose to remember that) and are now firmly part of the official view of how primary schools should develop. Coordinators in this sense are expected to formulate schemes and guidelines, to oversee their implementation, and to advise and work alongside colleagues requiring support in specific areas of the curriculum.

At first sight it might appear that the Leeds PNP coordinator is a happy amalgam of these two nationally endorsed concepts. In some respects this is so; but the Leeds idea is very different in certain vital respects. Where HMI, the Select Committee and DES tend to see the coordinator as a specialist, in Leeds, as we show above, *curriculum specialist* is but one of a number of possible curriculum-related roles the coordinator can undertake, and the Authority's documentation tends to give much greater prominence to the idea of the coordinator as an exemplary *generalist*. Similarly, where the Select Committee sees virtually every primary teacher as needing to be both a class teacher and a coordinator of an area of the curriculum across the school, in PNP there is usually only one coordinator in each school, and this person works with other colleagues who may have posts of responsibility for particular curriculum areas. One of the main implications of this comparison is that, as we have already noted, schools need to sort out the coordinator role in the context of an overall review of management roles and relationships, including those of staff with curriculum responsibilities.

The other implication is more fundamental and problematic. The general use of the same term 'coordinator' to denote similar but also distinctive professional roles in primary schools may seem to be fortuitous. We doubt this. For 'coordinator' neatly, and deliberately, implies a role which supports everyone and threatens nobody. It offers no suggestion (unlike 'specialist') of undermining the class teacher system with its celebration of the curriculum generalist's capacity to educate 'the whole child'. It implies no status differential of the kind that erodes the traditional senses of equality and community among a primary school's staff; indeed, the Select Committee advocates the day-to-day exchange among staff of the roles of 'adviser' and 'advised', so that there is 'no question of hierarchy'. Nor does the term 'coordinator' seem to impinge on the managerial territories of head and deputy. This sense that the innovative role of coordinator nevertheless preserves the professional status quo is reinforced by the strong advocacy — by both the Select Committee and, for its own distinctive version of coordinator, Leeds LEA — of 'working alongside' as a key strategy. In the Select Committee's words, the (curriculum) coordinator works 'with others and not on them'.

However, it should be clear from this report that one does not avoid controversy simply by using uncontroversial labels. The idea of a coordinator, whether within the special needs, Select Committee or Leeds LEA definition, directly confronts precisely those deeply rooted professional traditions in primary schools that the label and associated philosophy appear at first sight to defend. That is to say, it *does* signal the limits to the generalist class teacher's whole curriculum/whole child capacities; it *does* denote different levels in the staff hierarchy; it *does* overlap the head's role as traditionally defined; and it *does* raise questions about what, once the division of labour between head and coordinator is determined, there is left for the deputy to do.

Our evidence suggests that the potential impact of enhanced staffing in the form of coordinators on the quality of children's learning may be considerable, and in Leeds the role already appears to be facilitating important and impressive changes and improvements. Without doubt these are due to the skill, energy and dedication displayed by many coordinators and existing staff in PNP schools. Notwithstanding this, the role (especially its working alongside element) appears to be much more difficult for an incumbent, and problematic for a school, than bodies like the Select Committee and Warnock, and perhaps Leeds LEA, may have realized. Leeds coordinators, especially those in Phase 1, have effectively been testing the validity of a prescription which may have seriously underestimated the strength of the professional culture it seeks to change. That change was inevitably bound to be painful and slow. The way forward would seem to require, as minimum preconditions, that these issues are honestly and openly acknowledged and discussed, in the LEA and in the schools, and that they feature prominently in the programmes of support which are offered to staff in PNP schools. Beyond innocent labels like 'coordinator' and the comfortable language of 'working alongside' are some tough realities.

6
Change from Without: Local Authority INSET

Introduction

The PNP coordinator's role was devised by the LEA to promote change in its primary schools *from within*. We turn now to a second major change strategy, this time designed to influence practice from outside, or rather, from above: the LEA's programme of centralized in-service (INSET) courses. The link between the two strategies, the device used to ensure that co-ordinators did not end up pulling in a different direction from that required by LEA policy, was the LEA's advisory service.

In common with most LEA advisers and inspectors, those in Leeds undertook a large number of very diverse tasks simultaneously (see Bolam, Smith and Canter, 1979; Winkley, 1985), ranging from numerous administrative office chores to day-to-day pastoral and professional work in their particular schools, the appointment of new staff and the running of courses. Like HMI, their Janus-like role of servicing both employees and employers made them vulnerable to suspicion from both groups.

In the present context advisory staff (among whom we include, as explained in Chapter 1, advisory teachers) had a major part in the short-listing and appointment of PNP staff, in defining their roles, drawing up their job specifications and inducting them into the LEA's view of good primary practice. Advisers were also involved, as part of their general brief, in the appointment of senior staff. The advisory role was thus pivotal to the implementation of LEA primary policy in general and its Primary Needs Programme in particular. The present chapter looks at one major aspect of that role in some detail, and we shall be examining others in the second volume.

In concentrating here on centralized in-service courses we would not wish to convey the impression that this was the only form of in-service activity associated with the Primary Needs Programme. Professional development is achieved by many different routes, and is a highly complex and subtle process, much of it being inseparable from everyday experience, from the culture of the classroom and school, and from the personality of the individual teacher (Nias, 1989; Alexander, 1988). Even at the formal level LEA courses are but one of a range of possible INSET activities, many of them taking place within the school rather than at a centralized venue, and even the much-abused term 'school-focused' is capable of sustaining a large number of operational definitions (Alexander, 1981). Moreover, a range of contextual and personal factors ensures that in-service activities vary enormously in their impact on individuals and institutions (Henderson, 1978; Ruddock, 1981).

Leeds was no exception in this regard. Nevertheless, the centralized LEA short course was a key component in the Authority's strategy for generating change, and for this reason it had to feature in the evaluation. Over the three-year period of fieldwork our project monitored some twenty of these courses, usually through a combination of survey, observation and interview (the last involving both course tutors and their teacher clients).

The present chapter contains a case study of just one of these courses. It had the title 'Developing a Flexible Approach to Classroom Organization' and was chosen in preference to the others for five main reasons. First, it had a very clear and direct relevance to the PNP emphasis on flexible teaching strategies and a broadly-based curriculum. Second, the importance of its message to the LEA was apparent from the fact that, unlike the other courses, it was mounted four times within the space of a few weeks, and on several occasions subsequently. Third, this repetition gave full scope for the course's organizers to modify its style and content in the light of experience. Fourth, its importance to the LEA and PNP was further demonstrated by the seniority of the advisory staff involved. Finally, it exemplified issues common to many of the LEA's courses.

The study deals with the first stages in the evaluation process: the content and dynamics of the course itself, and its immediate impact on those who attended. Part of the follow-up study of the course's longer-term impact on classroom practice is incorporated in Chapter 8.

Evaluating an INSET Course

The simplest and most basic way to evaluate an in-service course is to hand out a questionnaire during its final session, or to waylay teachers on their way out, to ask them what they thought of the course's content and the way in which it was presented. There is a commonsense validity in this approach, for the value of any in-service support programme must be closely bound up with the extent to which the teachers it serves find its content relevant and interesting and its presentation attractive and informative.

However, these two techniques will scarcely do on their own. From the point of view of the people organizing the course, it is not enough that the teachers who attend it come away thinking what a pleasant and interesting time they have had. The principal aim of such courses is presumably to modify attitudes and to change practice. However well mounted they are, they cannot be judged successful if their message is not accurately remembered and widely discussed in schools afterwards, and if there is not some subsequent influence on daily practice. It follows that the evaluation of a course must concern itself with its longer-term effectiveness as well as its immediate impact.

At the same time practising teachers may validly have questions of their own about the in-service support they are offered, especially if they tend to have very little say about its form or frequency. In most other settings advice is something we seek out only when we feel we need it. We are free to get it from whatever direction we choose, and we steer well clear of people who insist on offering it when we haven't asked for it. Teachers in the employ of a local authority, however, may be in a very different situation. Although some of them may be able to opt for the precise level of advisory support they think they need, others may find barriers put between themselves and the advisers they would like to consult, or at the other extreme they may be sent willy-nilly on all manner of courses, with the inescapable implication that there must be something very wrong with their present practice. They may be given a lot of advice which they would never have sought and which they have no intention of following.

Even that is not all. As well as the questions of how welcome the message of a course may be, how well it is delivered and how effectively it is subsequently implemented, there is also the matter of the message itself. If it is designed to change the practice of trained professionals, maybe we need to examine it closely and ask a number of questions about it. What, precisely, does it say? Whose interest does it serve? Where did it come from and what are its credentials? Is it sense or nonsense; and if it is nonsense, is it dangerous nonsense or just meaningless nonsense? The problem is that although all these questions are an essential part of a detailed evaluation, some of them can be answered only in subjective terms which take us little further; for just as the message to be conveyed on a course ultimately reflects the opinion, the judgment and even the competence of the people who planned the course, any verdict about the quality of the presentation reflects the opinion, the judgment and the competence of those who were there to see it. Even if they cannot all be definitively answered, however, questions about LEA messages and orthodoxies must be raised, for there is another kind of professional development which is not necessarily mediated by outside agencies and which does not start from an official message at all.

Before members of the PRINDEP team first went to look at practice in Leeds primary schools, they worked out and agreed upon a set of strict rules about their role and the nature of their task. They were very clear that they were not visiting classrooms as inspectors or advisers, and that it was no part of their brief to offer opinions about how things *should* be done. A major emphasis in their own practice and in the preliminary training of teacher-associate fieldworkers was the need to be aware of their own prejudices and preconceptions so that they could make sure they were being as neutral as possible. They were visiting schools, in short, not to evaluate but simply to observe, discuss and make a written record of what seemed to be going on in a large number of ordinary classrooms. Any evaluation would come later, and would be based in part on the neutral and purely factual information they had collected.

As the weeks went by several of them reported the same striking experience. On their second or third visit to a class the teacher would say that she had been thinking a lot about what she had said last time, and that as a result she had now started to do things differently. It must be stressed that this change in practice had not come about through the handing on of an LEA message about how things should be done, nor because of something the visitor from PRINDEP had suggested on her own initiative from her own experience. It had happened simply because the teacher had allowed a neutral outsider to see what she was doing with her class and had then gone on to describe it and its rationale in detail. In making her practice intelligible to someone else she had found herself reflecting on it in more detail than ever before, and this examination of her own day-to-day activities had become the starting point of a major development in her thinking about the precise nature of her objectives and how she could best achieve them. She had generated productive and powerful new insights without any advice or guidance at all.

There is nothing new in the idea that a detailed examination of one's own behaviour can provoke far-reaching changes and increased efficiency. In the present context, however, it highlights the fact that there is more than one way to set about professional development. The principal role of an advisory team is presumably to ensure that teachers move in the direction in which the authority wants them to go, and its main task must therefore be to develop a rational and clearly articulated message and then deliver it with all the aplomb it can muster. On the other hand, if part of its aim is to foster independent personal and professional development, its members will often find themselves wanting simply to provoke teachers into a detailed examination of their own practice. For advisers and advisory teachers, this second approach poses particularly tricky problems. The role of *neutral catalyst* implies (and must incorporate if it is to be genuine) no value judgments at all and no preconceptions about what is good and what is bad in present or proposed practice. The very titles *adviser* and *advisory teacher* on the other hand imply advice; and this in turn implies that there are good and bad (or acceptable and unacceptable) ways of doing things, and that the advisers know which are which. The nature and the seriousness of the dilemma are clear if we imagine a situation where an advisory teacher took on the role of neutral catalyst and stimulated a teacher to an enthusiastic and detailed examination of her own practice as a result of which the teacher changed her teaching style in a direction which was quite contrary to the professional philosophy of the advisory teacher and the team within which she worked.

It would not be surprising if the possibility of such an outcome were to lead any advisory team to feel more comfortable when handing out specific advice rather than when encouraging teachers to question their own practice and find their own way forward, even though this must present problems of credibility to those teams which are dedicated to the principle that teachers serve their pupils best by fostering independence and self-reliance.

The delicacy of this situation is illustrated by the comments of three of the teachers who attended the course which forms the main subject of this report. It will be recalled that the theme was 'Developing a Flexible Approach to Classroom Organization', and in a follow-up questionnaire they were asked what had been the main message of the course for them. They answered as follows:

Reassurance that whatever style of teaching you use, if it is successful it is not wrong.

No one method is right; a mixture is better.

You'll teach this way, like it or not.

Here is striking confirmation of the difficulty of formulating a simple message and putting it over unambiguously. Perhaps we assume too readily that people subjected to the same stimulus are all undergoing the same experience, but this is transparently not so (which is one of the reasons why whole-class teaching nearly always fails to teach the whole class). In this particular example representatives of the advisory team had been treading the fine path between encouraging self-reliance on the one hand and handing on an LEA message about the officially approved approach to classroom organization on the other. Three of the teachers who had been there went back to their schools afterwards with totally different notions of what they had heard, for among them was one who thought she had been encouraged to teach in any way that works, another who thought she had been given strict instructions on how she should behave from now on, and a third whose understanding of what she had heard fell somewhere between.

This brings us back to the evaluator's need to consider the way in which things are said as well as the intended message of the person who says them. Messages can be and often are misunderstood, not only in the settings under discussion here, but by any of us in any situation. They are sometimes inappropriately formulated or inattentively received. In addition they are invariably suffused with a multitude of unspoken meanings which vary along with the cultural orientation and the emotional, intellectual and personal qualities of both the speaker and the listener.

Because of factors like these, accurate information about the *intended message* of the PNP in-service support courses can come only from the course organizers, while authentic information about *how the message was understood* can come only from the people who received it. It becomes clear that, in examining a particular course in detail, we shall need to consider several different issues one by one:

> What was the advisory team intending to convey (what was the principal message from the authority to its teachers)?
>
> How did the advisory team set about the task (what happened at the sessions)?
>
> What was in fact conveyed to the teachers who attended?
>
> What impact did this have on their daily practice?
>
> What factors helped or hindered them in implementing the message of the course?

The Course and Its Intended Message

The subject of this detailed study could equally well be described as four courses or as one course mounted four times. The title, the theme and the programme of events were the same on each occasion; there were some differences of emphasis and presentation as the organizers grew increasingly familiar with their material and became aware of how audiences reacted to it; the course's support staff were not always the same, and the audiences themselves were completely different each time. On each occasion the course timetable was as shown in Figure 6.1. This timetable alone gives a good preliminary indication of the message to be conveyed by the course, and of the way in which the course staff intended to set about the task of conveying it.

DEVELOPING A FLEXIBLE APPROACH TO CLASSROOM ORGANISATION
Day One:

9.15 am	Introduction by the Course Leader
9.30 am	Discussion Exercise
10.30 am	Break
11.00 am	*The marks of effective organisation*
	Course Leader
12.15 pm	Lunch
1.30 pm	*Classroom provision*
	Support Staff
2.40 pm	Break
3.00 pm	Discussion Exercise
4.00 pm	Finish

Day Two:

9.15 am	*A personal view of classroom organisation*
	Visiting speaker(s) (local teachers)
10.30 am	Break
11.00 am	Discussion Groups
12.15 pm	Lunch
1.30 pm	*Moving towards a flexible approach to teaching*
	Course Leader
2.45 pm	Break
3.00 pm	Final Plenary Session
4.00 pm	Finish

Figure 6.1. Timetable of a PNP In-Service Support Course Held Four Times during the Summer Term of 1987

It is clear from the timetable that in its simplest terms the basic message is something to do with flexibility: the course starts from effective organization in the classroom, and then moves on to examine the links between the way in which a classroom is organized and the range of teaching methods that are possible within it. There is a strong implication that a flexible approach to teaching is a desirable state of affairs, and that a flexible approach to classroom organization is a necessary precondition. There is no indication on the programme of what flexibility means in this context, but that is scarcely surprising. It is presumably something to be explained or explored in the sessions themselves.

The timetable also makes it plain that the message is to be conveyed partly through formal talk sessions and partly through discussion: if we assume that the final plenary session is mainly discussion, and that the session on classroom provision is to take the form of a talk or demonstration, then the working time over the two days is intended to be divided into a rather evenly balanced 55 per cent for lectures, talks and demonstrations, and 45 per cent for discussion. However, for a clearer and more detailed picture of both the message and the means by which it was in fact delivered it will be necessary to look elsewhere.

Two substantial handouts were produced by the course staff and used each time the course was held. Between them they provide a very detailed summary of the messages to be conveyed. They are too lengthy to be reproduced here in full but abbreviated versions appear in Figures 6.2 and 6.4. The first handout consisted of a series of general questions upon which teachers were invited to reflect, and these are listed in Figure 6.2.

PERSONAL ATTRIBUTES
1: Do you deserve children's respect?
2: Do you respect children?

RELATIONSHIPS
3: Have you established a good working relationship with your children?
4: Have you established warm open relationships with children or individuals?
5: Do you generate a sense of security amongst the children you teach?
6: Do you enjoy good professional relationships with your staff colleagues

PROFESSIONAL SKILLS
7: Do you have a clear understanding of objectives for the groups and individuals you teach?
8: Is work well matched to each child's stage of development?
9: Do you use class/group/individual types of organization based on the needs of the curriculum and the children as appropriate?
10: Are you making the most efficient use of teaching spaces?
11: Do you provide a stimulating and challenging environment for your children?
12: Do you use a range of teaching styles?
13: What use do you make of audio-visual resources?

EVALUATION
14: How successful are you in achieving the objectives for the groups and individuals you teach? short term/long term.

DEVELOPMENT
15: Are you concerned about your professional development?

Figure 6.2. Principal Questions on a Handout from the PNP In-Service Support Course on Classroom Organisation, Summer Term 1987

On the original handout each question was followed by a list of anything up to nine specific points to be considered in formulating an answer. Purely by way of illustration, one of the questions, together with its full list of points for consideration, appears in Figure 6.3, but for reasons of space the rest have had to be omitted.

This is precisely the kind of handout that provides a useful trigger to discussion and detailed self-questioning. In terms of the intended message of the course it provides something else as well. Except for questions 13 and 14, all the items in Figure 6.2 are yes/no questions to which the 'correct' answer is 'yes'. Faced with such an item as 'Do you deserve children's respect?' or 'Do you provide a stimulating and challenging environment for your children?', it is inconceivable that a teacher might suppose she was expected to say, 'No, certainly not'. At the same time she is in a tricky situation, for to reply 'yes' may suggest a degree of arrogance and self-deception that could hardly be appropriate in a person responsible for the education of a group of impressionable children. Although framed in a slightly different way, questions 13 and 14 are just as transparent in relation to the kind of answer which they seem simultaneously to demand and preclude; and to some extent the same can be said of many of the subsidiary questions attached to each main question and illustrated in Figure 6.3.

11:   Do you provide a stimulating and challenging environment for your children?

Consider:
    11.1   Are there displays of 2D and 3D materials from which work is arising?
    11.2   Have you recognized the need to supplement commercially produced materials with your own materials?
    11.3   Have you considered the importance of display?
        a)   for children's personal satisfaction
        b)   as a means of setting/encouraging good standards
        c)   as a focal point of classroom activities
        d)   as a centre of interest for children, parents and visitors
        e)   as a visual communication in its own right
        f)   as a major element in the creation of a total environment for learning.
    11.4   Do you sometimes stand back and consider the impact which your classroom makes?
        i.e.   the need to be selective in terms of appropriateness and quantity of work displayed
        the suitability, quality and arrangement of furniture

---

Figure 6.3.   Specimen Question from the Handout Summarized in Figure 6.2, Together with Its List of Points for Consideration

The effect is that, as well as being a list of questions or themes for reflection, the handout is also a list of statements about the ways in which primary school teachers would be thinking and striving to conduct themselves if they shared without reservation all the values of the people who compiled the list. It is plain that the course's message about organization is to be set within a broader but no less insistent message about the kind of professional persona to which teachers are encouraged to aspire.

The main course handout, summarized in Figure 6.4, is much more directly concerned with the overt theme of classroom organization. It is very lengthy, but taken as a whole it forms not only a forceful general message about an approved style of classroom organization but also a detailed account of the steps by which the desired state of affairs can be achieved.

MOVING TOWARDS A FLEXIBLE APPROACH TO TEACHING

1. Some General Points about Organizational Style

Efficient classroom organization should:
- enable the teacher to meet the wide range of educational needs and match work at an appropriate level
- provide opportunities for actual teaching at group level
- be flexible enough to provide opportunities for teaching at individual, group and class level, according to the demands of the activity
- minimise 'transition time' and make the best use of space and resources
- provide opportunities for pupils to work co-operatively or individually

2. Stage One — Preparation and Training

There are four important areas of preparation and training:
- The establishing of efficient resource areas with materials, work cards, books etc neatly stored and labelled
- Grouping children — either mixed ability or variable ability groups
- Training in the use of materials and class organization
- Establishing discipline and control
- Working in a co-operative way with support teachers

At the end of this stage children should be able to:

- Work individually in groups constructively and sensibly
- Organize themselves within reason — collect own materials, work with them, put them away again when finished
- Accept teacher's authority in an atmosphere of controlled freedom and have achieved a measure of self discipline in the interests of others
- Have begun to understand the principle of moving from one task to another without intermediate reference to the teacher
- Gain the benefit of working with support teachers on tasks related to their whole work programme

3. Stage Two — The Beginnings of Work Programmes
A short period — e.g. an hour/hour and half — is set aside each day for each group to complete two set tasks. The children *may* be allowed to decide the order in which they are tackled. For example:

[Here follows a detailed example filling one side of A4]

At the end of this stage the children should be able to:
- Complete one task and move to another without specific direction
- Organize their time in order to complete their tasks in a given period
- Take account of the need (sometimes) for the number engaged on certain activities to be restricted
- Recognize that there may be another adult to whom they can go for help

4. Stage Three — Extending Work Programmes
This is where stage two is extended as management skills, resource banks and organization, etc. develop, Essentially:
- The period of time of integration can be extended
- The number of tasks to be completed is increased

[*Here follow an example and further detail*]

5. Stage Four — A Fully Flexible Day

[*Here follows a list of activities for which time must be allowed*]

Work programmes can be:
- written on the flip chart/whiteboard/blackboard
- produced in the form of individual assignment sheets/cards
- a mixture of written instructions/discussion

Very careful planning is needed in order to create a balance between:
- activities involving movement
- chair based activities
- even use of spaces
- even use of resources
- those activities which are 'teacher intensive' and those which are not
- direct teaching to all levels of ability in fair proportion

This stage of organization can be extremely effective where:
- the apparatus and materials are well stored
- assignment cards, work books, tasks are carefully graded and 'matched'
- the pupils are well disciplined and used to the 'system'
- the teachers have a clear sense of direction and are prepared to give time to planning and preparation
- the record keeping system is efficient and comprehensive

Figure 6.4. Abbreviated Version of a Second Handout Used on the Course

At the end of the course this handout was taken away by teachers, and a number of them reported later that they had found it extremely useful. It is certainly hard to imagine a more comprehensive summary of a course's message. However, the broad range of its content is achieved only at a price. Inevitably, since handouts cannot go on for ever, many of its details are compressed to the point where they begin to be highly ambiguous. They would require a good deal of expansion and firm definition before their meaning could be determined precisely enough for a teacher to know whether she was succeeding or failing in trying to put them into practice. To give a single example, at one point the list states that by the end of a particular stage: 'children should be able to . . . accept teacher's authority in an atmosphere of controlled freedom and have achieved a measure of self-discipline in the interests of others.' At a simple, straightforward level this makes very good sense, and its meaning seems perfectly clear. However, as soon as we try to come to grips with it — to ask ourselves whether it reflects the state of affairs in our own classroom, for example — we are faced with quite genuine and difficult problems of definition and interpretation. What does 'accepting a teacher's authority' actually entail? Is it an all-or-nothing thing or does it allow some leeway for negotiation? What is 'controlled freedom', and how much control must it involve before it stops being freedom altogether? What does the term 'self-discipline' imply when used in connection with a young child? Is it really something children need to develop *in the interests of others* or is it also, and perhaps primarily, *in their own interests* that we want them to develop it?

All these issues not only merit but seem to demand detailed discussion and all are extremely relevant to the daily work of primary school teachers. Indeed they would probably furnish ample material for an intensive and highly illuminating in-service course in themselves; yet they all arise from a single one of several dozen subsections in only one of the handouts used on the course.

The difficulty with such an abundance of concepts all crowded together is that even the most alert and attentive reader cannot cope indefinitely with the frustrating task of looking for precise meanings when these are never explicitly stated. Before long she has to give up that task and settle instead for a diffuse, general impression which may come as much from her own preconceptions as from anything on the list of items itself (a call for controlled freedom, for example, is uncritically taken to match her own sentiments about freedom and control, and before she has had time even to wonder if other people would agree, and whether controlled freedom is in any case a helpful concept for a class teacher, her eye has moved on to the next topic and a quest for precision and clarity seems less and less appropriate).

In the setting of the course itself time can be set aside at the outset for participants to reach a clear agreement on their definitions of such terms, so long as there are not too many of them for the time available. If that does not happen, the chances are that those participants who are aware of the problem will all wait for somebody else to ask for clarification and, when nobody does so, each individual will get the uneasy impression that all the others have a clear understanding of the material under consideration. As the session proceeds it will become increasingly difficult to question what everyone else seems to be taking for granted. After all, it takes courage to risk looking a fool.

It must be emphasized that the handouts quoted here were not intended to stand on their own; if they had been, the course that went with them would have been entirely redundant. As indicators of the message intended by the course they give a picture which is rich in detail but sometimes lacking in precision, and that may be not so much a defect in the hand-outs as an accurate reflection of the message itself. Some of the other PNP INSET initiatives have had a very sharp focus on themes which are easy to define and easy to treat in isolation, and consequently their messages have been simple and straightforward. Classroom organization is not such a theme. It is elusive yet all-embracing. Certainly it involves the arrangement of furniture and the storing of equipment, but it also has implications for teaching styles and strategies, for staff deployment, for the curriculum itself, and for all other aspects of a teacher's daily work. *It is the way things are made to happen*, and it is underpinned by a teacher's own understanding of what, why and how children should learn.

It follows that a course advocating a flexible approach to organization will be concerned with a dauntingly wide range of possible topics, and that no selection will exhaust the possibilities of the overall theme. In these circumstances the formulation of a single, clear, precisely defined message may seem too difficult and hence somewhat inappropriate. It is when we turn to an examination of what happened on the course itself that we shall begin to see the extent to which the material on the handouts was discussed, clarified and developed into a series of specific messages which could be confidently grasped and unambiguously implemented.

What Happened at the Sessions

On each occasion the course began with a brief introductory talk in which the course leader welcomed the group. His account of the purpose of the course was summarized by one of the PRINDEP observers as follows:

> ... to home in on those skills which make you efficient as a teacher.... Hopefully, by the end of the day you'll understand more about: flexible approaches to teaching; a stimulating and challenging learning environment; and first-hand experience.... I hope you'll find the course practical (with things you can apply in your own classroom), reassuring (that an awful lot of what's happening in your own classroom is OK) and challenging (to make you rethink some of the things you do).... (An observer's notes made on the third occasion)

He went on to mention the model classroom which was to be used as a kind of life-size visual aid for the course. He explained how it came to be set up, and emphasized that it was meant to make a number of practical teaching points.

The opening session was followed by what was described on the timetable as a 'discussion exercise', presented by the course leader.

> The audience was split into groups of two and, later, groups of four. Groups were asked to look at a draft of an architect's plans for a school and to decide what were the good and bad points of the design. Groups were made up entirely of course members, and reporting back was done by general discussion afterwards . . . . (An observer's notes made on the second occasion)

The basic form of this opening activity did not vary from one occasion to another, and the main difference among the four occasions was in the balance of time allocated to the various parts of the exercise.

After the first occasion the time spent on discussion in pairs was cut by a third (from twenty-eight minutes to nineteen) and thereafter did not vary by more than a minute from one occasion to the next. The large group discussions fluctuated widely in length without any discernible pattern. On two occasions they took less than half as long as on another occasion when they lasted for fifteen minutes. The time spent on reporting back and summing up also varied but tended to get longer each time (although it was cut short prematurely on the last occasion because members of another course were clamouring to get into the room to use the coffee machine).

All in all there was a decided move away from discussion in pairs, which is an essentially private and hence relatively unthreatening activity, towards a more public discussion of issues, which some participants find difficult but which nevertheless gives presenter and participants much greater scope for interaction and shared understanding.

As for the presentation itself there were no major changes from one occasion to another, although there were some differences of detail. For example, at the first reporting back session the course leader 'mentioned that the ideal way of doing this would have been on an OHP transparency so that amendments could have been marked on a plan for all to see . . . ' (An observer's notes made on the first occasion). On subsequent occasions an overhead projector was used during the reporting back sessions, although not quite in the way that had been suggested: 'A brainstorming technique was used in the discussion period after group work. The course leader used an OHP to write down various suggestions called out by the audience. Thirteen suggestions were offered and written down . . . ' (An observer's notes made on the second occasion).

At the end of the exercise the course leader summed up:

> He said that the purpose of this exercise had been to get people

thinking about the physical organization of the school. The process of introducing flexible teaching was one of evolution not revolution and he hoped the course would reassure people. (An observer's notes made on the first occasion)

The lecture which followed the coffee break was based on a handout and a series of OHP transparencies, and was essentially the same on each of the four occasions. The speaker was again the course leader. The average length of the session was an hour and a quarter, and it began each time with the distribution of the handout summarized in Figures 6.2 and 6.4. However, the speaker spent only a short time on this, saying that it was mainly for people to take away and reflect on later. He then went on to his main theme which was the need for change and the characteristics of effective organization. On each occasion he paused from time to time to invite questions or comments, but he did not devote a large amount of time to this, and the number of questions asked was always small.

The first session after lunch was the one part of the course which differed markedly from one occasion to another. A model classroom had been set up, with approved furniture and equipment arranged and displayed in recommended ways. The aim was for two support staff to explain the rationale of this classroom to course members. The problem was that, whatever its merits in other respects, the room was a completely unsuitable setting for a joint learning activity involving up to thirty adults: it was much too cramped; the chairs were far too small; and the layout was such that from many of the chairs it was quite impossible to see other parts of the room.

On the first and second occasions the whole of the session was spent in the model classroom:

> The course participants were asked to sit on the children's chairs. It was very warm in the room and the traffic noise outside on the inner ring road meant that there were occasions when the speakers could not be heard . . . . (An observer's notes made on the first occasion)

> The setting was the model classroom. Furniture was children's chairs arranged around children's desks. It was quite a squeeze for thirty adults. (An observer's notes made on the second occasion)

The course support staff clearly had a problem here: the model classroom was their subject matter and hence indispensable to the session, yet it was sabotaging what they were trying to achieve. By the third occasion a partial solution had been found in the form of a twelve-minute preliminary talk by one of the support staff outside the model classroom. This ended as follows:

1.45: 'Spend some time now burrowing in that classroom. Look for the evidence of the factors I've mentioned. You won't be asked to report back. I'd like an interactive discussion . . . '. 1.57: We all have to sit down in the classroom. 'Now [my colleague] and I are going to spend about forty minutes talking you through the organization of this classroom. Do please ask if you want to; please feel free to butt in . . . '. (An observer's notes made on the third occasion)

This new way of doing things eased the situation a little but still left large people sitting on small chairs for an uncomfortably long time. By the fourth occasion the process of moving out of the model classroom had gone even further:

1.33: Setting: again the lounge with informal seating. [Presenter:] 'Make groups of three and poke about in the model classroom.' 1.42: Informal discovery of model classroom. [The presenter] decided the group could discuss things for as long as they were 'involved in education-related topics, because talk is good talk.' (An observer's notes made on the fourth occasion)

The overall length of this session varied from just over an hour to just over an hour and a quarter (from sixty-four to seventy-nine minutes).

The final session of the day was a discussion exercise, first in small groups and then in a plenary session:

The course members were asked to get into groups of four, to fill in a schedule. The group I joined did not talk very much about the schedule. One said he found it difficult to think when he was so green with envy. Another said she was wondering how she could split herself into six to look after six groups. Another said her classroom was too odd a shape and anyway she hadn't got that sort of furniture. The schedule was partly filled in . . . . (An observer's notes made on the first occasion)

3.11: The groups were now allowed to wander around and try, poke or examine things in the classroom . . . . 3.38: Moved to lounge for feedback session. Chairs arranged in rows with two presenters at the front . . . . (An observer's notes made on the second occasion)

At the end of the first day the discussion groups reconvened into a plenary session. This final discussion lasted longer and longer each time the course took place: on the first occasion it took only thirteen minutes, and on subsequent occasions fifteen, thirty and thirty-seven minutes. This was the second example of a shift away from small group interaction to a more public discussion in a single large group.

For the opening session of the second day, a local deputy-head gave a personal view of classroom organization. On three of the four occasions she was accompanied by a colleague who took part in some of the discussion and dealt with some of the points raised by the audience. A major problem with this session was the setting:

> The course members were asked to go into the model classroom and sit down. It was not obvious where the speakers were going to position themselves so there was some confusion about where to sit. [The course leader] introduced the two speakers and they stood between the workbench and the sink. As I had managed to get into the 'cosy corner' I was at a bit of a disadvantage because there was a screen between me and them . . . . (An observer's notes made on the first occasion)

> The session took place in the model classroom on chairs designed for children. Everyone was asked to sit around the tables and most found it unsatisfactory . . . . (An observer's notes made on the fourth occasion)

The style of the presentation was quite informal, and the speaker(s) tended to avoid abstractions and generalizations on the one hand and trivial detail on the other. The presentation visibly caught and held the attention of

---

DISCUSSION GROUP TOPIC

- The following are a possible list of topics you could use with a mixed ability 4th and 5th year primary class.

    Holidays
    Power
    Around Our School
    Growth
    Games and Pastimes
    Group Choice

- Prepare a planning chart to illustrate how this work might develop with your group of thirty pupils in the various curriculum areas.
- Choose one of the elements of your chart and plan *in detail* the organizational implications of the experiences/content you have listed.
- Be prepared as a group to make a short illustrated presentation to course members in the form of a printed chart(s) or an overhead projector transparency.

Figure 6.5. Handout Used as a Stimulus for Group Discussion

the audience, and generated a very large number of questions and comments. After coffee a handout was distributed, and the audience was divided into three groups for discussion. The handout is reproduced in Figure 6.5.

The three discussion groups were unsupervised, although the course leader went from one to another. There were marked differences in the ways in which different groups set about organizing themselves, and although some began the task quickly and successfully, others experienced major problems:

> Some minutes were spent reading the discussion sheet and people didn't look up from the sheets until one of the group bravely broke the silence by saying, 'I think we'll have to agree on a topic'. It was agreed that holidays would be interesting, and there ensued a discussion about which countries could be included, until one teacher said that since she taught children who had never been abroad for a holiday, she felt that sand and sea and transport would be more appropriate for them. The others let her talk about this for a while but when the discussion resumed they continued to talk about holidays abroad. It was as if she had never spoken. At this point another teacher . . . volunteered to draw up a flow chart and there followed a ten-minute discussion about who would talk about it in the reporting back session. No conclusion was reached and the talk drifted back to what should go on the flow chart . . . . (An observer's notes made on the first occasion)

> When the group turned its attention to the third section of the handout, it proved impossible to reach an agreement on what the task meant, and whole-group discussion broke down completely. A number of subgroups formed, each carrying out its own conver- sation . . . . (An observer's notes made on the third occasion)

Immediately after lunch one member from each of the three discussion groups reported back to a plenary session. The time devoted to this exercise varied considerably with no discernible pattern, being as short as twenty- eight minutes on one occasion and as long as forty-four on another. After each group had reported back, the rest of the afternoon was devoted to a lecture by the course leader, based on the handout summarized in Figure 6.4 and interrupted by a tea break. At the end of the session, the course leader summed up and ' . . . asked participants to spread it about and if possible come down to the Primary Schools Centre with colleagues to look around the model classroom . . . ' (An observer's notes made on the third occasion). This parting invitation was not an empty social nicety, but an important and innovative aspect of the course. After each occasion arrangements were made to enable interested participants to bring groups of colleagues to the model classroom, and for an advisory teacher to be there to help explain its features to people who had not seen it before.

The point has already been made that although there were minor shifts of emphasis, the course as a whole did not change markedly from one occasion to another. The allocation of working time to different activities is summarized in Table 6.1.

Table 6.1. Percentage of Working Time Devoted to Different Course Activities on Four Occasions
(A, B, C and D)

	A	B	C	D
Talks by course leader	34	30	33	31
Talks by support staff	14	13	12	15
Talks by visiting speakers	14	15	14	14
Small group discussion (twos and fours)	6	6	5	7
Large group discussion (three groups)	21	19	18	16
Plenary sessions (including reporting back)	11	17	18	17
Total working time	100	100	100	100

The proportion of the time given to talks was broadly similar throughout, and hovered around 60 per cent. About a third of the time was for talks by the course leader, and a little under a third for talks by other people. The remaining 40 per cent was devoted to discussion in one form or another. Small group discussion in twos or fours took up about 6 per cent of the time. Discussions where the participants were divided into three groups working in three different rooms were a more prominent feature of the course, although the time spent on this activity dropped from about two hours on the first occasion to an hour and a half on the last; to be precise, the time taken on the four occasions was 116, ninety-three, ninety-three and eighty-eight minutes.

Plenary sessions, on the other hand, accounted for an increasing proportion of the total time. Table 6.1, in which all plenary sessions are treated together, shows a big jump from the first occasion to the second, followed by a plateau. However, if the plenary discussion at the end of the first day is treated separately, there is a dramatic and steady increase over the four occasions, the time taken on each occasion being thirteen, fifteen, thirty and thirty-seven minutes.

Thus, although the overall proportion of time devoted to discussion did not vary, there was a marked shift away from largely unsupervised group discussion towards plenary sessions where the course leader could keep a close eye on what was happening and deal personally with whatever issues arose. The advantages of this shift are immediately apparent, especially in view of the obvious difficulties experienced by some of the groups in their attempts to organize themselves into any kind of useful activity. The price paid was in the loss of smaller group discussion with its enormous potential for interaction and involvement.

The other noticeable change in the course as time went by was in the use of the model classroom. The visiting speaker's presentation took place in it on each of the four occasions, but the support staff were able to devise a system whereby they could conduct at least a part of their session outside the room, so that the time they spent in it on the four occasions steadily dropped from seventy-six minutes on the first occasion to fifty-two minutes on the last. It is perhaps relevant to note that subsequent courses on the same theme have used a different model classroom in a rather different way.

The content or subject matter of the course remained remarkably constant over the four presentations, and it must be assumed that this was because the course staff found it at least a relatively satisfactory solution to a difficult problem. A comprehensive treatment of all aspects and implications of classroom organization would have been quite out of the question in a two-day course, and if it had been attempted, it would inevitably have led to a level of superficiality that could have satisfied nobody. Instead of selecting areas of the general theme at random there seems to have been a policy of shifting the vantage point, as in a series of photographs taken from a variety of distances from long-shot to close-up. Some parts of the course dealt with very broad issues and others with tiny details: for example, at one time the participants were considering an architects's plans for a whole school, and at another they were being invited to consider putting pieces of foam rubber into the bottom of their pencil tins to stop the pencils rattling. Sensitively handled, this examination of a theme from several differing distances can lead to an exhilarating sense of familiarity with all its aspects. The risk, however, is that some of the less reflective participants will go away pre-occupied by the tiny details but oblivious of the issues behind them, and the only way to discover whether this is happening is to ask participants after a course what kind of message they received.

The Message as Received

A basic decision had to be made about timing when we asked teachers about the kind of message they had received from the course. It was clear that the material would be freshest in their minds if they were approached on the day of the course or very shortly afterwards. On the other hand, it can be sensibly argued that the only important part of any message is the part which is remembered for long enough to exert a lasting influence. It was therefore decided to approach teachers after a delay of several weeks, and to combine questions about their recollections of the course's message with a more detailed enquiry into the ways in which their daily practice in the classroom had been affected by it. With this in mind, a short questionnaire was sent to the eighty-six teachers who had attended on the first three occasions; the fourth occasion was so near the end of the school year that any changes in practice seemed likely to be deferred until the beginning of the following year. Respondents were asked to answer the questions anonymously to guard against the possibility that any of them might think their personal views would be made known to individuals within the Authority.

Teachers were asked first to indicate briefly what the main message of the course had been for them personally. The commonest theme in their replies was 'organization', although the word itself was not always used. Typical responses were: 'Organization is the key . . . '; 'reorganize your class-room . . . '; 'make the best use of space and resources . . . '; 'good classroom management . . . ' and so on. In one form or another a message about the importance of classroom organization had been perceived and remembered by just under two-thirds of the people who answered the question, and the proportion remained remarkably constant over each presentation of the course.

The single word which appeared most frequently in comments about the message was 'flexible'; it was used by just under half the respondents. The message was nearly always summarized quite simply as 'be flexible', although the same word was used as part of slightly different messages too, for example: 'the "flexible day" approach to teaching'. This concept of flexibility was the single example of a marked difference between teachers' perceptions of the three presentations of the course. Virtually everyone who had attended the first presentation saw it as a course about flexibility; hardly anyone who had attended the second presentation saw it in this way; with the third presentation the balance was midway between the other two.

Some way behind flexibility as a concept which had stuck in people's minds was 'group work'; it was mentioned by nearly 40 per cent of respondents, although the messages in which it appeared varied considerably: 'group work is always practicable . . . '; 'teach in groups . . . '; 'group by ability . . . '; 'importance of working with different sized groups . . . ' and so on.

Almost a fifth of the respondents said that the main message of the course for them had been about the 'self-sufficiency or independence of pupils'; typical responses here were 'encourage independence . . . '; 'children must be active in their learning . . . '; children should have choice wherever possible . . . '; 'encourage self-sufficiency in the children . . . '.

No other responses were common to substantial numbers of respondents: a handful of people mentioned the curriculum (though not all in the same way); a few mentioned the importance of evaluation; two or three mentioned collaborative or team teaching; and then there was a very long list of messages which had been perceived (or at least reported) by only one or two people. Ten such messages, chosen virtually at random, are listed here:

> Be a problem solver . . . .
> Match work to ability . . . .
> Create a stimulating environment . . . .
> Structure topic work to develop specific skills . . . .
> Set high standards . . . .
> No style of teaching is wrong if it is successful . . . .
> Practical application of basic skills . . . .
> Have high expectations . . . .
> Staff discussion leads to continuity . . . .
> Importance of first-hand experience . . . .

In view of the complexity and even diffuseness of what might be termed *the actual message*, it is scarcely surprising that what was recollected and seen as important differed so widely from person to person. Perhaps the extraordinary thing is not what people said but what they didn't. We have seen that nearly two-thirds of them said that the course had been chiefly about the importance of classroom organization — but that means that *more than one third of them didn't*; nearly half had been forcibly struck by the course's emphasis on flexibility — so *more than half hadn't*; nearly 40 per cent mentioned groups or group work — so *more than 60 per cent didn't*; nearly a fifth mentioned the independence or self-reliance of pupils — so *more than four-fifths didn't*.

The overall picture would undoubtedly have been very different if the question had been posed on the day of the course itself when the terms and concepts which had been used were all still fresh in people's minds. After a few weeks the questionnaire respondents were tending to see the course's value in terms of the changes they had been able to implement rather than in terms of a necessarily rather abstract 'message'. This goes some way toward explaining how a teacher could sit through the complex series of interrelated messages which made up this particular course and then report a few weeks later that its main message for her had been 'Be a problem solver'. Surprising as this perceived message may be, there is no reason to suppose that she had missed the point of the course; it is quite possible that the complexity of the real set of messages about flexibility, classroom management, group work, self-reliance and the like had left her with the generalized feeling that her own practice needed changing but that she would have to work out the nature and pace of the change for herself — in short she would have to become her own problem-solver.

To penetrate to the level of the course's influence on everyday practice, teachers were asked if it had included clear guidance or instruction about what they and their colleagues should be doing in their own schools and, if so, what the guidance or instruction had been. Well over 90 per cent of the respondents said that clear guidance or instruction had been given, although many of them were not very explicit about its nature. Some answered the question solely in terms of the techniques used by the course staff, without describing the guidance or instruction itself: e.g. about a quarter mentioned the sessions in the model classroom but gave no indication of what they had learned there; and about the same proportion mentioned either a lecture or a handout without indicating its content. Those respondents who did summarize the guidance itself tended to concentrate on three themes: the material organization of the classroom, advice about group work, and guidance on how to plan a topic or project.

Taken as a whole, the questionnaire responses serve to confirm a common experience. When we think back to anything that happened to us several weeks ago, however striking it may have been at the time, we tend to recall a very basic and generalized impression coupled with a few seemingly random details. However important a course may be to its organizers, the people who attend it have many other concerns and preoccupations. The course may affect them deeply and even transform their classroom practice, but this does not necessarily mean that they will be able to summarize its messages in a very coherent way later; and if some relatively trivial detail strikes them at the time as a splendid idea, it may loom much larger in their recollections than it did in the course itself.

The Impact on Daily Practice

The power of a message must ultimately be judged by its influence on people's thought and practice; however entertaining and instructive a course may be, it can hardly be judged a success if we all go away and carry on exactly as before. It is plain that in evaluating a course's effectiveness the timing of the enquiry is a very important variable. The sooner the questions are asked, the less chance there is that changes will have been fully implemented; yet the longer the questions are delayed, the less chance there is that the effect of the course can be separated from the effects of other things that have happened in the intervening time.

In the present enquiry the time lapse of four or five weeks was thought by several respondents to have been too short; they indicated that more time would be needed before they could introduce radical changes in a way that would help rather than confuse the children.

The most common change in practice during the weeks after the course involved the shifting of furniture and the rearrangement of materials: 'I have moved some furniture...'; 'I have improved my labelling system...'; 'I have defined working areas more clearly...'; 'I have made materials more available to children...' and so on. Nearly three-fifths of the participating teachers had taken some action of this kind, although it is too soon to determine in how many cases this was the first step towards an integrated system of flexible classroom organization in its wider sense.

On a less basic and material level various other suggestions for organizational change had been enthusiastically put into practice: ten examples are listed below:

> More classroom activities are going on at once . . . .
> I have tried to reduce transition time . . . .
> I now use activity cards . . . .
> I am planning my work differently . . . .
> I try a wider variety of techniques . . . .
> Better preparation . . . .
> More integrated work approach . . . .
> More role play . . . .
> I have reorganized existing groups . . . .
> I am extending topic work . . . .

A few of these activities refer to specific suggestions made on the course; most are variations on the theme of flexibility; all reflect a willingness to try things out, and this was the prevailing mood conveyed by the questionnaire respondents. However, there were exceptions to this. Nearly a quarter of the respondents said that their practice had changed very little or not at all, although it must be stressed that this was generally not because they rejected the messages conveyed by the course; in nearly every case they were at pains to say that they had been *doing it all anyway*.

Factors Helping and Hindering Change

Teachers were invited to comment on the likelihood of their being able to follow the guidance or instruction given on the course in their own school. Nearly three-quarters thought there would be no serious problems in this area, and nearly all of them mentioned other adults as the likeliest source of help and support. The head was seen as the strongest single influence, although other colleagues were also mentioned frequently. A few teachers listed other helpful factors ranging from new furniture and suitable equipment to the course handouts and their own personal conviction. The same pattern of responses appeared when teachers considered factors which had already helped them in changing their practice. The head came top of the list, with other colleagues close behind. Other factors ranged from flexible school organization to cooperative pupils.

However, there were hindrances as well. The head and other colleagues featured on this list too, although other factors now played a much bigger part. Perhaps because of the emphasis during the course on furniture and equipment, more than half of the respondents said that they were prevented from carrying out recommended changes because of unsuitable or inadequate furniture, equipment or accommodation: 'lack of resources ... '; 'my classroom is used for lunches ... '; 'wrong size of furniture ... '; 'the roof leaks ... ' and so on. Pupils were also seen by some teachers as an unwittingly sabotaging element: 'children find it difficult to talk and listen to each other ... '; 'children's unfamiliarity with this type of organization ... '; 'children's lack of previous training in making choices ... ' and so on.

While some of these comments about pupils indicated an obvious form of scapegoating (for of course children make choices and talk and listen to each other all day long), it was refreshing to note that nearly a fifth of the respondents had had the courage to identify their own anxiety, lack of confidence or lack of energy as a major stumbling block. Teachers who are fortunate enough to possess this degree of insight have already taken the first steps toward a transformation of their practice; others may lag behind. All of them might benefit from the opportunity to follow up the experience of attending the course with some continuing interaction with the other people who were there. The questionnaire responses indicate the isolation which some teachers feel and the open hostility towards the message of this course which others perceive in their colleagues. In such circumstances, and without a well-defined network of support, even the most enthusiastic supporter of flexible teaching strategies is likely to become disheartened and discouraged in time, and it might be helpful if some kind of informal follow-up arrangements could be built into courses of this kind.

Long-term Effects of the Course

In the nature of things the long-term influence of the course cannot be investigated in detail at this stage; it took place too recently. However, teachers were invited to speculate on the long-term changes likely in their schools as a result of their attending the course, and they expressed a range of differing views.

More than a quarter of them were to some extent pessimistic, citing the reluctance or hostility of colleagues or their own lack of power and influence within the school. However, almost a quarter were quite optimistic, saying that it would be slow or difficult (or both) but that the goodwill was there and that the staff of their schools were willing to give it a go. The three key themes which emerged in this part of the enquiry were:

> the organization and pooling of materials and resources;
> the introduction of a more flexible attitude to teaching methods;
> the introduction or development of group work.

In terms of lasting impact, the rich assortment of ideas and themes within the course was thus simplified and pared down to a very basic trio of likely changes, and it will be interesting to see the extent to which these are implemented when more time has passed and a longer-term follow-up becomes possible.

Conclusion

This report is a case study of one course which formed part of the Authority's PNP in-service support programme during 1986–87. We have explained why we chose to focus in such detail on this particular course, the central role it played in the in-service programme and the way it exemplified issues common to most or all of the courses which PRINDEP monitored. We have also indicated that our evaluation of this and the other courses is continuing and that we hope to report on them and their longer-term impact at a later date.

There seem to us to be three ways in which this case study can be helpful to the Authority. One is quite specific to the course in question, in the sense that those running it and perhaps preparing to mount further versions of it may profit from the particular analysis which this report provides. Second, because the course has so much in common with others in the Authority's PNP in-service support programme, the 1986-87 experience and our analysis of it raise questions and issues which can usefully be applied to other courses besides the one under review. Third, this case study provides perspectives for reflecting upon staff development in a more general way, in so far as it exemplifies a particular *style* of in-service activity which offers both advantages and disadvantages and needs to be contrasted with alternative possibilities.

At this stage we cannot offer the final word on any of these matters: partly because the issue is too vast, complex and sensitive to be dealt with in one relatively short report, and partly because PRINDEP's study of this aspect of the Primary Needs Programme has some way yet to go. The general discussion which follows, therefore, provides pointers of an interim rather than a final kind.

One caveat needs to be entered first. It may be assumed by some that a report on courses mounted by the Authority is of interest only to those who organize and run them. We trust that teachers in the Authority's schools will resist such a view. They are, after all, the recipients of these courses, and the people through whom the INSET programme's messages are translated into the kinds of classroom practices whereby the Authority hopes to achieve its goal of improving the quality of primary schooling in Leeds. At the same time the teachers concerned are not mere agents or operatives in this process, but professionals with ideas of their own. This being so, it is unlikely that they would wish to opt out of discussion of their own professional development.

The first of our three proposed ways of using this report — for reflecting on and perhaps modifying one specific course — needs no further discussion. The report is divided into sections, each of which clearly identifies a number of issues, and the overall discussion agenda for those concerned is self-evident.

The main issues which apply more generally to the full range of courses that PRINDEP has been monitoring seem to be as follows. First, the idea of *message*. This is a fundamental matter, given the approach to in-service development the Authority has chosen to adopt. We have seen that central to this approach is the conveying of a particular view of what 'good practice' looks like, coupled with the expectation that teachers will internalize that view and change their own practice accordingly. If this is indeed the preferred approach, then the case study provides important lessons for those concerned.

We have seen, for instance, that there can be a considerable difference between a message as *intended* and as *received*. We have seen that the same message is received and interpreted in widely differing ways, and it is clear that in some cases the interpretation may even be the opposite of what was intended. Exactly the same thing happens, of course, in the primary classroom: teaching raises the same kinds of issues at every level from schools to adult education. We can analyze the causes of the discrepancy in three possible ways.

The first is to look at the recipient of the message — in this case the teacher attending the INSET course — and consider what it is about him or her as an individual which has made for difficulty in understanding or has led to a particular interpretation of a message. It may have something to do with past experience, general attitude, ability, or any one of a very large number of other factors. The second way is to look at the message itself and examine the extent to which it is clearly and unambiguously expressed. The third is to look at the person or people delivering the message and the way they do it. Two of the relevant questions here are whether their status and style are such that their overt message becomes tangled with messages at other levels, and whether they have the credibility to convince their audience that what they are commending is valid and workable.

This takes us to the next general issue concerning not just the case study course but others as well: the *methods* used. The courses monitored by PRINDEP combined a number of methods: formal delivery by a course presenter; the use of handouts and checklists; simulated activities and model classrooms; question and answer sessions led by a course leader and/or support staff; small group discussion and other tasks, some led by course staff, others run by course members on their own. Each of these has advantages and disadvantages. Moreover, as with different teaching methods in the primary classroom, they do not suit all teachers and all learners equally. Some course presenters are happier interacting with a large group, while others come into their own in small group work; exactly the same is so for course members. As teachers in primary schools we would acknowledge such variation and build in sufficient variety to maximize the chances of all children finding learning circumstances with which they are comfortable. Do INSET courses reflect the same principle? Should they?

Then there are points about specific methods. What is the most productive way of delivering a complex message about classroom organization (or any other aspect of teaching)? What is the best way to handle large group question-and-answer sessions? What exactly *is* the function of a handout or checklist: to prescribe exactly what the recipient should do, or to raise questions and promote self-appraisal? Is it sometimes a case of one appearing in the guise of the other, of an ostensibly 'open' document being in fact a closed agenda? Or, taking another common method, if course members have difficulty in sticking to the task set or the focus provided in discussion groups, why is this, and how can it be dealt with? Are the instructions clear enough? Is small group discussion among teachers a skill which cannot be taken for granted and which needs some degree of training? The evidence from the present study suggests that this is indeed the case.

We need not pursue these examples further: the general point is that in the particular course which is the subject of this report, various methods were used which also feature in other courses run by the Authority. This being so, the case study can provide perspectives for examining the validity and effectiveness of such methods in a wide variety of in-service contexts. Among these are not only venues like the Primary Schools Centre or the John Taylor Teachers' Centre, but also schools themselves, since heads frequently use exactly the same range of strategies to promote staff and curriculum development.

Finally, we come to the much more fundamental matter of the assumptions about professional development which courses like the one in this report seem to reflect, and the issues which such assumptions raise. We noted near the beginning of the report that the activity of getting teachers to analyze and describe their practice, which the PRINDEP team has been undertaking as a necessary part of their PNP evaluation programme, also happened to be a powerful tool for professional development in its own right. We went on to suggest that this might validly prompt certain questions about the approach to professional development which is embodied in the Authority's INSET programme.

There are many different approaches to professional development, and a single INSET activity can combine several of them, but all tend to require the resolution of the following choices:

Target: General/Specific

Some in-service activities are open to any teachers who apply for them; some are restricted to particular categories or groups; some are for particular individuals. If follows, therefore, that the more general and diverse the target group of teachers, the more the in-service activity involved becomes — whatever its quality — something of a hit-or-miss affair.

Definition of Needs: From Above/From Below

The question of who defines the professional needs of teachers is a fundamental one. At one end of the continuum is the view that those in authority (advisers at LEA level, heads at school level) know best what teachers need by way of professional development and construct INSET activities accordingly. At the other end is the view that the individual teacher is the best person to make that judgment, or at least should be invited to do so. In between is the idea that defining needs is best seen as a consultative, negotiated process.

Mode of Development: Training/Self-Development

Some in-service activities reflect the assumption that 'development' is something one person does to another, and that a teacher is most likely to change if there is an irresistible external impetus or incentive together with external agents to devise the in-service programme and instruct or train the teacher in the required direction. The contrasting view is that true change comes only when the individual concerned is committed to bringing it about and is actively involved in devising and implementing the means by which this is done; by this view professional development is something we do for ourselves rather than something others do to us.

Putting these sets of choices together provides a three-dimensional framework for thinking about different approaches to professional development. It will be clear that the courses under discussion in this report tend towards a particular combination of choices. They are aimed at total populations of teachers rather than at identified individuals; they reflect an LEA view of 'good practice' and what teachers need to achieve it; and, at least in the first instance, they mainly feature an external agent like an adviser or advisory teacher acting on the teachers rather than the teachers acting on themselves.

The thinking behind this approach can be readily appreciated. There are about 2400 primary teachers in Leeds and a primary advisory staff of only sixteen, all of whom have many other jobs to do in addition to running in-service courses. They are charged with the responsibility of implementing an extremely ambitious and wide-ranging policy for primary education, some of which incorporates ideas and procedures which may be unfamiliar to some teachers and indeed perceived as alien and threatening by them. It is not surprising if the Authority judges that the quickest way to achieve results in the largest number of schools is to mount a substantial in-service programme in which an enthusiastic set of messages is delivered to large numbers of teachers in the hope that though some will inevitably remain unaffected a fair proportion will return to school ready and able to bring about change in their own and their colleagues' practice.

It can be argued that, given the nature of the policy to be implemented, and the scale of the challenge in relation to the resources available, the approach adopted is the only one possible. It can also be shown that as a strategy it is delivering results, and PRINDEP's own evidence, in this and earlier reports, begins to confirm this. Nevertheless, as the framework above indicates, there are at least as many alternatives as there are permutations of the various dimensions (far more, in fact, since the framework is a very simple one). The essence of a comprehensive and flexible in-service policy, one might suggest, is that such alternatives should exist as practical opportunities for an Authority's teachers. Nor should the possibilities be polarized, as so often in INSET debate they have been, into the stark choice between so-called 'top-down' (LEA-controlled/INSET centre-based) and 'bottom-up' (teacher-controlled/school-based) approaches. Presenting the debate in such adversarial terms is both simplistic and unhelpful, since the questions of who should control a teacher's professional development and how and where it should take place can only be resolved by taking into account the experience, expertise and needs of that teacher, the circumstances and needs of his or her school, the policies and facilities of the LEA and other critical factors.

This would dictate an approach to INSET in which courses firmly steered along LEA policy channels run alongside activities encouraging a high degree of teacher autonomy and self-determination; in which both training by others and opportunities for self-development are readily available; in which 'basic' INSET, where teachers acquire new knowledge and skills, runs in parallel with the kind of advanced provision that takes the accumulated expertise and insight of the talented teacher to even higher levels of refinement; and in which advisers, lecturers and heads learn from classroom teachers, as well as the other way round. The undeniable fact of diversity in teachers and schools requires diversity in provision for teacher and school development.

Since the Authority's total provision combines courses like the one discussed here with one-to-one adviser-teacher consultation at school level, opportunities for teachers to attend a wide variety of full and part-time courses elsewhere, support for school-based development programmes and many other comparable initiatives, its endorsement of the diversity principle seems very clear.

However — and this brings us back to the sequence of 1986–87 PNP in-service support courses with which we started — if diversity is valid as a guiding principle at the level of an Authority's in-service provision as a whole, then it may be no less valid as a criterion for appraising provision at the level of the individual course. How far does each course meet the range of needs of its member teachers and their schools? How far can it? To what extent does it acknowledge the inevitably wide variation in member teachers' experience and expertise? Does it respect, build upon and learn from professional talent as well as locate and remedy professional inadequacy? More fundamentally, where is 'good primary practice' to be found: in policy statements, in the educational literature, on courses, or in classrooms? What is the most productive way to link these: in a hierarchical relationship or a dialectical one? These are the kinds of question which, alongside the issues raised earlier, PRINDEP's analysis of the Authority's PNP inservice support programme is beginning to generate, and which we hope will in turn encourage discussion and appraisal within both the Authority and its schools.

7
Teachers Teaching Together

Introduction

In comparison with other sectors of education, primary schools have always been very tightly staffed. Not only have pupil-teacher ratios been higher, but primary teachers have usually had to accept the absence of 'free' periods — something their secondary colleagues would never have tolerated. The most recent figures available at the time of writing, those from HMI's 1987 Primary School Staffing Survey (DES, 1988b) show primary class teachers having about forty minutes a week non-contact time or eight minutes a day. This is an average figure: most primary teachers, as HMI pointed out in their subsequent 1987–88 Annual Report, 'teach for 100 per cent of the time available' (DES, 1989a). Even senior staff with substantial cross-school responsibilities for year groups or infant/junior departments have under an hour a week non-contact time, as do many deputy-heads.

The historical reason for this, in part the legacy of the 'cheap and efficient' elementary system, is that primary schools have been staffed on the basis of the simple formula of one teacher for each registration class, plus the head. In smaller schools, of course, the head can be expected to teach anything from a few hours each week to full-time. The generalist class teacher system has allowed this formula to persist unchallenged: if each teacher is capable of teaching everything, then the logistics of staffing a school are satisfyingly straightforward. Thus, unwittingly, the primary profession's strenuous defence of the class teacher system has ensured the continuation of conditions much less favourable, in this respect at least, than those enjoyed by their specialist secondary colleagues.

Quite apart from the pressure this creates for all involved, it is a system which offers very little flexibility. The basic act of teaching a class dominates the teacher's day, and the other tasks of which teaching is necessarily constituted — planning, assessment, record keeping, curriculum development, staff development and so on — take place 'out of hours': or rather — under the 1987 conditions of service — either during 'directed time' (the difference between the hours spent teaching and the 1265 hours per year a teacher is required to work to the head's instructions) or in the teacher's own time.

It has always been argued that the short working year allows ample time for the full range of 'non-contact' professional activities, and in a sense this is true. But this argument also ignores one vital consideration, namely that many of these activities need to take place during the school day. This is particularly significant in the present context, for two reasons. First, the pressure of unrelieved full-time teaching is felt particularly acutely during periods of impending or actual change. It is at such times that the routines which work well during periods of stability are placed under increasing stress. Second, as many of the witnesses to the Commons Select Committee argued, among the most effective tools for coping with or generating change is collaborative activity within the classroom:

> First, it provides an opportunity for the inservice training of the class teacher; second, it offers the opportunity to concentrate available teaching skill on the group of children who for the time being require it; third and fourth, because (the 'visiting' teacher) will acquire knowledge of what is happening in other classes than his or her own, it should be easier to develop continuity from class to class, and to adapt the programme more nearly to the needs of the children and the capacities of the staff. (House of Commons, 1986, pp. 133–4)

Such collaboration, it need hardly be added, is virtually impossible within the conventional staffing formula, and it was with these and other needs in mind that the Committee went on to assert more strongly: 'The inescapable conclusion . . . is that primary schools cannot be expected to make much further improvement unless there are more teachers than registration classes' (House of Commons, 1986, p. 141).

The Primary Needs Programme addressed this problem directly by making enhanced staffing its main investment. The figures in Chapter 1 show the scale of the commitment, particularly to the seventy schools in the first phase. All these schools acquired staff to take their establishment above the usual ratio, and in a few schools the numbers of extra teachers were very substantial indeed (up to nine or ten above normal establishment).

Since this achieved precisely what the profession had been insisting on for decades — more teachers — it might be supposed that the initiative opened the floodgates of collaborative innovation on a grand scale. But this would be to ignore the very important fact that since the schools had no experience of anything other than the traditional staffing formula, this had powerfully shaped not only their pattern of organization, but also their professional culture and thinking down to its deepest levels.

Thus while it may be true that collaboration is an essential part of the primary ethic, such collaboration has almost always taken place outside rather than inside the classroom. The important study of primary teachers by Nias (1989) bears this out. Though a climate of 'mutual dependence' was highly valued by her respondents, its focal point was usually the staffroom. In fact, many primary teachers have little experience of observing each other's teaching and thereby beginning to enter in a more fundamental sense into each other's thinking, let alone of actually working together in the same classroom. Some, indeed, may fiercely defend their privacy and autonomy, and see such mutuality of endeavour as undesirable or unnecessary. (The patterns of organization adopted in some open-plan schools are a notable exception.) So in the first instance what a programme like PNP offered teachers was not so much an opportunity as a challenge. What would schools *do* with these extra teachers? How would a culture which attaches so much significance to 'ownership' of a class respond?

This sense of the problematic nature of classroom collaboration emerged very early and powerfully in PNP. It was, as we explain below, one reason why Kay Kinder undertook this study. It may also explain why her term 'Teachers Teaching Together' (abbreviated TTT) and her analytical framework were so rapidly adopted by the LEA for in-service purposes and why 'TTT' became part of the city's primary orthodoxy. Given the strength and pervasiveness of the tradition being confronted by TTT, the problems of its introduction probably could not have been anticipated.

We believe that where opportunities for classroom collaboration exist elsewhere, the decisions to be confronted and the problems to be sorted out will be very similar, if not identical, to those we have noted in Leeds. One such context is that of special needs, where since the 1981 Education Act a number of LEAs have introduced special needs support teachers to work alongside primary class teachers. HMI's survey of these practices points up similar problems to those we record below, encapsulated in their finding that many of the claimed cases of team teaching were 'little more than the presence of two teachers in one classroom' (DES, 1989b, p. 10).

The analysis in this study is somewhat different from that contained in other chapters. Though it is empirically grounded, its thrust is less towards the presentation of 'findings' than the generation of a conceptual framework. The follow-up study, which consolidates the framework through further classroom data, is incorporated in Volume 2.

Background

Teacher collaboration featured very prominently in the responses of PNP Phase 1 staff to our preliminary survey of July 1986. Teachers at all levels, from class teacher to head, ventured strong and often conflicting opinions about the impact, value and practicability of working together in the classroom. The questionnaire responses confirmed that there was a wide variety of practices, and also considerable variation in the perceived success rate of these collaborations. During the early stages at least, teachers did not always find it easy to work together, however valuable the notion seemed in theory, and this in itself justifies a search for any common factors which helped or hindered collaboration.

The questionnaires revealed another variation. Teachers were using a diverse array of terms to name the collaborative practices they felt so strongly about. While 'team teaching' was the phrase used most frequently, it was applied to many different kinds and degrees of collaboration. Other teachers referred to 'support teaching' and 'working alongside' (the terms used by the LEA), stating categorically that team teaching was not occurring in their schools.

Because of this confusion we have invented our own term, 'Teachers Teaching Together' (abbreviated to TTT), hoping that such a neutral phrase will capture the informal, flexible and in many cases experimental collaborations which seem to be occurring, while allowing us to characterize what was actually happening free of existing connotations. The term 'team teaching', in our view, refers more properly to formalized staffing arrangements where large groups of children are the shared and full-time responsibility of a permanent group of teachers, as in the American and British experiments of the 1960s and 1970s (Shaplin and Olds, 1964; Taylor, 1974). The medley (or muddle) of current terminology raises a further question: does this lack of consensus about the terms for describing teacher collaboration reflect a similar confusion about what TTT might actually entail?

This report is a preliminary account of the TTT practices currently being undertaken in Leeds primary classrooms. It makes use of interview and observation data gathered in both Fieldwork A and B schools. It considers the different types of TTT which have emerged so far and their function, the problems and advantages of TTT, and possible future developments.

Types of TTT: Overview

> PNP is about teachers working together.... This is the message our head has brought back, but there's no guidance about how we should tackle it. (Scale II postholder in a Phase 2 school)

It is evident that currently TTT is a teaching arrangement of considerable variety, variability and versatility. As teachers decide, or are asked, to work together a number of aspects are involved. First, there is the question of the *participants* or who the collaborating teachers are. Most examples of TTT involve a class teacher and one or more support teachers. Each participant's teaching experience, status, subject expertise and length of service within school may all influence how they work together. Second, there is the issue of the intended *purposes* of the collaboration. Teachers have identified three major purposes of TTT, not necessarily seen as mutually exclusive: special educational needs, curriculum enhancement and the professional development of one or other of the participants. These different purposes will affect the collaboration also. Third, there is the question of the different teaching arrangements within the collaboration (what we have come to call *collaborative style*). Teachers have tended to speak of two main styles of collaboration — 'withdrawal' and 'working alongside'. Included here are issues of where each teacher works, how much teachers liaise before, during and after a session with the children, and how often they actually work together. Fourth, there is the issue of *pupil organization*, or the ways in which pupils are allocated to the collaborating teachers. Various patterns have emerged: equal division, no division, and small groups/individuals and the rest of the class.

With all four of these aspects operating at the same time, a wide range of practices results. For example, we may find any of the following patterns:

PARTICIPANTS: support teacher (coordinator) and class teacher
PURPOSE: special educational needs
STYLE: withdrawal
ORGANIZATION: small group and rest of class

PARTICIPANTS: support teacher (coordinator) and class teacher
PURPOSE: curriculum enhancement
STYLE: working alongside
ORGANIZATION: equal division

PARTICIPANTS: support teacher (curriculum leader) and class teacher

PURPOSE: professional development of class teacher
STYLE: working alongside
ORGANIZATION: no division (support teacher gives 'key' stimulus and instructions)

There are many other possible permutations. By examining more closely each of these four aspects, we hope to clarify further the types of TTT being undertaken.

Participants

Most teachers who are involved in TTT arrangements comment on the strains as well as the strengths of working together. They refer to 'relationships' as the key to successful collaboration. Commonly heard assertions that 'it's a bit threatening' or that 'it's all down to personalities' clearly signal, but do not properly explain, what the tensions underlying collaboration are.

Of course, some teachers have a considerable adjustment to make when engaging in TTT initially. For it is certain that, in the traditional staff deployment of the primary school, a class teacher has a high degree of autonomy — she is, so to speak, queen of her own castle. Whatever the direction offered by the school's curriculum guidelines and policies, usually she alone takes responsibility for selecting, planning and delivering the day-to-day curriculum experiences of her children. And she does so in private; she plans in private, and usually teaches secluded from other professionals. It is not necessarily easy to disclose the detail of one's professional thinking and practice to others: TTT can make quite rigorous demands on the participants to reveal that which has previously been unspoken and unobserved.

The class teachers with whom we have talked have had other points to make about TTT. Some speak of a sense of implied or overt criticism of their classroom management styles and the curriculum they offer to children. This can be a very undermining experience. Several class teachers confided that they 'had lost confidence' and 'no longer felt valuable'. Some refer to the difficulty of planning for a support teacher's occasional visits. They speak of a sense of 'being tied down' and 'losing the opportunity to respond spontaneously to children's interests'. Some confess they have difficulty 'letting go of the children in their care'. TTT involves an adjustment of the powerful bonds of affection between a class teacher and her class, and a modification of her sense of exclusive professional responsibility.

Support teachers, on the other hand, have a rather different perspective on TTT. Some speak of the problems of gaining access to classrooms. They encounter an unwillingness on the part of the class teacher to put herself on display either while teaching or at the planning stage. Some mention the difficulty of exerting a lasting influence on teaching style or curriculum. Some express a sense of unsatisfactory 'bittiness' about their role. They feel that their peripatetic existence could inhibit the consolidation of their relationships with children as well as the work undertaken with them.

Many of these reservations have been expressed by teachers during the early stages of their collaboration, and they are telling and perhaps inevitable comments on the problems of adjusting to a classroom life which no longer offers complete self-determination for either participant.

Teachers who perceive their collaborations as successful have identified four main reasons for their success. They mention:

flexibility;
time to plan and evaluate;
complementary styles of teaching;
willingness to learn from each other.

They also acknowledge that they share the same educational values. They make, or are given, the opportunity to discuss their roles and responsibilities within the collaboration. They clarify instructional goals and decide on organizational procedures for achieving them and, not unimportantly, they like and respect each other.

Such liaison is a radical departure from the traditional professional relationships between many teachers. They may talk informally in the staff-room about their classroom practice, but in that setting their talk tends to be anecdotal. They allude to what they have been doing rather than discuss it comprehensively.

TTT may require new kinds of professional discussion, where classroom management and curriculum practices are more rigorously confronted and appraised, and participants may find it necessary to create new opportunities and contexts for such discussion to occur. Undoubtedly TTT involves a recognition that collaborating with colleagues can be an exacting experience. As one commentator has said, it involves 'the acceptance of criticism, the realization of weaknesses and an acknowledgment of the superiority of others in certain areas'.

Purposes

This aspect refers to the different learning objectives which TTT, with its enhanced teacher provision, might pursue. Teachers have mentioned three main reasons for working together:

special educational needs;
curriculum enhancement;
professional development.

In each of these three purposes we can identify some of the broad aims of PNP.

Special Educational Needs. Although a stated aim of PNP is to 'meet the identified needs of pupils', many teachers interpret this as referring solely to children with learning and/or behavioural difficulties, and in several schools these children are perceived as needing the majority of a support teacher's attention. The in-service programme has provided training for this role with courses on LISSEN. We have seen several schools which were operating something like an old style remedial service, with the support teacher removing children for separate work programmes, which were not in any way connected to their work in class, nor negotiated with the class teacher.

However, there are now strong messages being delivered by the Authority's advisory team that this is not how PNP provision is to be used and the SEN provision must be 'in the context of general classroom provision'. This is consistent with national trends since Warnock, and we noted that several schools are carrying out the kinds of practices referred to in the Thomas Report on ILEA primary schools:

> Special tuition...should be linked to the child's main programme of work.... The whole work of the child should be the concern of his class teacher and both class teacher and incoming teacher should take care to use and build on what the other is doing. At least some books and materials should be used in the presence of both teachers. (ILEA, 1985, p.43)

The implication that close collaboration is a prerequisite for successful SEN provision is unmistakable. The TTT arrangement which employs the remedial approach has, whether deliberately or otherwise, avoided establishing liaison, and participants may have to analyze reasons why this should be so.

Curriculum Enhancement. Another stated aim of PNP is 'to develop a broadly-based curriculum, within a stimulating and challenging learning environment'. Certain schools are using TTT as a strategy to spread the curriculum strengths and expertise of key staff members, who may or may not be recently appointed PNP staff. Existing postholders or senior staff can have an important role to play here. In a thematic cross-curricular approach these teachers offer suggestions for their subject area at the planning stage and also contribute to its delivery in the classroom. In this way it is said that there is an 'enriched curriculum' for the children and expertise is passed on informally to the class teacher. Science, CDT, drama, music, maths and computers are some specialisms being taught by curriculum leaders alongside their colleagues. Alternatively, in some collaborations the whole of the class theme is jointly planned by the teachers involved.

It is clear that the integration of curriculum specialisms into the class theme again requires time and opportunity to plan: in some cases teachers perceived themselves as being relieved of the responsibility to consider the curriculum area of the specialist. Effective liaison here meant substantial amounts of planning and evaluation: half-termly and weekly, often lengthy sessions involving decisions on appropriate content, resources and the kinds of skills which the children should develop.

Professional Development. While special educational needs and curriculum enhancement suggest that the target for improved provision is primarily children, in some examples of TTT a parallel (and sometimes major) purpose of the collaboration is *professional development*. This can either be 'renovation' of practice for long-standing members of staff or guidance and support for the less experienced, e.g. probationers. In several of the TTT arrangements in our sample schools, support teachers felt their role was primarily to give advice on classroom organization and appropriate curriculum content. In effect they were trying to help their colleagues to achieve the PNP objectives of developing 'flexible teaching strategies' and 'a broadly-based curriculum' by establishing what we might term a consultant/client relationship.

In these cases it would appear that *status* becomes an important issue. Those professional development collaborations which are seen by the participants to operate with most success have some or all of the following four characteristics. First, there is a clear recognition of the professional development function and an accompanying status differential. Typical examples of this might be a senior member of staff supporting a probationer, or an advisory teacher working with a class teacher. Here the consultative role is overt and acceptable to both sides. On the other hand, there is evidence of problems in an advisory collaboration between staff who are supposed to be of equal status. Second, the consultant teacher has the acknowledged backing of the headteacher's authority. Advisory collaborations are said to be facilitated by strategies such as joint consultations in the presence of the head or provision of non-contact time for planning and evaluation. Third, the consultant teacher needs to have negotiating skill, tact and sensitivity.

Offering advice and direction obviously requires considerable interpersonal skills. Many support teachers recognize that they must prove themselves as classroom practitioners and some choose to adopt a low profile within the collaboration initially. There might be a contradiction here. Certainly it indicates that professional development through working with colleagues is a slow process. Some Phase 1 staff are beginning to feel, by the end of their fifth term in schools, that their influence is at last evident. Fourth, the client teacher has to be amenable and to accept TTT as a strategy for her own professional development. For some teachers, involvement in this use of TTT is felt to be a stigma. TTT needs to be viewed as a valid and valuable type of in-service activity, equivalent to attending courses and reading educational literature.

Our observation of TTT as a professional development strategy raised a further interesting issue. In some examples, which purported to assist the client teacher's understanding of curriculum or classroom management, it was difficult to know what she could really learn from her colleague when both teachers were fully involved with their own groups of children. The opportunity for the client teacher to observe the consultant teacher in action may be of benefit here.

Collaborative Style

This aspect refers to different kinds of collaboration as they are realized in the classroom. The terms 'working alongside' and 'withdrawal' are used frequently by teachers themselves and tend to describe the degree of their collaboration as much as where each participant is actually working. For example, we have seen teachers who are withdrawing children into one area of the classroom and engaging in quite separate and unnegotiated teaching activities, while physically located alongside another teacher. Alternatively, a teacher may be working with a group of children out of the classroom, and yet this group work is part of a carefully integrated and jointly planned class theme.

The advisory service makes a useful distinction here between withdrawal and working alongside: withdrawal is when one teacher takes responsibility for the learning of a group of children, but the other teacher is clearly informed about the intentions and outcome of that withdrawal; working alongside is a more complex relationship, where the teachers share the planning and delivery of learning experiences for a single group of children.

It is evident from our fieldwork that both these styles of collaboration are not always quite like this in practice. In some cases withdrawal is done with minimal liaison. Support teachers have reported being given a group of children (often with learning or behavioural problems) 'to do whatever you want with', and indeed one class teacher said to us, 'There is no need to plan together; it's self-evident what is needed.' This may be a tactic for preserving the comfortable privacy and autonomy which either the class teacher or the support teacher actually prefers. Another reason given for minimal liaison is that certain areas of the curriculum which follow a structured scheme, like maths or reading, are quite comfortably operated without detailed joint planning or feedback. We have also seen examples of curriculum leaders withdrawing groups for the specialist teaching of science or drama, with no feedback to their class teacher either offered or requested. The fieldwork has provided examples of working alongside where the planning is done exclusively by one teacher, who determines the content of the children's learning and plans for the use of her support teacher in 'something like an NTA role'. Several support teachers refer to being 'only an extra pair of hands' or giving 'practical help' in the classroom. Both these extremes have been employed deliberately by support teachers as tactics or transitional stages to ease the 'sense of threat' and help the long-term development of the kinds of professional relationship upon which collaboration depends.

A further issue in this aspect of TTT is how often the participants work together. Some support teachers have commented that they are 'spread too thinly'. Teaching in many classrooms for short periods obviously affects the contribution they can make in each; they feel working for extended periods with fewer colleagues facilitates much closer collaboration. Working alongside then becomes something more like a *partnership*, allowing each participant a sustained and substantial role in both planning and teaching.

Pupil Organization

This last of our four main aspects of TTT refers to the ways in which participants share out the teaching of a group or class or children. In our fieldwork we have noted three main variations.

Equal Division. Here two or more teachers operate independently with a smaller number of children, creating virtual mini-classes. The children are then grouped, so that each teacher has responsibility for perhaps two groups. She may then employ the 'flexible' class management strategy of interacting intensively with one group and monitoring the more self-occupying work offered to the other children. Alternatively, a teacher may operate as a monitor of children who are undertaking individual assignments, the lower pupil numbers involved enabling her to ɑ this more effectively than with a whole class. Responsibility for the children and their work is delineated at the planning stage.

No Division. Here the major input or stimulus is given by one teacher and then each monitors how the children cope with the learning task that follows. This is a TTT version of a whole-class activity/class-lesson. Special needs support teachers have commented that this arrangement is a useful way to observe and interact with their charges.

Small Group/Individual and Rest of Class. Here one teacher may have a lengthy interaction with a specific group of children, while the other maintains the rest of the class with their assigned work. Although the class teacher might be expected to undertake this maintaining role, some collaborations are exploiting the opportunity for the class teacher to take on specialized small group work — SEN provision, outside visits, craft or computer work, baking and practical maths are some examples referred to.

Clearly TTT offers teachers the opportunity to try out many class management techniques as well as guaranteeing children more attention. The security of operating with smaller numbers can encourage experimentation. In this way schools are recognizing that TTT can help both staff and pupils become familiar and comfortable with what the Authority calls 'flexible teaching strategies'.

Advantages and Problems of TTT

TTT's advantages and problems have featured throughout this report: as with all worthwhile educational innovations, teachers are finding collaboration at the classroom level both productive and challenging. When asked specifically, they have stated that TTT is beneficial because:

It allows teachers to share ideas.
It enables them to implement more ambitious programmes of work.
It gives children more 'teacher time'.
It provides children with the opportunity to observe the cooperation of adults.
It enables children to interact with more than one teacher.

At the same time, however, they have indicated three major problems:

Differences of opinion about educational ideas and practice are highlighted.
Handling smaller groups of children is challenging.
Available resources and teaching space are inadequate for TTT.

Each of these comments raises important issues about the implementation and viability of TTT and therefore is worth examining in detail.

First, on the matter of teaching facilities, it is clear that the classrooms and teaching areas of some schools are far from ideal places in which to undertake ambitious TTT enterprises. Yet the ingenuity and resourcefulness of some collaborating teachers are very impressive. It is difficult to avoid the suspicion that in some other cases architectural constraints may be a justification for non-collaboration rather than the real cause.

On the matter of teachers exemplifying cooperation, our fieldwork confirms the view held by those teachers who are enthusiastic about TTT: there appears to be a specially purposeful and contented classroom atmosphere during some examples of teachers teaching together. Pupil discipline and time on task visibly improve. Teachers feel able to cope better with the inevitable classroom crises. They work with less stress. We observed that interaction between the teachers involved was intermittent in that it mainly took the form of occasional supportive comments on the work of each other's pupils. But in general the teachers convey a congenial respect for each other and in so doing it is likely they present a powerful and positive model for children to follow.

This brings us to the two final, and indeed central, issues of TTT which teachers have raised: that there are both benefits and difficulties accompanying the sharing of ideas and working with smaller numbers of children. TTT has clearly demonstrated that agreement among collaborating teachers about curriculum content and teaching methods cannot be assumed or taken for granted. To some extent the differences of opinion about educational ideas and practice, referred to by TTT participants, are inevitable: education is a value-laden enterprise and teaching is as much about implementing ideas and beliefs as it is about exercising class management skills. Yet ultimately the 'sharing of ideas' can only be meaningful and productive where there is an underlying consensus. In other words, TTT can operate, somehow, with limited resources and in cramped conditions, but without unity of purpose and consistency of practice between the participants its benefits are likely to be limited.

This has important implications for all staff in a school — senior management as well as the teachers who are teaching together: at classroom level TTT can be seen as a test of the wider professional climate of the school. There are inherent dilemmas here — consensus is necessary but differences in educional values are inevitable and to a certain extent healthy; teaching is a highly personalized activity so educational beliefs and practice are unlikely to be changed simply by orders from above. We hope to discover how school staff tackle these complex matters, which TTT both highlights and potentially resolves.

The other aspect of TTT where advantages and problems are interlinked is teacher-child interaction. TTT provides teachers with longer periods of uninterrupted time for interacting with smaller numbers of children. But it also requires them to exercise particular teaching skills which the solo teaching of a large class may not have allowed them to develop. Working with a group of children for extended periods is not simpler than managing a class: it is different but no less demanding.

Thus the teacher who commented that group teaching could 'get quite boring because once the children are working there isn't enough to do' seems somehow to have missed a fundamental point. Working with small groups requires and encourages a high level of refinement in teaching skills: there may be some teachers who need to develop a greater range of questioning styles, or sharpen their powers of diagnostic observation, or become more alive to the subtle social dynamics of children working together. Some teachers have found that taking smaller numbers of pupils challenges their own expertise in certain areas of the curriculum, since sustained questioning and discussion require the teacher to have a clear framework of the kinds of understanding she wishes to promote.

This brings us to the final point about TTT and teacher-child interaction: several teachers have expressed the view that children gain a great deal from working closely with more than just one teacher. Traditionally primary children establish a working relationship with only their class teacher during the course of a school year. (This fact may account for some support teachers initially encountering problems of status with their pupils.) While the solo class teacher arrangement undoubtedly provides emotional security for the young child, it must also be acknowledged that its exclusiveness may not always be entirely advantageous. TTT enables children to encounter and build firm relationships with a number of teachers in a variety of learning contexts. Each of these teachers will offer a unique combination of personal and professional experience that children can relate to and learn from. In this way, it is argued, TTT is of considerable benefit to primary children's personal and social development as well as their intellectual growth and academic progress.

Future Developments

At a national level what started with the 1978 primary survey's concern about lack of specialist curriculum expertise has now produced firm recommendations for primary schools to appoint curriculum leaders/consultants/co-ordinators. As well as curriculum planning, preparing guidelines and so on, part of the envisaged role of such staff is to 'undertake specific teaching' alongside class teachers. The outcome of this must be that primary teachers will increasingly be expected to work together and open up their professional practice and thinking as never before.

Most of the current emphasis nationally is on collaboration at the school level — in the staffroom rather than the classroom. Yet it is clear that classroom-based collaboration (which in the Leeds PNP context PRINDEP has termed TTT) is an essential and expanding part of any serious attempt to improve curriculum and teaching through collective action.

We shall need, therefore, to move beyond the easy rhetoric or 'working alongside' and 'working together' to the reality — the problems and potential — of collaboration at the classroom level. In particular, it seems important to ask (and encourage others involved at both LEA and school levels to ask) two basic questions:

What can two or more teachers achieve together with a group of children that one teacher alone cannot?

Precisely what difference does enhanced staffing make to the quality of teaching and learning in the classroom?

The present report is an opening-up of the idea of TTT and some of the issues that it raises. It is based on a relatively short period of preliminary fieldwork at the start of a four-year evaluation project. It is 'preliminary' in another sense too in that TTT, having been facilitated by the enhanced PNP staffing, is at a very early stage of development in most of the schools concerned. As collaborations mature, there will probably be a significant advancement in the teaching skills and curriculum expertise of the participants, as well as in children's curriculum experiences and learning outcomes.

This discussion is structured round four central aspects of TTT: participants, purposes, collaborative style and pupil organization. There are probably other, equally central, aspects which will emerge as we gather more extensive information, and it is possible that the framework for discussing TTT may look somewhat different in a year or so: that, in part, is the nature of a *formative* evaluation like PRINDEP's. Meanwhile, we intend to use the framework as we move to the next phase of this part of our programme.

The present framework also translates easily into four basic sets of questions which can be asked about either existing or proposed forms of TTT in a school (and to which some of the possible alternative answers are suggested in the appropriate sections of this report).

Participants. What does each of the collaborating participants bring to the TTT situation? How can they achieve shared understanding of the educational and practical issues involved? What is the status of each in the collaboration? What authority/backing does each have?

Purposes. What educational and/or professional goals do we hope to achieve through TTT? Curriculum enhancement? Special needs? Professional development? Other?

Collaborative Style. What is the role of each teacher in the collaboration — in action in the classroom and in planning and review? How useful is the withdrawal/working alongside distinction?

Pupil Organization. How are the children to be allocated to the collaborating teachers? Equal division? No division? Small group/individual and the rest of the class? Other? What teacher roles does such allocation dictate? What learning outcomes is this organization designed to achieve?

There is little doubt that TTT is one of the most innovative and potentially rewarding aspects of the Primary Needs Programme, and for this reason it will be a recurrent theme in PRINDEP's evaluation.

8
The Classroom: Messages, Decisions and Dilemmas

Introduction

However wide-ranging, complex and ambitious a programme of educational reform may be — and the Leeds initiative was certainly all of these — its ultimate test must always be the same: its impact on classrooms, teachers and, above all, children. It is easy enough and proper to voice such a sentiment, rather more difficult to devise the research procedures which will deliver the evidence required, even assuming we can agree on the criteria by which the impact of an initiative should be judged.

The study which follows is part of an attempt to explore the kinds of classroom practice associated with the Primary Needs Programme. Our aim was to look at practice in one classroom in each of sixty (about a quarter) of the primary schools in Leeds. The study was conceived as having three 'levels', each one more concentrated and detailed than the last. The first two of these are discussed in this chapter, while the third and most substantial is reserved for Volume 2. Level 1 (forty classrooms) was to involve a single classroom visit and interview; Level 2 (ten more classrooms) a visit, one lesson observation and two interviews; Level 3 (a further ten classrooms) an intensive programme of interviews and systematic observation of teachers and children at work over a two-week period. Further details about the methodology appear in Appendix B.

The teachers at Levels 1 and 2 were chosen because they had all attended one of the courses on classroom organization which formed the subject of Chapter 6 and were therefore all in possession of the ideas about practice which were central to the Primary Needs Programme. Those at Level 3 were chosen because their classroom and/or ways of working were very clearly affected by PNP support in one or more of its various forms: extra teachers, classroom refurbishment, additional equipment and so on. All sixty teachers, therefore, were not only teaching in PNP schools but had also been directly influenced in some way by PNP's messages or resources.

The study as a whole was underpinned by a number of principles, of which three need to be mentioned here.

1 *'Good practice' can be defined only if practice is properly understood.*

From the casual way the term 'good practice' is used one could be forgiven for assuming that everyone (a) knows and (b) agrees what it means. In fact, neither is the case. The use of the word 'good' indicates the true state of affairs, namely that 'good practice' is an expression of value, and that different people, therefore, have different views of what it looks like. Moreover, the evidence about the efficacy of particular classroom procedures is still fairly scanty. In this enquiry we were seeking not to impose our own or anybody else's version of 'good practice', but simply to study, describe and discuss 'practice' as a phenomenon. The question of what kinds of practice are effective, let alone whether they are good, can be addressed only once they have been made explicit in this or some other way.

2 *The influences on practice are many, various and sometimes hard to discern.*

Each teacher's practice is shaped by a unique combination of events and circumstances: the particular school and classroom, its children, staff and parents; the teacher's biography — childhood, education, training, professional experience; the teacher's personality, competence, values and so on. There is a comparable array of unique factors at play at the level of the school as a whole. This means that we have to be extremely cautious in the way we attribute cause and effect — asserting that teacher X works in a certain way because of head/adviser Y, for example, or that a school's practice has changed for the better (or worse) as a result of involvement in a programme like PNP.

3 *Teaching is thought as well as action.*

We repeat here a point made at greater length in Chapter 1. The practice of teaching involves the interplay of ideas, knowledge, skills and on-the-spot judgments, and the quality of children's learning depends on how the teacher thinks as well as on what he or she does. The point is obvious enough, banal even, and at a commonsense level few would dispute it. Yet neither professional discourse in primary education nor some classroom research always acknowledges it. On the one hand this produces the aggressive rhetoric of indifference or resistance to ideas which is a powerful part of the culture of teaching; on the other it produces a tendency for some classroom research to fall into the mutually exclusive camps of recording action while ignoring intentions and decisions, or of recording thoughts and opinions while ignoring events. For us, the interdependence of thought and action had one simple methodological consequence: all observation had to go hand-in-hand with interviews seeking the actors' intentions and meanings.

The last of these three principles leads us to one of the study's central themes, that of primary teaching as a job characterized by private doubts, dilemmas and compromises which contrast starkly with the doctrinal certainties delivered in public. The theme is developed more fully elsewhere, particularly in Alexander (1988, 1989), and relates closely to the perspectives of writers like Argyris and Schön (1974); Schön (1983, 1987), Berlak and Berlak (1981) and Nias (1989). It is an idea to which we shall need to return when we undertake our more general appraisal of the Primary Needs Programme as a whole in Volume 2 since it relates critically to the ability of teachers in classrooms to put into practice handed-down educational policies and philosophies.

The chapter is in three parts. Part 1 is a survey of the classrooms and accounts of practice of the thirty-eight teachers from the original forty at Level 1. Its material is predominantly factual, but it focuses increasingly on the problems teachers encountered in responding to the LEA's versions of 'good practice'. Part 2 is a set of case studies of five individual teachers from the ten observed and interviewed at Level 2, and here we look in greater detail at some of the central decisions they faced on a daily basis and how they responded to them. Part 3 explores some of the main issues raised by the Level 1 and 2 data, and identifies four ways in which the material might be used in the context of the formative evaluation of PNP. The last two of these centre on fairly fundamental questions about how teachers can be helped to improve their practice and how, indeed, practice should be defined.

The Level 3 material, which, as we have said, will form a major part of this book's companion volume, is considerably more concentrated and systematic than that from levels 1 and 2 and will enable us to develop and more thoroughly substantiate the view of primary classroom practice towards which the present chapter leads.

We turn now to Level 1 material — that derived from a visit and teacher interview in just under forty classrooms. The headings we use when presenting this material may look somewhat arbitrary: in fact, they reflect the emphases of the LEA's course on classroom organization which all these teachers attended and of which this part of our study constitutes the longer-term follow-up evaluation presaged in Chapter 6.

Part 1: Message and Response — The Level 1 Survey

The Teachers

As indicated in Appendix A, the proposed sample of forty teachers shrank by two to thirty-eight. In the main the teachers were very experienced: more than three-quarters of them had been teaching for over ten years, and more than half for over fifteen years. A third of them were working mainly or exclusively with 7–8-year-old children; the rest had pupils of various ages from 5 to 11. Thirty-six of the thirty-eight teachers had classrooms of their own. Two of them shared with other teachers on a long-term, full-time basis, and in all three-quarters had support teachers in their classrooms for part of the time.

The classrooms themselves held as few as seven and as many as fifty-two pupils, although only eight of them housed fewer than twenty, while eight others had more than thirty. Seven of the teachers (about a fifth of the sample) had the use of areas outside the classroom to augment their teaching space and to store bulky equipment.

Influences on Practice

The development and spread of new ideas through an LEA occur in many ways and take place over a number of years, quite independently of any courses which may subsequently be mounted to advance them. According to the teachers in this sample, the main influence on their practice came from their colleagues at school. Just over two-thirds of them said that this influence was substantial, and they singled out the head and the PNP coordinator for the most frequent mention. In only a few cases was the influence negative: one teacher claimed that her colleagues were powerful models of poor practice, making her determined to be as different from them as possible; and half a dozen others said that they had been discouraged by lack of support from their colleagues in implementing the kinds of change associated with PNP. Staff meetings were a common way in which colleagues exerted their influence, and were mentioned by two-fifths of the sample. All but one of these references were positive.

Only a third of the teachers in the sample said they were influenced by what they read, and of these only three spoke of specific books or research reports in the area of primary education. *Child Education* and *Junior Education* were mentioned, and one or two teachers said that they had been helped by *Bright Ideas*, course handouts, documents circulating in the school and so on.

A little under a third of the sample said that they had been influenced by courses other than the classroom organization course, about half of them mentioning attendances at outside institutions, sometimes for fairly straightforward and conventional INSET activities, and sometimes for lengthy and formal courses of study leading to higher degrees or diplomas. It is important to note here, however, that teachers' attendance at such courses is dependent not only on their wish to take part but also upon the opportunities they are offered to do so.

A quarter of the sample said that members of the advisory service had influenced their practice. One teacher said that a particular advisory teacher had had more influence on him than anything else, and another that an adviser's visit had started her thinking positively. A small minority — four other teachers — spoke in very negative terms of the same service, one claiming that she had been given wrong advice which had affected her career prospects, two saying that they had asked for help but received none, and the fourth expressing the view that visits from advisory staff were more of a threat than a help, and that in any case advisers gave conflicting opinions about the nature of good primary practice.

Perceived Influence of the Classroom Organization Course

Although the teachers' perceptions of the long-term influence of the classroom organization course varied a good deal, most of them fell into six main categories.

Type A: Eight teachers said that they had already been working along the lines advocated by the course, and their subsequent account of their practice suggested that this was indeed the case. For some of them the course had seemed somewhat redundant, while for others it had provided reassurance by confirming their existing practice.

Type B: Seven teachers were enthusiastic converts. They had made major changes to the layouts of their classrooms, and adopted the teaching strategies recommended on the course. In general these teachers praised the course highly, and several of them said that they had been inspired by it.

Type C: Five teachers were partial converts. They had been impressed with the course proposals, had made some changes and were contemplating others; but they were experiencing difficulties of organization and were feeling their way carefully.

Type D: Nine teachers had made token changes but made it clear that they were in fundamental disagreement with some of the main recommendations of the course. Seven of the nine felt strongly that each pupil should have his or her own place, with a chair; and of these, two had tried the more informal seating arrangements proposed on the course, but had quickly reverted to the old familiar system on the grounds that it made the children feel happier and more secure.

Type E: Three teachers said that they could not make the kinds of organizational change recommended on the course because of cramped and unsuitable conditions in their classrooms.

Type F: Six teachers had rejected the course entirely. They reported no changes of any kind: their classrooms, their daily practice and their basic beliefs and classroom organization were all exactly as before. One reported that the course had had a short-term effect on her in that it had worried her and made her reappraise her practice; however, she had decided that she was not going to change.

By their own accounts the course seems to have affected three groups of teachers: those of the Type A respondents who claimed that they were already working along the lines it advocated, and that the course was redundant; those making Type E responses, who protested that it did not apply to them; and those making Type F responses, who rejected its messages entirely. Although some members of these three groups said that they had enjoyed the course or had been reassured by it, it cannot be claimed that it had played a significant part for any of them in furthering the aspirations and objectives of PNP. This could be as much a reflection on the teachers concerned as on the course, since an interview response tells as much about the respondent as about the topic of the interview.

The relative sizes of the six groups are shown in Figure 8.1. Just under a quarter of the teachers made responses of Types E or F, all indicating that the course had been in some way unsuitable for their current needs. A slightly smaller proportion made Type A responses, indicating the course's confirmation of their practice. The rest can be divided into two groups. Those making Type D responses accounted for just under a quarter of the sample; they had embarked upon relatively superficial changes, and for them the success of the course remains a matter of doubt. Finally, there were those who made Type B or C responses, indicating major changes in their organization and practice as a direct result of their attendance at the course. Some of these teachers were experiencing difficulties and reservations, but all were con-

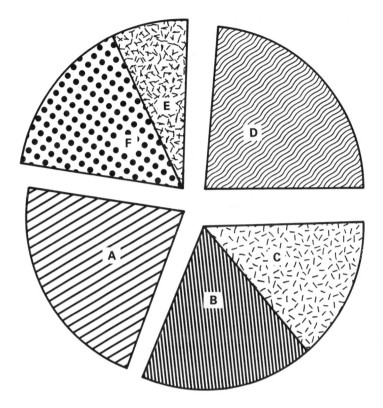

Figure 8.1. Teacher Response Types

vinced that the changes they were making were for the better. There can be little doubt that for this final group, constituting a little under a third of the sample, the course had been an outstanding success.

In general the teachers' accounts of their practice revealed that *flexible teaching strategies* within *a quality environment rich in stimulus and challenge* had found a place in the common parlance of primary education in Leeds, and that other more specific prescriptions had been adopted by at least some of the teachers in the sample, often working with unpromising accommodation and equipment. In all, just over half of the sample complained that they were hampered to some extent by the shape, size, age or location of their classrooms.

The Rooms

Architecturally the rooms in question showed a wide variety of styles, ranging from the solidly Victorian to the uncompromisingly modern. One was a school hall, and three others were huts or prefabricated structures. In about half of them the windows were too high for the children to be able to look out, and in five of them they were so small as to make the room seem dark. In general the rooms were in a reasonable state of repair, although one had crumbling plaster and another a leaking roof. In ten rooms there were partitions or alcoves, sometimes resulting in substantial areas which were out of the teacher's line of vision from the main part of the room. More than half were fitted with a sink of one kind or another, and three rooms had tiled wet areas.

A model classroom, furnished and laid out in accordance with the advisory service's specifications, was a central feature of the classroom organization course. It was therefore not surprising that the course had exerted its most immediately apparent influence on the rooms themselves, and only three of the teachers claimed to have made no changes to their rooms at all as a direct consequence of their attendance.

Display. The most visually striking features of the classrooms were the displays, many of which were clearly influenced by the advisory service's policy on this matter, with its discussion of features like draped fabric, double mounting and neutral colours. More than two-thirds of the rooms contained large and elaborate displays: every room had something on show on the walls, and just over half had additional material displayed on tables, shelves or other flat surfaces. Three-dimensional items had been incorporated into the displays in all but five of the rooms, and ten rooms had mobiles hanging from the ceilings.

In every room examples of children's work formed part of the display. About half of them included items which were there not because they were of a particularly high standard, but because whatever their quality they represented special effort on the part of the children who had produced them. More than four-fifths of the rooms had examples of the teacher's work as well, often of an informative nature, and sometimes as a model of excellence. In about a third of the rooms the displays incorporated commercially produced visual aids.

It is perhaps not surprising that art accounted for a high proportion of the work on display, but maths came a close second, with topic work not far behind it. In thirty-one of the rooms the displays bore some obvious and unambiguous relationship to the current work of the children, and in eight rooms they were related to other material on show elsewhere in the school.

About three-quarters of the displays looked fresh and new. In twenty-six of the rooms at least some of the displays were examples of work in progress, developing and changing with the passage of time. Techniques of presentation varied a good deal, from ambitious set pieces involving hessian, drapes and double mounting, to very basic and straightforward arrangements of sheets of paper on a pinboard.

Equipment. In twenty-seven of the classrooms items of work equipment were set out in plain view. Again they varied in both age and state of repair, and they were displayed in ways which ranged from the elaborately methodical to the apparently haphazard.

A quarter of the teachers had introduced equipment which had been recommended on the course, and a fifth had made their classroom equipment more easily and directly available to the children. To this end seven teachers had changed and expanded their system of labelling. In just over half of the rooms there were specific items of equipment which could not be seen by the observer although their presence was apparent from labels on boxes, doors and so on.

However, in view of the heavy emphasis placed by the advisory service on labelling as an aid to children's independence in the classroom, it was striking that in almost a third of the rooms there were no labels of any kind to indicate the nature or location of equipment.

Furniture. Like the classrooms themselves, the furniture ranged from the outdated to the very modern, and from the somewhat neglected to the carefully maintained. In all, a third of the teachers were experiencing problems with old, heavy, inadequate or immovable furniture; for example, one room was dominated by an enormous old science bench complete with gas taps. However, there were other rooms which had been entirely refitted with brand new furniture of the type recommended by the Authority's advisory team and used in the model classroom. Three-quarters of the rooms were at least partially carpeted, though this was not infrequently with carpets brought in by the teachers themselves.

Classroom Layout

Fifteen teachers (two-fifths of the sample) said that they had rearranged their furniture as a direct result of suggestions made on the course. Even here there were occasional problems. One teacher claimed that she could not make the changes she wanted because the caretaker liked all the furniture to be against the wall. Whether this was a convenient excuse, or an example of the kind of seemingly trivial difficulty that in the real world can completely sabotage genuine human effort, is hard to determine.

A few of the suggestions made on the course about the deployment of furniture had been fairly generally rejected. In three of the classrooms the teacher had dispensed with the convention that each pupil should have his or her own place, and had moved over to the much more fluid arrangement where there might be fewer chairs than children, and where children simply used the most appropriate place for the immediate task in hand.

The possibility of dispensing with the teacher's desk provoked a mixed reaction, although a substantial minority of teachers were giving it a try: a fifth of the sample had no desk or table at all, and another fifth were using their desks for display or other purposes not traditionally associated with this item of furniture.

In other ways, however, many of the layouts echoed that of the model classroom, notably in the disposition of the furniture into work bays. These bays were generally, though not invariably, dedicated to specific areas of the curriculum; in some classrooms their function was nothing more than to break up the available space and provide cosy corners in which groups could work without too much distraction.

Four Layout Types. Only three of the classrooms had no work bays at all. For the purposes of the analyses which follow, these have been termed Type 1 classrooms, and a specimen plan (along with examples of three other classroom types) will be found in Figures 8.2, 8.3, 8.4 and 8.5.

Exactly half of the classrooms observed in the Level 1 survey had only one work bay each, and in every case this was a class library or reading corner. These eighteen classrooms have been allocated to Type 2. Type 3 classrooms, of which there were fourteen, each had several work bays, although there was in every case a substantial part of the room not laid out in this way. A single classroom, the sole representative here of Type 4, was very much like the Authority's model classroom. It had been entirely set out in work bays for various aspects of the curriculum, and contained seven of them.

Key to Figures 8.2–8.4:

A	—	Armchair	Ms —	Movable screen
AVA	—	Audiovisual Aids	Msh —	Maths shelves
BC	—	Bookcase	MTU —	Maths tray unit
BSU	—	Built-in shelf unit	P —	Plant stand
C	—	Cupboard	S —	Sink
Cu	—	Cushion	Sh —	Shelves
DTB	—	Daily task board	Tb —	Tub-like container on castors
DU	—	Display unit	TD —	Teacher's desk
LC	—	Low cupboard	Tr —	Trays
MET	—	Maths equipment table	Tu —	Tray units
			⌐¬ —	Built-in tray units

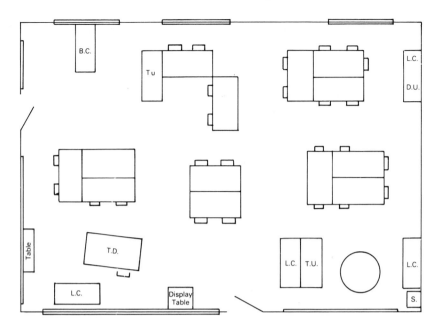

Figure 8.2. Type 1 Classroom Layout

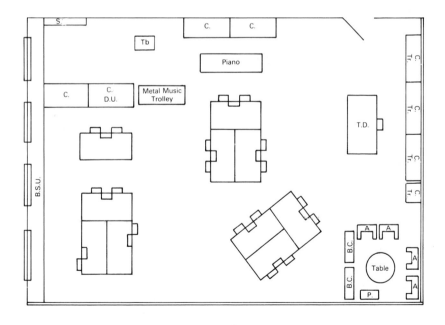

Figure 8.3. Type 2 Classroom Layout

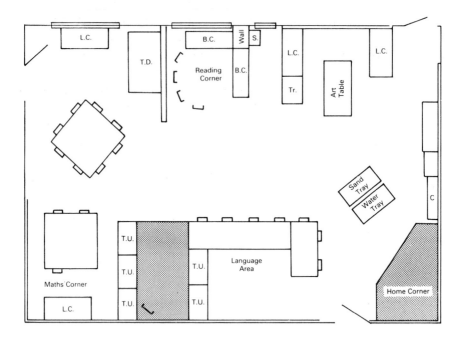

Figure 8.4. Type 3 Classroom Layout

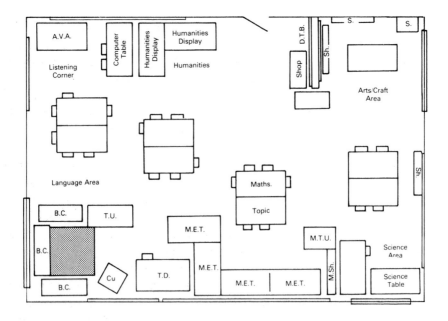

Figure 8.5. Type 4 Classroom Layout

Not surprisingly, the teachers who claimed to have accepted what they saw as the main messages of the course tended to have classrooms more like the model classroom than teachers who said they had not been able to implement its messages, either because of their own convictions or because of such external problems as unsuitable furniture. The extent of the relationship between the teacher's reactions to the course (response Types A to F, discussed earlier) and the layout of their classrooms (layout Types 1 to 4) is shown in Table 8.1. It should be noted that the two support teachers in the sample have been omitted from this table since they were not responsible for the layout of the classrooms in which they worked.

Table 8.1. *Classroom Layout and Teachers' Perceptions of the Influence of the Classroom Organization Course*

| | Teacher Response Type | | | | | |
	A	B	C	D	E	F
Classroom Type 1	—	—	—	1	1	1
Classroom Type 2	—	2	3	7	1	5
Classroom Type 3	7	4	1	1	1	—
Classroom Type 4	—	—	1	—	—	—

The relationship between the reported impact of the course and the physical appearance of the classroom is unambiguous and statistically significant. The importance of this finding lies in its confirmation that in general those teachers who said they had been influenced by the ideas developed in the course did have classrooms which showed the impact of those ideas; while those teachers whose classrooms were closest to the PNP ideal generally acknowledged the influence of the course on their thinking and practice.

There were, however, a few anomalies. Two teachers who made Type B (or enthusiastic converts) responses to the course had Type 2 classrooms in which the only concession to the recommended style of layout was a reading corner. Elsewhere, one Type D (or fundamental disagreement) and one Type E (or unsuitable conditions) response came from teachers in Type 3 classrooms which had several work bays and a number of other features that were reminiscent of the model classroom. Although infrequent, these anomalous responses illustrate the sizeable and significant gaps which can exist between expressed beliefs and observable behaviour, and confirm the advantage, in an enquiry such as this, of a combination of interview and observation over either on its own.

Classroom Layout and the Curriculum

Since attending the course, ten teachers had allocated or reallocated parts of the classroom to specific curriculum areas, even though the chairs and tables usually had to double as pupils' regular places. These curriculum-specific work areas were often, though by no means always, housed in work bays formed by the physical arrangement of cupboards, bookcases and other items of furniture; and the extent to which the classrooms had curriculum-specific work areas (either in or out of work bays) is shown in Table 8.2.

Table 8.2. Curriculum-specific Work Areas in Thirty-six Classrooms

Areas per room (f)	Number of rooms (x)	Number of areas (fx)
0	3	—
1	9	9
2	5	10
3	6	18
4	8	32
5	2	10
6	2	12
7	1	7
Total	36	98

It is clear from this table that in spite of the suggestions made on the course, backed by the example of the model classroom, a third of the teachers (3 + 9 = 12 out of 36) had either rejected the idea of curriculum-specific work areas or had restricted themselves to one such area in the classroom (in every case a reading corner or class library). At the other extreme a few teachers had organized their classrooms entirely into these areas, forming as many as six or seven of them. Across the sample as a whole the average number of areas per classroom was 2.7, and this remained fairly stable over the different age ranges, showing only a slight and statistically insignificant increase in the classrooms of older children.

A common arrangement involved four curriculum-specific work areas, and in seven of the eight classrooms where this arrangement occurred the four areas were devoted to reading, art, maths and language. The comparative frequency with which the various areas of the curriculum were allocated space of their own is indicated in Figure 8.6, and major discrepancies are immediately apparent.

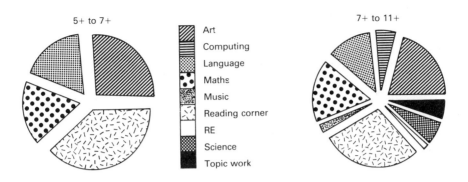

Figure 8.6. Curriculum-specific Work Areas

First, the pattern of allocation was markedly different between younger and older pupils. In the classrooms of children of up to 7+ there was not a single example of a curriculum-specific work area devoted to anything other than reading, art, maths or language. In contrast, a fifth of those provided for older children were devoted to a range of other curriculum areas: computing, science, topic work, music and RE.

The reasons for this difference are clear enough when one considers the scope and character of the curriculum as conventionally devised for older and younger primary children. Similarly, the pre-eminence of reading corners at all ages is hardly surprising, given the priority it has always had in primary education: in these particular classrooms it was allocated more space than anything else, accounting for no less than one-third of all curriculum-specific work areas.

However, the allocation of space to other aspects of the curriculum is less straightforward, and a comparison of art and science is particularly instructive. In the present enquiry art came second in prominence only to reading, with more space devoted to it than to maths or language, accounting for just over a quarter of all curriculum-specific work areas for younger pupils, and a fifth of those for older pupils. In contrast, and in spite of the examples set in the Authority's model classroom, only four of the ninety-eight curriculum-specific work areas in these classrooms were devoted to science.

There are two main reasons why an aspect of the curriculum acquires space in this way. One is its perceived importance, and the other is the kind of activity it entails. In the case of art the latter reason seems paramount; art can be messy, requiring running water as well as a wide range of special materials and equipment, and the strategy of segregating both the activity and the children doing it seems sensible. However, science too involves practical activity which makes use of apparatus and equipment, even if not on the scale of art and craft, and for this reason one might expect it to feature more prominently in the physical layout of classrooms, particularly given both the recommendations of the Authority and its high profile in national policy.

We suggest that this anomaly captures primary classrooms and the primary curriculum in a state of transition. Though never a 'basic', art has always enjoyed high standing in primary education. In contrast, although science is now a National Curriculum core subject, it is a relative newcomer, and the messages about its primacy in the curriculum are taking some time to become reflected in classroom practice. A similar time lag was noted in the analysis of schools' curriculum development priorities and strategies in Chapter 4, with science lagging well behind mathematics and language in terms of posts of responsibility, review, development and expenditure. All this is now changing rapidly as a result of the 1988 legislation. Nevertheless, if the physical arrangement of a classroom is indeed — as the Authority has argued — a reflection and embodiment of educational principles and priorities, then it would seem sensible for schools and the LEA to keep this matter under review, monitoring the relationship of policy, layout and practice, and helping teachers to keep the three in step.

Grouping and Group Work

Teachers asserted that the course's major influence on their daily practice was the encouragement of group work, although individual teachers also mentioned a move towards an integrated day, the introduction of whole-class activities, and an experiment in cooperative teaching. Group work was now playing a greater part than previously in the classes of a third of the teachers interviewed; and four other teachers, who had not increased the amount of group work in their classes, had none the less revised their grouping systems.

In a little over two-thirds of the classes groups were formed on the basis of the teachers' perceptions of their pupils' ability. Most frequently the aim was to make the groups as homogeneous as possible, and groups formed in this way generally remained relatively stable, moving as a whole from one activity to another. In a very small minority of classes, however, ability groups of this type were formed only for specific activities (generally maths) and disbanded for the rest of the day. An alternative way of grouping by ability was to ensure that there was a relatively wide range of ability in each group. A third of the teachers in the sample made use of this kind of mixed-ability grouping, and again there were a few examples of the formation of such groups for specific activities only.

Six teachers reported that they switched from one of these two grouping strategies to the other as the activities of individuals and groups of pupils changed. Such a policy would clearly have presented an organizational problem to any teachers who were dedicated to the orthodoxy that at any one time each group should be working in a different curriculum area; but by no means all the teachers in the sample subscribed to this view. In addition to these grouping strategies, an eighth of the teachers opted for friendship groups for at least a part of the time, and one teacher grouped her pupils by age.

It should not be supposed that the pupils of these thirty-eight teachers spent the whole of their time working in groups. One teacher had no groups at all but organized her pupils so that they always worked either on their own or as part of a class lesson. For the rest, nearly two-thirds favoured the balance of individual, group and whole-class teaching recommended by the Authority.

The changing activities of the day and the fluctuating numbers of teachers in many of the classrooms meant that the formation of appropriate working groups could be a complex problem, and teachers tackled it in a wide range of different ways. For example, one teacher of a class of 5–6-year-olds reported that her pupils were organized in groups based mainly on friendship, but that a small number of less able children were grouped together for language work. The grouping was flexible, but she usually had two groups doing practical or written work in maths, two groups doing writing or another language task, and two groups doing activities such as Lego or jigsaws. Group work usually took place during the mornings, and art and craft, PE, reading, stories and library work took place in the afternoons. The class came together for stories, RE, PE, singing, work with flashcards and a daily conversation session.

Another teacher, whose pupils were a year older, tackled things very differently. In the mornings all her pupils did maths at the same time, and then moved on to English. She organized the children into ability groups for maths, but because they had different objectives she expected them to work individually within their groups. English usually involved using a story card to write a story, and when the children had finished their stories, they were expected to read. She liked to ensure that every child did some reading each day. Children who did not finish their maths and English tasks in the mornings continued with them during the afternoons, which were officially given over to art, craft and other activities. Topic work was done as a class activity. She said it consisted of looking, talking, drawing and writing.

A third teacher, whose pupils were 7 and 8 years old, rejected the idea of group teaching altogether: 'I don't see the point of wasting time saying the same thing to five or six different groups when I can say it once to one large group . . . .' She asserted that keeping her pupils together as a whole class maximized her time for teaching as opposed to merely monitoring what the children were doing, and she was confident that her pupils learned more when she taught them all the same thing at the same time. She said that she had found the classroom organization course very short of hard evidence that children were learning better under the prescribed methods.

These three examples cannot be fully representative of the others in the sample, and their strategies are outlined here chiefly to give an illustration of the complexity of the task of grouping children for a day's work, and of the very different ways in which the task was tackled.

We might describe the first of these three teachers as 'convinced'. She was attempting to change the essence as well as the trappings of her classroom practice, but she was facing a number of difficulties as she became fully aware of the repercussions of the changes she was implementing. She had opted for friendship groups but found it necessary to preselect a small number of children for a low ability group, even though this inevitably meant that they had to be deprived of the freedom to choose their own companions. She also ran maths and language groups alongside groups working with Lego and jigsaws, thus ensuring that not all the children were engaged in activities which required much of her attention or intervention. This proved to be a common strategy: it is one which has been observed in other studies, and is a topic to which we shall return in more detail later.

The second teacher can perhaps best be described as 'ostensibly convinced'. She had changed the appearance of her classroom to make it blend in with what she perceived to be the new orthodoxy, yet she had made no alterations at all to her long-established ways of working. She used groups simply as a form of seating arrangement, firmly rejecting any suggestion that different groups might be engaged in different tasks, or that the children within each group should work cooperatively. Her pupils were all engaged on the same curriculum area at the same time, often sitting in groups, and sometimes sitting in ability groups, but always working either individually or as part of a class lesson.

It is clear that the third teacher was 'totally unconvinced'. She attended the course, heard its message, and then persisted with a familiar way of working that suited her purposes, justifying her stance on the grounds of the success she was enjoying with her pupils, and asking for a lot more in the way of hard evidence if she was to be expected to make major changes.

Even so, most of the teachers had made some changes, and this being so, it is scarcely surprising that four-fifths of the teachers also reported changes in the children themselves. Almost a third said that their pupils were becoming more independent, and several remarked on the increased quantity and better quality of their work, on the smaller delays between different activities, on the new, quieter atmosphere in the class and on improved social integration. On the other hand, one teacher somewhat ruefully remarked that the course's chief influence on her pupils was that their reading had suffered.

Planning

The teachers' planning varied in three basic ways: in its time scale, in its degree of formality, and in its structure. The time scale ranged from the very short-term to the comparatively long-term: from daily to yearly, with many intermediate steps. The degree of formality ranged from elaborate and schematic written documents to a simple mental rehearsal of what would happen next. The structure also showed considerable variation. Some teachers' planning involved a *comprehensive* awareness of the balance of different lessons and their place in the curriculum as a whole, as well as a very clear concern with progression, continuity, the acquisition of underlying skills and the achievement of goals. Other teachers adopted a more *incremental* approach, planning as they went along. They were much less concerned with the details or wider curricular context of future activities, and much more interested in trying out ideas in practice before moving on to further planning.

To a very large extent these three basic variables appeared to operate independently of each other; thus it was possible to be a comprehensive yearly or termly planner, drawing up elaborate written schedules, but to plan informally and incrementally on a day-to-day basis; or to plan comprehensively for the day-to-day details but within a fairly vague framework which might or might not be written down.

There were very few teachers in the sample who did not make some written plans in advance. Twelve of the thirty-eight had a powerful incentive to do so, since their headteachers looked at their plans of work regularly, at least once a term; five teachers submitted their work plans to their headteachers every week. One teacher reported that each day she planned her number, reading and written work for the following day. The head usually took the less able children and planned his own activities. In maths and reading this teacher followed published schemes, so that to a large extent the work was already planned for her in those areas. At the end of the week she entered an account of the children's work in a record book. Her headteacher liked his staff to plan as far ahead as possible for topic work. She had had to tell him what her topic for the summer term would be before the previous Christmas, and she had planned this topic in the form of a flow chart. There was also a whole-school topic which was planned at staff meetings. Other teachers prepared written plans of work even though nobody demanded it of them, and several prepared long-, medium- and short-term plans, often in parallel. In all, half of the sample made detailed and comprehensive written plans for each week, and a fifth made daily plans; fifteen teachers planned by the term, and twelve by the half-term.

As described by the teachers, some of the planning was very elaborate. One described how he wrote a fortnightly forecast of his programme of work, and then made a daily plan for each group. He wrote the daily work plans on the blackboard, and also read them out to ensure that even the poor readers would be fully aware of their programmes. All written work was collected at the end of each session so that he could monitor what the children had done. A profile of each child was kept, together with a record of his or her progress in maths and reading. At the end of each fortnight he commented upon his last fortnightly forecast in the class record book. He planned a subject-based programme half-termly, and at the time of the interview he was trying to organize more time for discussion with the support teacher about this pro-gramme. All his records were given to the headteacher half-termly, and returned with the head's comments.

Discussion and collaboration with colleagues played an important part in the planning of fifteen of the teachers. For example, one teacher had an outside commitment which took her away from the school for one and a half days a week, when her place was taken by a colleague. On one afternoon each week she swapped classes with another colleague so that she could take his class swimming. In addition, the PNP appointee worked with her class for two half-days each week. For this teacher, as for many others, effective planning could not be done in isolation. The long-term planning for her class took place at half-termly year group meetings attended by the PNP appointee (who also discussed the work programme with the class teacher on an informal basis whenever the need arose). The support teacher met the class teacher once a month to discuss the topic work: the support teacher had responsibility for the art and craft side of this work, while the class teacher dealt with the language and maths involved. Notes were left on the teacher's desk to pass any urgent messages between them. The children were told at the beginning of each session what they were to do, and on Friday afternoons the class teacher ensured that they had completed the week's work.

In contrast, a few teachers did the whole of their planning in a very informal and entirely incremental way. One said that she knew the children so well that she was aware of their needs and could plan as she went along. Another gave an account which blurred the distinction between planning and record keeping, saying that in maths and reading she kept formal check-lists to give an indication of what the children could do, but that for all other planning she tended to play it by ear, basing her judgments on the children's successes and failures in their topic work.

This partial amalgamation of planning and record keeping was by no means infrequent. Many of the teachers in the sample used checklists of tasks already accomplished as the starting point of their plans for the following day or days; and from there it was perhaps a natural short cut for some of them to begin to see the record of what had already happened as the plan for what would happen next. Conversely, one teacher claimed that her fort-nightly forecasts for the headteacher acted as 'a kind of record' of work done, and although this may have been the case if she was very good at forecasting, it was clearly not necessarily so.

Record Keeping

Only the teacher who had reported that she could plan as she went along claimed that she kept no records of any kind. The records kept by all the rest varied from the elaborately formal and comprehensive, involving a good deal of work, to the admittedly casual and labour-saving. Some were limited to checklists of work completed, while others were equally concerned with the acquisition and improvement of underlying skills.

There was one teacher who kept what she called 'mental notes' throughout the day as she worked with the children in their groups. At the end of the day she sorted through the trays of finished work, and then updated a set of tables which showed the specific work activities completed by each child in each of the main curriculum areas. The published maths and language schemes which she used provided ready-made records, although she felt that in maths particularly these needed augmenting with other things outside the scheme. She thought that the school as a whole should move towards a system of records based on objectives and skills. She kept a reading record for each child, with details of the books they had read, and a commentary. She was not altogether happy with her system as it stood, and was considering ways to improve it.

Another teacher, while acknowledging the importance of records, had found an easier and far less rigorous solution. She said that by organizing the class so that everyone was working on the same subject at the same time she could keep track of what the children had done without spending a lot of time on written records. She thought her pupils (at 7+) were too young to make a record of their own work, so she kept a notebook and once a fortnight she wrote down what the children had been doing and anything else of note. She said that she found it easy to talk about the children because she knew them so well, but that she found it hard to write down what she knew.

Level 1: Summary

The Level 1 enquiry gave a clear picture of a complex situation. There was no doubt that the LEA's principal PNP messages had been heard and considered by a high proportion of the teachers interviewed. The classroom organization course had played its part in this process, but it was naturally only one of many sources of information about PNP. There was also a great deal of both formal and informal consultation among colleagues during which key PNP ideas were handed on, discussed at length and sometimes modified before finding their way into everyday practice; and many of these colleagues had heard their version of the PNP message from other sources entirely. Wherever it came from, and however they understood it, most of the teachers found the PNP philosophy congenial, although many had reservations, and a few found it lacking in persuasiveness or substance.

In their own classrooms the teachers were in settings which were sometimes very unlike the model classroom of the course. They were also experiencing varying degrees of freedom to accept or reject the LEA's messages, and varying amounts of support. Any help was almost universally experienced as coming not from the LEA but from within the school itself. However, problems and difficulties, although occasionally stemming from the hostility or scepticism of colleagues, were far more often seen as a matter of inadequate accommodation, furniture or resources.

For the most part the Authority's PNP documents cover a wide range of material, dealing with both broad, abstract ideas and specific practical matters. The classroom organization course also followed this pattern, ranging in its subject matter from fundamental organizational strategies to tiny details of equipment and display. The clear advantage of this breadth of content is that it maximizes the likelihood that every reader or listener, irrespective of initial attitude or previous experience, will find something relevant to his or her own situation and needs. However, this advantage was purchased at a cost, in that it left the maximum leeway for individual teachers to claim, quite truthfully, that they had implemented a good many of the Authority's suggestions, even though their basic beliefs and practice had sometimes remained relatively untouched. Similarly, there were teachers who said that they had already been doing most of the things discussed on the course, but who went on to describe their practice in a way which revealed similarities of peripheral detail yet profound differences between their own organizational preferences and those espoused by the LEA. In general, however, there was a clear tendency for the warmest agreement with the messages of the course to be expressed by those teachers whose classrooms were set out along the lines it had recommended.

The course's emphasis on grouping was almost unanimously accepted by the teachers interviewed as the obviously right way to organize children's learning experiences, although about two-thirds of them favoured a balance between individual, group and whole-class teaching (a view which is endorsed by the Authority itself).

However, the arrangement of the classroom into bays dedicated to specific curriculum areas presented a number of challenges. Although most of the teachers found it an attractive idea, some of them found it hard to reconcile with their belief that every child should have a place of his own. Others perceived the idea of curriculum-specific seating as meaning that different curricular activities should be going on simultaneously, and this interpretation complicated things further for those teachers who strongly felt that they could keep a firmer grip on their classroom organization if everyone in the class pursued the same curriculum area at the same time.

Consequently, a common pattern was for teachers to adopt some of the suggestions from the classroom organization course while rejecting others. Sometimes this selection was productive. At other times there could be a certain amount of muddle as they tried to balance the conflicting demands of many different activities going on simultaneously, of a wide variety of grouping strategies, and of curriculum-specific work areas together with pupils' 'own places'.

Some teachers were endeavouring to ease the situation by ensuring that at least some of their groups were engaged in activities which rendered them unlikely to need much help or attention; but since help was perceived to be required only when difficulties arose, such a solution could lead to the use of somewhat undemanding tasks.

The confusion of partial change also had repercussions in the areas of planning and record keeping, areas where only a third of the teachers were working under any kind of supervision, although a somewhat higher proportion were collaborating with colleagues. There were teachers in the sample who were grappling with several complex long-term and short-term schedules and forecasts at a time, and others whose only apparent work plan was to set up a succession of ad hoc activities with little long-term coherence or progression. At the same time there were teachers who were keeping no methodical record of what had been going on in their classrooms, as well as others who were devoting quite extraordinary amounts of time and effort to the problem.

The overall picture was of a very mixed group of teachers, stimulated by new ideas and making a genuine effort to bring about quite complex changes in their classroom practice, but often thwarted by mundane practical difficulties, and sometimes floundering as they encountered conflicting demands and pressures. The Level 1 study also confirms much of our earlier discussion of the character and fate of LEA messages about educational practice: the problems of ambiguity and misunderstanding, for example; and the tendency for any idea delivered by an authoritative source to be treated as a requirement, even when its status is clearly no more than an option or suggestion. For many recipients of such messages, therefore, the force of an idea resides less in its substance than in the status of its purveyor.

Part 2: Decisions and Compromises — Cases from Level 2

Helping teachers to change their practice is a complex and delicate process. Since the inception of PNP, the LEA has shown a long-term commitment to improving its teachers' classroom delivery of the broadly-based curriculum, emphasizing teaching style as well as curriculum substance. The PNP messages about flexible teaching strategies have been reinforced by an INSET programme which has annually featured courses on the organization of children's learning in the classroom. In addition, the work of the primary advisory team in schools has encouraged teachers to evaluate their own classroom practice. Finally, the creation of the innovative role of PNP coordinator has provided each PNP school with a relatively senior teacher whose job description and INSET training carry a strong implication that they exemplify good practice. Together, these various strategies for bringing about change might be expected to form an irresistible combination of imperative, suggestion and example.

However, LEA strategies have to operate in the context of individual schools, where the leadership style and the overall professional climate exert their own pressures on teachers to keep pace with — or to ignore — the LEA's current thinking on curriculum delivery and classroom management (see Chapter 4 for the range of heads' attitudes to PNP messages and Chapter 5 for the factors influencing the impact of the coordinator on teaching approaches). Beyond the school context, as Chapter 6 indicated, it is ultimately classroom practitioners themselves who have to decide whether to accept and how to operationalize recommended teaching approaches.

Level 2 of the present enquiry involved a study of each of the ten teachers who had attended the classroom organization course and were also working in the PRINDEP representative sample (Fieldwork B) schools. Five of these case studies have been selected for discussion here. The teachers at Level 2 were asked to talk about their preferred classroom procedures and the reasons behind them. In discussing organizational issues such as grouping, curriculum content and planning, they revealed the very wide variation that exists in teachers' views about what is important in children's learning and what is achievable in the classroom. The observations of their classroom practice showed how such personalized curriculum priorities were usually delivered in the style that seemed most acceptable and comfortable to the individual teacher. The studies also illustrate the teachers' varying degrees of readiness to implement the LEA messages about good practice. Some were faced with an enormous challenge in being asked to change what had always seemed appropriate classroom management, a challenge that could seem invigorating or overwhelming. Others believed they had had their current practice reassuringly reinforced.

Above all, the case studies indicate a fundamental problem for every primary practitioner. Teaching in a primary classroom is essentially a series of compromises. The teacher alone is responsible for delivering the whole curriculum to perhaps thirty children, and usually has to do so in the context of less than perfect classroom resources and facilities. This necessitates selective decision-making in several major and closely connected areas:

> what the children will learn that day;
> which children's learning will receive the teacher's attention at any one time;
> how the working environment can best facilitate that learning.

In the case studies which follow, each teacher is, in effect, talking about her solutions to these problems.

The studies are concerned with three major aspects of practice. First, under the heading of 'Classroom Organization' there is an outline of the kinds of decision which the teacher generally made before (and sometimes after) working with her pupils: issues like classroom layout, organization of children and curriculum, record keeping and planning. The teacher's views on how — or if — these decisions had been influenced by the classroom organization course are also recorded. Second, under the heading of 'Management of Learning' the teacher in action in the classroom is described, and a brief outline of a single observed lesson is given. Here the main focus is upon the kinds of teaching interactions which resulted from her earlier organizational decisions, and also upon the nature of the activities provided for the children. In a third section, entitled 'The Wider Context', school influences upon the teacher's practice are considered, and reference is made to the PNP coordinator's role as well as the perspective of the head-teacher. A discussion of the teacher's particular and unique set of compromises concludes each study.

It is important to stress that the following portraits of practice cannot validly be used as the basis of general statements about teachers as a whole. They do no more than illustrate something of the variety of teaching behaviours and teacher viewpoints in the Authority's primary schools. Equally, the studies should not be seen as definitive portraits of the five teachers involved: their attitudes, intentions and actual classroom practice were considered in a series of two interviews and one observed lesson in the spring term of 1988, and it would devalue the complexity of primary teaching to claim that this had comprehensively captured their repertoire of teaching approaches or was the sum of their professional thinking. Nevertheless, common issues do emerge and these are presented as general points, or propositions, in the summary which follows the case studies.

Case Study 1

Mrs A was a 48-year-old redeployed middle-school teacher, with twenty-four years' teaching experience. She had a class of eighteen 8–9-year-olds in a Phase 1 school.

Classroom Organization

In terms of the classroom layout types proposed earlier, Mrs A's classroom was of Type 4. There were clearly defined areas for language, reading, maths, practical maths, topic work, science and art and craft. The old-fashioned desks had lift-up lids, but they had been pushed together to make groups of tables, and covered with thick pieces of cardboard to create reasonable writing surfaces. To provide maximum mobility for her groups, Mrs A did not allow the children to use the desks for storage: books, pencils and equipment were located elsewhere in the room, and all clearly labelled.

Mrs A explained that her groups had formerly been determined by the children's mathematical ability, but that since attending the classroom organization course she had reorganized her class into four mixed-ability topic-based groups. She described her way of working as a roundabout system: she wrote on the board the order in which each group should undertake art, language, topic work and maths, and divided the working day into four sessions to accommodate this range of activities. She said that the system was the result of much experimentation, and that she now made sure that all the children had work they could go on to if they finished one task before the designated time to change activities.

She completed the school's maths and language records, which were entirely based on the Peak and Ginn schemes, but was also experimenting with her own topic-based checklists. Here she was attempting to keep a record of the new skills and understanding which children were acquiring instead of simply noting their completion of prescribed activities, but she was finding this a very complex task. While aware of the view that language and maths should as far as possible be treated in a cross-curricular context, she acknowledged that much of the children's work in these two areas was dictated by the school's maths and language schemes. Nevertheless, she stressed that her preparations for topic work always included activities designed to incorporate some language and maths. These preparations were under way many weeks before the children were introduced to the topic.

Her response to the classroom organization course was of Type B: she had found it 'absolutely splendid', and had afterwards totally reorganized her classroom layout during the summer vacation. As well as altering her system of grouping children, she had changed from single-area to mixed-curriculum teaching. She acknowledged that there had been difficulties of adjustment, including 'traffic jams' when children from different groups had needed attention simultaneously, but she felt that she was overcoming them and that the children were now able to work more cooperatively and independently. She herself was enjoying greater contact with pupils, in groups and individually, and she felt she was working in a 'more intense way'. She had got into the habit of questioning her practice at all times.

Management of Learning

When Mrs A was observed at work in her classroom, she had organized four activities for the children: maths worksheets and Peak workbooks, worksheets for topic work and language and a cooperative topic-based craft activity. In one hour of observed teaching she spent twenty-six minutes working with children doing maths, fifteen with each of those doing topic work and language and four minutes with the children doing craft. The great majority of these interactions were with individuals and at least half of all work-related interactions were initiated by pupils. Mrs A acknowledged that she worked mostly in this responsive way: the class size assisted this teaching style, and she did not think that the high number of problem children in the class would be able to cope with the situation if she gave her attention exclusively to single groups for extended periods. However, she was convinced of the appropriateness of mixed-curriculum teaching: 'It's much better . . . . The children are more motivated and I think teacher time is better used.'

The Wider Context

Mrs A was described by her head as willing to try new ideas, hard-working and open minded, and she had made considerable adjustments to her practice after encountering LEA messages on classroom organization. However, it is possible to identify other school factors which also contributed to her teaching approach.

She herself mentioned the externally appointed coordinator, who had operated in a support teaching role and whose expertise she had willingly accepted: 'The PNP coordinator has worked with me in the past, and through that and talking with her, I have been greatly influenced in my approach and teaching style.' She also said that her head had given her support, and for his part the head said that his policy was to praise rather than pressurize his staff to make changes.

With regard to the influence of other staff, Mrs A expressed some sense of isolation in the school because of the location of her classroom in the building, and the reservations of a neighbouring colleague about undertaking collaborative teaching with their two classes. Nevertheless, she indicated that colleagues were beginning to discuss classroom organization, and referred to a staff visit to the model classroom. She also felt that the size of her class was ideal for experimentation, and that as this was her second year as their teacher, she was in a doubly advantageous position to undertake major organizational changes.

However, the head also admitted that implementing LEA messages on classroom organization and teaching style was left in the hands of the individual teacher, and this meant that Mrs A had to devise her own methods for organizing her class and training the children to work in a new way. In addition, the head's curriculum management strategy did not include a major commitment to delegated curriculum leadership so that Mrs A received very little support in this area, and had to sort out for herself the complexities of a curriculum delivered through the medium of topic work.

Her isolation was intensified by the PNP coordinator's involvement in an unsuccessful collaboration elsewhere in the school. It would seem that in general the coordinator's support role was never entirely successful in influencing the practice of colleagues (with the exception of Mrs A and one or two others) and she subsequently undertook a new role as a full-time class teacher. In this way Mrs A effectively lost a potentially valuable consultant on classroom practice.

Against this background it is not difficult to understand Mrs A's decisions about what her pupils should learn, which children would get the bulk of her attention, and how the classroom itself could best facilitate the children's learning. Although the classroom gave clear evidence of a 'broad' curriculum, with science, CDT and practical maths as curriculum-specific work areas, the structure and guidance to Mrs A's work came mainly in the 'basics' of maths and language, and by and large from publishers' schemes in these areas. Even so, she demonstrated her commitment to an integrated curriculum: teacher-devised topic-based activities were a prominent feature on the day of observation. She was one of the few teachers in the sample who said she read educational books, as opposed to magazines: she mentioned the work of Joan Tough and several authors on the subject of reading extension. These had exerted a noticeable influence on her questioning technique and the worksheets she prepared. The classroom itself illustrated her resourcefulness in creating a working environment which complemented her commitment to curriculum breadth and grouping.

It would seem that the extra teacher time which Mrs A believed mixed-curriculum teaching had created was spent almost exclusively on children engaged in maths and language activities, with maths receiving substantially more of her attention than any other curriculum area. She had chosen mixed-ability grouping and she had a favourable teacher-pupil ratio; this combination of factors undoubtedly contributed to the success of the individual and responsive work interactions that characterized her teaching approach on the day she was observed, as well as encouraging and enabling her to provide intellectually challenging activities for all her pupils. She said she would have to change her approach the following year when she would have a larger class, and referred to the necessity of providing 'occupying' work for children: the implication being that groups of children could not as easily be stretched and challenged if a teacher was any less accessible than she was at that time.

Case Study 2

Mrs B was a 40-year-old primary-trained teacher who had taught children with special educational needs in a previous post. She had a class of thirty-one 7–9-year-olds in a Phase 1 school.

Classroom Organization

Mrs B's classroom was a portacabin in the school playgound, with a Type 2 layout. It had a carpeted reading or quiet area, a space at the front of the room for watching TV, and resource areas for maths and art. There was no sink. The desks had lift-up lids, and had been pushed together to make five tables. The arrangement of the room had been worked out with the PNP coordinator after Mrs B had attended the classroom organization course.

Mrs B explained that the children were grouped by reading ability and remained permanently at their places because of lack of space. She said they all worked at maths, language and 'activities' every day. She now insisted that they did not interrupt her when she was teaching a group, and they had the materials for plenty of extra activities stored in their desks for use when they finished or were stuck. Each day she planned to work with the groups that had the most difficult task or needed most oral work.

She planned topics half-termly, and often linked them to TV programmes. There was no completed maths or language scheme in the school, although schemes were being systematically developed at staff meetings. At present she was following what she described as a basic number progression for basic maths. When asked about record keeping, she said that she recorded the names of the books children had read from the reading scheme, and the results of spelling tests; and that these records helped her plan her language work. She also recorded the activities undertaken by each child in her half-termly topic plan.

Her response to the classroom organization course was of Type B: she said it had given her the confidence to make changes in the way she taught. She no longer devoted the afternoons to activities but now devoted the whole day to mixed-curriculum teaching. She was now less anxious about the need for children to record their maths work in books, and was subsequently undertaking more investigative work in maths. She was enthusiastic about the results:

> This way of working has enabled the poorer ones to have a bit more confidence, because I'm not always at their beck and call . . . . The brighter ones can do problem-solving . . . they know they're not going to get told off if they talk.
>
> It's a much more enjoyable way to teach, especially when there are

two [teachers] in the room. It's how we should teach; it's how we should spend our day . . . and it just looks so nice when you go to schools and see children doing different things in bays.

Management of Learning

In the observed lesson Mrs B carefully presented each group's introduction to its work while the rest of the children read their reading books. First she set up some shape games and an activity involving the colouring of number bond patterns for a group who would work later in the session with a support teacher. Then she explained a task of matching words and pictures to a language group. Next she undertook some group teaching on the concept of maps (a theme that had arisen from a TV programme). Finally, she worked with an activities group, encouraging discussion of what the children had made in relation to some work on colour and light. In all she spent twenty-eight minutes of the one-hour lesson with this group (in two blocks of eight and twenty minutes). She spent fifteen minutes with the maps group, and ten minutes with the language group, hearing some children read and checking the results of their matching task.

In this way Mrs B created time for extended and uninterrupted interactions with one group at a time. Only about 5 per cent of her interactions were with pupils not in her current group, and they were invariably work interactions initiated by individual pupils themselves.

The Wider Context

There had been a marked change in Mrs B's practice since she had attended the classroom organization course. However, it is important to note that the school itself was experiencing a veritable *perestroika* in relation to primary practice at that time. Under its previous head it had been formal and insular, as evidenced by the initial marginalization of the PNP coordinator, by streamed classes and even by the fact that the children's desks were in rows. Since the arrival of a new head shortly after Mrs B attended the classroom organization course, several significant changes had taken place. The PNP coordinator had been appointed acting deputy-head, thus acquiring additional status, and now had a support role that allowed for involvement in the whole curriculum rather than an exclusive concern with special educational needs. The whole culture and discourse of the staffroom had been transformed.

Mrs B singled out the new headteacher, and the staff discussion she had generated, as the major influence on her practice; and for her part the head made it clear that she was working quite deliberately and systematically to exert precisely this kind of influence:

> I try to get people to think what their philosophy of education is. I'm trying to focus the staff's attention on the needs of children and how they learn . . . . I've said, 'If you believe children learn when they are motivated and involved, you have to decide what's the best way to organize the physical environment to get them to learn'.

> I use certain words when discussing curriculum. I've [talked about] 'themes' and . . . about 'integrating the curriculum'. I do *not* [talk about] 'the integrated day . . . '.

> I've discussed with staff the differences between teaching a class, a group, [and] an individual. I've talked about the greater response from a group, and [pointed out] that it's possibly harder because you do more teaching. I've probably advocated group teaching in these discussions: I've said [that] in group teaching you're able to monitor the effect you're having, and you are able to alter the strategy in response to this . . . .

> I've given everyone a piece of carpet [and] this has influenced classroom organization. I've used vocabulary such as 'work bays' and 'reading corners' [and] I refer to 'your art cupboard'. In other words I drop hints like bricks about what I expect teachers to have in their classrooms . . . .

The school's adviser had also been asked by the head to lead a staff meeting on classroom organization. Thus from a formal INSET course, from the staffroom, and in classroom collaboration too a consistent set of messages about practice was being delivered to this teacher. In relation to decisions about what children should learn and which children's learning would get her attention, her organization now demonstrated a commitment to mixed-curriculum teaching and to teacher investment in areas of the curriculum other than the 'basics', as the very lengthy interaction with her activity group demonstrated. She spoke positively about the value of investigative maths, problem-solving and group discussion, and in doing so she gave clear evidence of the impact of the staff's curriculum development work on her maths teaching and classroom organization.

The observed lesson demonstrated a further commitment to creating time for extended interactions with her groups, and this was no doubt facilitated by the presence of another teacher in the room. However, this teaching strategy was achieved only at a price. The children in her maps group were, in effect, left to decorate their worksheets with felt-tipped pens for almost half the lesson, and Mrs B herself expressed some regret at not being able to hear the language group read. Clearly, desk-bound children and cramped working conditions presented some limitations to the possibilities for independent working. Perhaps the permanent space for TV viewing, which appeared to feature strongly in Mrs B's curriculum planning, also contributed to the children's lack of mobility.

Despite all the positive support and reinforcement she was now receiving, Mrs B herself expressed a slight reservation about her new approach in the classroom: 'I've got so far, and it's difficult to go on. I'm still formally structured, and it's difficult to know how to progress . . . .' In this way Mrs B indicated how the goal of informality is more than a matter of rearranged furniture, regrouped children or a retimetabled curriculum. In her newly reorganized classroom a teacher faces further major tasks. She must acquire the necessary curricular expertise to set work appropriate to the children's apparent ability, especially if some of her groups are to be left unattended for long periods of time. She must also develop the skills necessary for small group teaching, and learn how to pace her own input.

Mrs B's observed lesson showed how successfully she had adopted a style of organization that gave her 'time for actual teaching at group level'. However, it was also clear from her group interactions and the tasks she set that an equal emphasis on curriculum and pedagogy should accompany discussion of classroom management. Mrs B stated that she did not read educational books: the only reading that had an influence on her practice was INSET handouts.

Case Study 3

Mrs C was a 36-year-old teacher with a total of seven years' teaching experience. She had a class of twenty-seven 5–6-year-olds in a Phase 1 school.

Classroom Organization

Mrs C's classroom had a Type 2 layout, with labelled storage spaces for maths equipment, textbooks, a library and other reading materials. There was an annexe at the back of the room which was used for painting and also served as a cloakroom. It was at the opposite end of the room from the child-level sink.

Mrs C explained that she did single area teaching at all times. The children were grouped by ability for maths and language. These two areas of the curriculum were undertaken every morning, and an NTA sometimes took a group for art at that time. Children who finished their prescribed activity before the end of the session were expected to read. In the afternoon, the children were allowed to sit in friendship groups while they worked as a class for topic work. The maths activities were usually taken from the Scottish Maths Scheme, and in language the children generally worked through various comprehension books, phonic workbooks and teacher-made workcards.

Mrs C explained that she kept all records in her head; she was aware of the children's ability and therefore knew what work to provide next. She said that she kept some very basic plans in her record book, but that planning ahead was difficult because she didn't know how quickly the children would get on.

When she was asked about the impact of the classroom organization course, she said that she had already been doing what the LEA advocated. However, her subsequent account of her practice made it clear that this was not really the case. She said that she had returned from the course feeling uplifted and enthusiastic, and had made workbays in her classroom. Soon after this, she had put her cupboards back against the wall because she didn't work an integrated day, and in any case the new arrangement had taken up too much space in a classroom that was already too small. However, the course had made her realize that it was better to keep the equipment and resources for each subject area together. All in all, this response to the course might reasonably be allocated to Type D.

Management of Learning

In the observed lesson the class was grouped by ability and each of the four groups was involved in a language activity. The top group worked through a textbook comprehension exercise, a second group used headphones to listen to a story, and Mrs C spent the majority of her own time teaching phonics to the third group, using an exercise from another workbook. The bottom group worked with the PNP coordinator / SEN support teacher on workcards, and Mrs C had no contact of any kind with this group or its teacher.

Some class discussion of phonics had preceded the deployment of children into groups, and, in all, the group activities lasted for three-quarters of an hour. During that time Mrs C left her phonics group to monitor the two other groups for just under ten minutes. There were only five occasions when children approached her about their work. The children worked quietly, although they became distinctly but discreetly restless by the end of the session.

The Wider Context

Mrs C's commitment to single area teaching, and her apparent adherence to teaching the 'basics' primarily through textbook exercises mark a considerable divergence from the LEA's messages about good practice. Given that her school had already had three years within the PNP programme, it is important to identify possible reasons for this incongruence.

In this context it must be significant that, according to Mrs C, there was no discussion about teaching style or classroom organization in her school. She said that at staff meetings everyone was too busy. She believed that her colleagues all taught differently, but that there was little chance of their influencing each other because of the isolated nature of their work. In addition, the PNP coordinator, who had been internally appointed, had a self-chosen and very substantial role in the area of special educational needs, and was hence unlikely to exert much influence upon her colleagues' practice. Indeed, she herself referred to her colleagues as a stable and experienced staff, not in need of much advice, but also added: 'I feel we are all in a comfortable rut . . . . We don't really want to make too much effort or change anything, [and] this is why it's so difficult to get anything off the ground . . . .' Similarly, the school's head said that she believed in adopting a very low profile when it came to influencing or dictating practice:

> I have no influence on the grouping of children, or on teaching style. I do not interfere. I don't try to interfere in my teachers' planning style either. If it is working and I can see the results, I think it is best to leave my staff to it and let them have the freedom to work as they see fit. Classroom layout is also up to them . . . [although] I sometimes suggest they change the pictures if they are getting tatty . . . .

Thus two possible sources of direction or guidance in the adaptation of classroom practice were not available to Mrs C.

As it was, Mrs C expressed clear reasons for the tightly controlled and structured organization which characterized her decisions about how and what her pupils should learn. First, she described the children in the part of the city in which she was teaching as difficult and different, and said that all her colleagues shared this view. She thought that such children needed stability, and that the way she structured their work session by session provided this. Second, she expressed the opinion that single area teaching also provided security because if more than one activity was occurring in the classroom, the children would become confused. She also liked to know what everyone was doing. Third, she thought it best that children of this age should do maths and language in the morning while they were still fresh.

In this way Mrs C justified her own curricular and classroom management priorities as coinciding with the needs of her pupils. Her commitment to control and structure, and the very high priority she gave to the 'basics' in her timetabling and classroom layout, seem markedly different from the LEA's messages on breadth, integration and flexibility. Yet she was relieved of the need to confront the disparity by finding elements in the Authority's version of good practice that appeared to reinforce and reflect her own, for example grouping and the organization of resources. Another factor was identified by the head:

> The course Mrs C attended was useful . . . in that it provided new ideas, and emphasized group work and discussion in the classroom. I can't say what she got out of it; each person takes out what is useful to them. Mrs C's classroom is certainly better organized, [and] her teaching seems a bit livelier. She had a bad class last year, and was jaded and lacking in confidence . . . .

If Mrs C had been experiencing problems of classroom control in the recent past, her position in relation to the LEA's messages on good practice becomes much easier to understand. Her initial willingness to implement some of the ideas she encountered, as evidenced by her reorganization of the classroom, needed careful nurturing and guidance, but there was no one in her professional sphere to offer this. She also commented that she could not recall reading anything which had influenced her practice. It is not surprising that she reverted to her original views on classroom and curriculum management: with little sense of either imperative or reward, changing her practice must have seemed simply too daunting, difficult or dangerous.

Case Study 4

Mrs D was a 35-year-old teacher with six years' primary teaching experience. She had a vertically grouped class of twenty-six 5–7-year-olds in a Phase 2 infant school.

Classroom organization

Mrs D's classroom had a Type 3 layout, with areas set aside for language and activities, a maths area which included a post-office shop, a reading corner and a home corner. A further two tables were described as being for overflow work from other areas, and tabletop work. Play activity materials, such as sand and wood, were located outside the classroom.

Mrs D's pupils were allocated by age to three groups: reception, middle infants and top infants. They were then often subdivided by ability for maths and language work. In each of three daily working sessions the groups worked at maths, language or activities. The order in which each group undertook its work in the three areas rarely varied; for example, the middle infants always started with activities and moved on to maths, while the top infants undertook activities in the afternoons. On each day a different aspect of language and maths was covered: number on Mondays, time on Tuesdays, money on Wednesdays and so on. Free writing, comprehension, phonics and handwriting were regular weekly components of the children's language work.

Mrs D said that she tried to work with one group at a time, but that children from other groups inevitably approached her, and the reception group needed her attention at least at the beginning of every activity she set them.

She kept detailed maths and language records for every child.

For topic work there was a whole-school theme: members of staff pooled their ideas, and then each teacher prepared her own termly flowchart. Mrs D also explained that when curriculum areas were reviewed, the staff discussed appropriate classroom organization and teaching strategies.

Mrs D felt she was already doing much of what the LEA suggested with regard to classroom organization. However, her response had elements of both Types A and B, in that the course had reinforced her particular teaching strategies of grouping and mixed curriculum teaching, while it had also inspired her to reorganize her room to create curriculum-specific bays.

Management of Learning

In the observed lesson Mrs D began with a comparatively lengthy whole-class discussion, undertaking incidental teaching about the maths involved in registration and dinner numbers, and the phonics and spelling of various objects the children had brought in for the phonics table. She also encouraged responses to the style and substance of stories written by some of the children the previous day. The immediate work programme for each group was then explained to all the children. Mrs D spent nearly all of the remainder of the session — some thirty-five minutes — sitting with her reception group where the children were all doing the same exercise from their maths workbooks to consolidate practical work undertaken previously. Her teaching role was, therefore, essentially *responsive*: she monitored these children's work by allowing them to show her their workbooks after each question, and constantly repeated the vocabulary of length as she did so. During this time she also took part in more than thirty pupil-initiated inter-actions with children from the top infant group who were story writing and who wanted to know how to spell particular words. An observational drawing exercise was the task for the middle infant group, followed by free choice play when they had finished. They were informed of this orally after they showed their completed pictures. In all Mrs D spent no more than five minutes with these children once their work was under way.

The Wider Context

The PNP programme had provided the school with extra staffing, and this made it possible for the deputy-head to take on the role of support teacher and PNP coordinator. She commented that working alongside colleagues enabled her to give practical help and advice, as well as making them more accountable: 'They have to plan and prepare more thoroughly when they know a senior member of staff is coming in . . . .' In this coordinator Mrs D had an outstanding practitioner working alongside her for a day and a half every week, teaching language to both the reception and top infant groups, and maths to a group of less able older children. Thus classroom support came from a high status but very familiar colleague. However, Mrs D did not mention this collaboration as a particular influence on her practice.

She said she did not generally have time for educational reading, but sometimes got the odd idea from *Child Education*.

The school itself was considered a model of good practice within the Authority, and had a consistent policy of grouping and cross-curricular approaches, reinforced by the headteacher's emphasis on whole-staff discussion:

> There is a common thread running through the school on organization and learning. All the teachers have an integrated day and work in groups; . . . if they did not I would tell them [to do so]. For our whole-school cross curriculum theme, all staff discuss and decide together. We all put in suggestions, but each teacher plans

her own class's work. I see plans and record books and I'm in and out of classrooms, [but] I don't give specific instructions as long as the organization and learning are flexible and reflect the needs of the children.

My staff are professionals. They think about their jobs, [and] it would be wrong of me to be dogmatic and tell them how to do things.... I see myself as the team leader, not a head. I encourage and praise and say things like 'I liked...' and 'I'd like to see more of...'.

Perhaps Mrs D usefully illustrates that, however supportive the professional climate of a school may be, innovations are most likely to occur after an authoritative external stimulus. Even so, Mrs D, rather like Mrs B, did not concern herself with the curricular and pedagogical issues implicit in some of the LEA's suggestions on classroom management. For example, although she had begun to encourage her pupils to select their own paper and materials for art activities, it was obviously difficult to find teaching time to discuss the options and outcomes of such aesthetic decision-making with them. It became increasingly obvious during the classroom observations as a whole that art was sometimes used as an organizational device to allow the teacher to devote her time to other activities elsewhere in the classroom — generally the 'basics' of the primary curriculum. Mrs D's practice was an example of this.

The observed lesson also showed the enormous pressure that teachers of young children face. Mrs D's management of learning necessitated two kinds of compromise, one child-related and the other a curriculum issue. She felt that vertical grouping was a definite advantage in her attempts to create extended periods of time to work systematically with a group. At the same time she acknowledged that when she was working alone, any such time tended to be given to the children in her reception group, unless they were involved in activities. In other words, the older children were likely to receive less of her attention while they were working, and this perhaps explains the compensatory attention given by the support teacher. With regard to the curriculum Mrs D's thorough and carefully structured weekly learning programme involved three subject areas: maths, language and art and craft. This meant that '... subjects such as science are fitted in; they can be part of the writing side of language or be linked to practical maths'. It is plain that within this kind of organization, important and topical curriculum issues such as children's scientific understanding, or the kinds of learning mediated by play and activities may have to occur without close monitoring by the teacher, or may not even be considered at all.

Case Study 5

Mrs E was a 37-year-old teacher with seven years' teaching experience, some of it gained in secondary schools. She had a class of twenty-four 10–11-year-olds in a Phase 2 school.

Classroom Organization

The class was housed in a very large old hall, in which Mrs E had created a Type 3 layout with what she called bays. One of these was fitted with a carpet and was intended for quiet reading, while equipment for maths and art was displayed in another. Mrs E explained that these bays were not used as working areas because of the large size of the room; there had been proper work bays in her previous classroom, but she had been moved from that room because it was unstructurally unsafe.

The children were organized by mathematical ability, based on the stage they had reached in their maths scheme. Mrs E said that in previous years the children appeared to have worked through the maths scheme workbooks individually, but that this year she had tried to create teachable groups. These groupings were flexible and therefore did not have names. She also had language ability groupings based on the stages children had reached in the two published language schemes she used. She explained that the rest of her language work was 'integrated into the curriculum', and that for this the groups were generally of mixed ability, as they were for topic work. She said that she liked to make topic work include language and practical maths, and that she tried 'to make it as cross-curricular as possible ... [and to] make it reflect the school's aims of first-hand experience'. She thought mixed-curriculum teaching was less demanding than single-area teaching, and she usually had maths, language and 'activities' under way simultaneously.

Every morning she discussed the day's work programme with her class, and the five tasks involved were also listed on a board so that the children could read them. Her rule was that the two or three high priority tasks at the top of the list must be done first, and that the rest could then be selected in any order. She acknowledged that meticulous planning was needed to succeed in this kind of organization, but also stated that the children were not bored; they were well behaved because they were in control of their own learning, and there were no queues. She spoke of other staff in the school, who commented on the good behaviour of the class, but she added, 'They don't seem to connect classroom organization with the way children behave in it'.

In maths and language the published schemes themselves formed the basis of her records of children's work, while for topic work she maintained a checklist of activities completed. She said the whole staff was unhappy about the current school records.

Mrs E believed that the classroom organization course had confirmed all that she was doing, although she singled out only one of its effects for special mention: 'Perhaps after the course I have felt more justified in having non-intensive activities like painting and drawing . . . .' With regard to the overall message of the course, her classic Type A response was that ' . . . whatever the circumstances and age of children, it's possible to make it work if you want to'.

This teacher was one of the very few in the sample who mentioned advisers and advisory teachers as a supportive influence on her practice. She added that her classroom was shown to advisory staff when they visited the school.

Management of Learning

Mrs E said that her intention was to be free-ranging during the session in which she was observed at work in the classroom, since she had spent her time with two maths groups during the previous session before play. However, she also said that she had organized things so she could concentrate on maths. Some of the children were finishing off a particular section in the published maths scheme, and were then moving on to other activities, including topic-related painting and clay work.

During the hour-long session Mrs E moved around the room quite rapidly from one table to another, and children approached her continuously. Usually from one to three children were beside her waiting for attention. In all she devoted half of the hour to individual children working at their maths. Much of this time was spent monitoring or marking, although it still involved some discussion of the task. Just over three-quarters of the maths interactions were initiated by pupils, and there was a very small number of extended interactions when particular children had problems. She gave her attention to the group undertaking art activities for nineteen minutes, and again most interactions occurred when pupils approached her. She did address this group about the procedures for mixing paint and the appropriate use of brushes, but made no teaching points to other groups.

The children collected equipment and stored completed work without reference to the teacher.

The Wider Context

When asked about the main influences on her practice, Mrs E mentioned two colleagues: a teacher who 'structured the day round a child's interest' and the PNP probationer with whom she had had many useful conversations. She did not specifically mention the PNP coordinator, who was working full-time as a class teacher and year group leader in another part of the school, after a period of support teaching which it was generally agreed had not worked successfully. Since then, the year group of two large classes had been made into three smaller ones, and the coordinator was teaching one of them. Mrs E and the coordinator were both described by the head as setting standards and giving a good example to the rest of the staff, even though Mrs E's classroom was on a separate site from most of the school.

Mrs E was generally unenthusiastic about school support in relation to either curriculum or record keeping, and felt that some of her colleagues were tokenistic in their attitudes to change: 'At staff meetings, they say what it's expected to [say] . . . and then go off and do their own thing . . . .' In effect, Mrs E felt obliged to bypass her school's professional culture, and seek out official LEA messages as the major guidance and reaffirmation for her practice, although she did also mention reading a number of books on topic-based approaches to learning.

In the observed lesson she successfully translated her intention into practice. She monitored the children (or as she — and the course — expressed it, 'free-ranged') in a classroom atmosphere of contented and quiet industriousness. As the teacher in the sample of fifty who was perhaps most attentive to the LEA's messages on good practice, she offered a clear rationale for her practice, using the language of PNP and the progressive educational tradition. Yet it was hard to avoid the conclusion that her assertions, when put against observed practice, could not always properly explain and capture the way she worked.

The successful management of this session seemed to depend on a number of factors. First, she felt comfortable with the idea of art as a low teacher investment activity. Second, in spite of what she said about the absence of queues, she effectively encouraged them by relying on children to approach her so that she could identify their learning difficulties. Third, although she explained that 'teaching at group level means I can work through new things with children at their own level, and then leave them to work on their own reinforcement . . . ', her concentration on children doing maths in the session indicates that her extended periods of teaching did not and could not replace the minute-by-minute diagnostic attention that her pupils, like all primary children, often required. Finally, Mrs E's session (and her grouping) was a clear example of the overriding importance which is often attached to children's mathematical understanding, even when the teacher has a genuine commitment to a broadly-based curriculum.

To pinpoint these discrepancies is not to undermine the commitment and talent of Mrs E herself. It rather implies that the official descriptions and messages of good practice were not always subtle or precise enough to help her represent — to others and even to herself — what was actually happening in her classroom.

Level 2: Interim Issues

The Level 2 enquiry was concerned with the ideas and practice of ten teachers from the sample schools who had encountered some of the Authority's central ideas about classroom practice in the context of PNP. Five of these teachers provided case study material for this report. Some of the initial insights generated by this part of our fieldwork have already been presented at the end of each study. Others are briefly mentioned here.

Changing a Teacher's Practice

In each of the ten schools the interviews and observation dealt in some detail with the ways in which the teachers were influenced to develop or modify their teaching. All the heads in the sample expressed their unwillingness to intervene too forcefully in their teachers' practice. At the same time most of the coordinators felt themselves incapable of affecting colleagues' teaching in the long term, while many of the teachers themselves asserted that no adviser had made any direct impact on the way they worked.

Since this latter valuation appears to contradict that offered by some teachers in the Level 1 sample, however, we must add that there are different kinds and context of adviser influence. Thus a significant proportion of the Level 1 teachers were clearly influenced by the advisory service's ideas as presented in documents and on courses, while the Level 2 teachers appeared to distinguish between such collective influence and that of individuals coming into their classrooms.

This combination of responses in respect of the three main groups with formal responsibility for teacher development in the context of PNP seems to imply a no-go area surrounding classroom practice, and one, moreover, which is tacitly accepted as such by all concerned. It raises the vital but troublesome question: how *are* teachers effectively helped to accept and implement change in pedagogy?

The general strategy seemed to be one of concentrating not so much on the *substance* as the *context* of teaching. Thus even the most interventive of heads in the sample attempted to bring about a desired pattern of teaching interactions in classrooms by making demands, not about the interactions themselves, but about classroom layout and appearance; in this she echoed an underlying assumption of the classroom organization course that changes in the physical character of the room would of themselves generate changes in organization, and hence in interaction and eventually the quality of pupil learning.

In general, therefore, the main basis for assessing teachers' practice appeared to be visual clues. These can undoubtedly tell knowledgeable and experienced observers a great deal, yet successful teaching depends on communications between teacher and pupil at which visual evidence can sometimes barely hint. For example, although it is clear that having groups of children simultaneously undertaking different activities discourages one form of communication — that of whole-class teaching — it does not of itself ensure the quality of the desired alternative — that of interaction with groups and individuals. Nor does the visual evidence of variegated group activities, attractive though they may seem, say much about the quality and effectiveness of the communications in which the success of such arrangements are claimed to reside. Nor, of course, are there firm grounds for supposing that a shift to such an arrangement will of itself transform the teacher's curriculum expertise and pedagogical skills, let alone his or her educational beliefs.

Planning

Of all curriculum areas mathematics was the one where teachers in the sample found the clearest structure and sense of progression. In this they were obviously aided by school guidelines and commercial schemes, which shape this area of the curriculum more thoroughly than any other. Such material not only provided much of the content for children's learning but also tended to determine teachers' views of their pupils' levels of progress and dominated the way they allocated the time and attention in the classroom. That being so, the quality of the guidelines and schemes used becomes a significant factor in the quality of practice overall, for such material can constrain or distort as well as structure and liberate.

In contrast, teachers did not always find it easy to describe their own curriculum planning. Written plans were frequently produced for the head and for themselves as a sort of visual map or prompt; but translating intentions into a readily communicated set of principles and procedures was less familiar, and this may account for some of the problems experienced by teachers teaching together (see Chapter 7).

Managing Learning

Grouping children was an organizational device as much as a teaching approach, a way of maximizing the opportunities for productive teacher–child interactions as well as a means of encouraging flexibility in curriculum and cooperation among the children. It raises important questions, therefore, about two kinds of activities: those allocated to children with whom the teacher expects to spend time, and those given to the others. The latter tends to be a neglected issue: if a child is to receive little teacher attention while on task, what kinds of work can he be asked and expected to do?

We have noted how frequently art and craft activities were defined and employed as needing little investment of teacher time and attention, once they had been planned and set up, thus inviting the question of whether they require less teacher–child interaction by their nature, or whether they were being made to serve as a device to free teachers to concentrate their attention elsewhere. Art and craft was not the only aspect of the curriculum to feature in this context, and the whole issue of children not under direct or constant teacher supervision generated major differences of opinion among the respondents.

Those teachers who favoured single curriculum area teaching (and there were several others besides Mrs C, the one in the case studies) consistently voiced the opinion that their pupils would be at grave risk of underachieving if the activities in the classroom were so varied that the teacher could not monitor them all effectively. In contrast, those teachers who advocated mixed curriculum teaching saw it as a device for securing greater manoeuvrability and flexibility. They tended to respond to the risk that some children might be underachieving in curriculum activities in which little teacher attention was investigated by arguing that working for relatively long periods unsupervised enabled other educational and social goals to be achieved — independence, cooperation, free expression and so on.

The multiple dilemma which this analysis exposes can be expressed as follows: the more accessible teachers seek to make themselves to all their pupils as individuals, the less time they have for direct, extended and challenging interaction with any of them; but the more time they give to such extended interaction with *some* children, the less demanding on them as teachers must be the activities they give to the rest; and the less demanding of their time and attention as teachers, the more the likelihood that the activity in question will demand very little of the child.

Teachers responded to this dilemma in different ways, but almost invariably they resolved it by making the curriculum the safety valve for releasing the pressure the dilemma placed on them: first establishing which curriculum areas mattered most and according them protected status, and then constructing low-demand/low-investment activities in the curriculum areas they deemed less important. Or, as one teacher honestly and succinctly put it: 'If a child leaves my class and can't paint, that's a pity; if he leaves and can't read, that's a problem.'

This dilemma is compounded by another, equally pressing. The teacher has to decide which children need close attention and which can be left to get on by themselves. In the face of the manifest requirement that she concentrate a great deal of time and thought on certain children in her class, the teacher has to be able to assume that others are able to make do with less. The most able, the oldest, the best behaved, girls — they may all, at different times, be seen as the 'undemanding ones' who can be left to their own devices, and the fact that they do just that, without drawing attention to themselves, is taken as evidence that this is both a reasonable expectation and a sensible strategy. However, the price that some of these children may pay for demanding little of the teacher may be that they are given work which demands little of them.

In the end, classroom practice, or educational beliefs in action, should perhaps be judged not only by the actions of the teacher herself and the children with whom she is working, but also by what she believes it is appropriate to give the rest of the class to do.

Part 3: Changing Classroom Practice — Issues for Schools and the LEA

Four Ways of Using the Material in Parts 1 and 2

So far we have discussed material from the first two of the three levels of the PRINDEP study of practice in fifty-eight PNP classrooms. The data presented and discussed in the present report come from interviews and observations of teachers in nearly forty schools. The common thread is the access which all of them had to PNP ideas about classroom practice as presented on one of the Authority's courses. There are four distinct ways in which all this material can be used by schools and the LEA, and these are considered below.

Looking at Variations in Classroom Organization and Practice

First, the material can be read as a record of some of the many variations in PNP classroom practice and can thus serve as discussion material on courses and in staffrooms. For example, a comparison of the typical classroom layouts will prompt questions about their purposes, advantages and disadvantages. Or colleagues can use the general findings about furniture, display, equipment, labelling and so on to focus their own thinking about these and other aspects of the physical organization of classrooms which make for both smooth running and an attractive learning environment. Or the various approaches to planning — written/unwritten, comprehensive/incremental, yearly/termly/weekly/daily — can each be explored and compared in order to address basic questions about the most appropriate and useful ways to plan for teaching and learning. Or the material can be used to address the matter of grouping: the familiar alternatives of ability, mixed-ability and friendship grouping, and the associated questions concerning the proper nature of activities undertaken in groups and of the balance of whole-class, group and individual teaching. And so on: each aspect of practice discussed here can be opened up in this way.

Following Up the Classroom Organization Course

Second, because all the teachers concerned were in various ways influenced by a particular course conveying the central PNP messages about classroom practice, Parts 1 and 2 can be read as the follow-up evaluation of that course. Again, the task is a relatively straightforward one. For example, colleagues can consider the implications of the six very different kinds of teacher response to the ideas presented on the course, from enthusiastic acceptance to outright rejection, with varying degrees of partial, reluctant or tokenistic adoption in between. They can explore the divergences between the classroom layout commended by the Authority and the arrangements actually encountered and exemplified in Part 1. They can look again at the issue of planning and its relationship to record keeping, noting and questioning the tendency for the latter to focus more on activities completed than learning achieved. They can consider the question, increasingly prominent in other research as well as here, of the efficacy of curriculum-specific bays, areas or

groups. Are they really the best arrangement? How far may the drawbacks —
for both children and teachers — outweigh the gains? These are just a few
examples of the many offered in the report which can and should provoke
discussion in both schools and the LEA.

Exploring Alternative Strategies for Improving Classroom Practice

Digging deeper, however, we come to the third and fourth uses of this
material. The third is to treat it as a springboard for considering not so much
the one course — which was, after all, only one of many and has in any case
been overtaken by events — as the *style* of teacher development which it
illustrates. This was why in Chapter 6 we examined it in such detail, and the
last part of that report raised important issues in this regard. For such an
exercise, the starting points might be the discrepancies between what some
teachers said they were doing and what they were actually doing; and the
way the course's ideals seemed to allow such discrepancies, focusing as they
did on material minutiae as much as on deeper principles, so that the former
could be implemented while the latter remained untouched, even though
the teacher could truthfully claim that the course had had a powerful
impact. Or we might look at some of the tensions presented when teachers
sought to implement different parts of the package of 'good practice' suggestions presented to them: the combination of curriculum-specific bays and
varied grouping arrangements discussed in Part 1 is a good example, and is
one of several.

This third kind of analysis will provoke consideration of fundamentally
important questions about the goals and means of improving classroom
practice which are at the heart of PNP. What, in short, are the most effective
strategies for bringing about change in ways that teachers work with
children? How, as we asked in Chapter 6, is the professional development of
teachers best conceived? As a generalized set of multipurpose messages for
all teachers or as strategies more sharply focused on individuals within their
unique working contexts? As ideas disseminated downwards from the LEA
or generated with and by the teachers themselves? As training or as self-
development?

Probing beneath the Surface of 'Practice'

Finally, and in similar vein, we can use the material, and perhaps especially
the case studies in Part 2, to begin to probe beneath the visible surface of

practice and to move beyond the cosy platitudes which all too often constitute the main medium through which such practice is discussed. Rhetoric is inevitable in any job as complex and exposed as teaching: it is a necessary device for preserving professional solidarity and morale. Ideals, too, are an essential part of the educational endeavour, for without them teaching becomes aimless and habitual, lapsing before long into time-serving cynicism. But beyond the words, what are the realities?

In this final section of the report we do not propose to say any more in relation to the first two of these four applications of the findings and issues we have presented. The factual material on classroom practice and on the classroom organization course is clear and self-explanatory, and apart from the general discussion pointers offered above it needs no further highlighting for schools and the LEA to use it productively. The third and fourth applications — strategies for improving classroom practice and alternative ways of looking at the latter — do require further comment, however, and this we now offer.

Strategies for Improving Classroom Practice

PNP is a programme which seeks to facilitate and enhance what is seen as good practice where it exists, and to promote it where it does not, whether that practice concerns teaching and learning, school management or relations between school, home and community. This purpose is reflected in the various complementary strands of the programme with which all readers of this report will by now be familiar: enhanced staffing, a raised advisory profile, increased and refocused INSET, refurbishment, increased capitation and so on.

The four strategies in PNP which bear particularly on the more specific task of improving practice *in classrooms* are:

the day-to-day work of advisory staff;
the range of centrally mounted INSET courses;
the opportunities created by enhanced staffing in general;
and the role of the PNP coordinator in particular.

At various points since PRINDEP's formative evaluation began in 1986 we have reported and discussed these strategies at work. Thus Report 4 (Chapter 7) examined the possibilities and problems of what we termed 'Teachers Teaching Together' — the various forms of classroom collaboration made possible by enhanced staffing. Report 5 (Chapter 5) looked in some detail at the work of PNP coordinators, identifying their various roles and activities, together with the factors influencing their success. Report 6 (Chapter 6) examined LEA-provided INSET, focusing for case study purposes on the pivotal PNP course referred to in the present report. Report 8 (Chapter 4) examined the range of school-based strategies for managing and developing the curriculum, adding heads and curriculum leaders to the list of change agents whose roles needed exploring in the context of the evaluation of PNP.

Alongside these studies of the various distinct strategies we have attempted to assess their impact. Thus Report 7 (Chapter 2) considered how the four specific versions of children's 'need' encapsulated in the Primary Needs Programme — special needs, ethnicity, gender and social/material disadvantage — were operationalized by the LEA as specific initiatives, and how far they were reflected in the ideas and practices of staff within the schools. Report 8 (Chapter 4) looked at the impact of the LEA's ideas about the curriculum in general and the notion of the 'broadly-based curriculum' in particular; and the present report examines the impact of the Authority's versions of good classroom practice on teachers working daily with children.

Common to all of these elements — the policies, the various change agents, their day-to-day roles, the strategies they adopt, and the influence which, separately and in conjunction, they exert — is the idea of *messages*: the verbal representations of good practice which are passed down the line from the Authority to its teachers, through the medium of policy documents, INSET courses, meetings, advisory staff, heads, PNP coordinators and so on.

Strategies: Further Observations

Putting together all these components — the strategies, the messages and their impact — in the context of the present report, what can we conclude? First, and most important, it is clear that what ought to have been an irresistible combination — progressive policies, substantial resources, specially appointed people geared up to making the idea of PNP work — has in fact had a somewhat uneven impact on classroom practice. The facts reported here and in several of PRINDEP's earlier reports speak for themselves. Though overall the picture is one of livelier classrooms and more open and forward-looking professional communities, the extremes on the continuum are a long way apart, with a substantial number of class teachers and heads apparently affected very little by the ideas about practice central to PNP.

Second, the present study confirms and strengthens our earlier findings about the formidable influence, both positive and negative, of each school's professional culture in relation to what individual teachers do in their classrooms. On the one hand, we find heads, coordinators and class teachers working together to promote and consolidate what they believe to be good practice, and generating a climate of excitement and commitment which develops its own momentum and makes each new initiative more likely to succeed. On the other, we have class teachers lacking support from head, coordinator or both; coordinators confronting inertia, complacency, anxiety or hostility; heads unable or unwilling to generate the climate of openness and collective discussion and commitment upon which progress seems to depend.

Third, this study reinforces and extends our earlier concern with the substance, manner and reception of the messages being conveyed. Any tendency to diffuseness or ambiguity makes possible a wide range of inter-pretations (as we showed in Chapter 4 in respect of the 'broadly-based curri-culum') and allows teachers and heads to assert, not untruthfully, that they are implementing the LEA's policies and principles. They can do this partly because some of the messages are generalized enough to allow virtually any interpretation — hence the oft-repeated claim 'we do this already' — and partly because messages may combine minute practical detail with very broad general principle. This, as we saw in the present report, allows teachers to change the surface appearance of their practice without altering its sub-stance.

We can now add two more comments on the matter of strategies for pro-moting change in the classroom.

The Need for Linkage

The first harks back to the reference above to the 'irresistible combination'. Taken separately, each element in the strategy — INSET, advisory support, enhanced staffing, coordinators and so on — has great potential. Too often, however, there is little or no *linkage* between them. Thus class teachers go on a course about classroom practice of whose contents their heads and/or co-ordinators may be unaware. Or they may be aware but not geared up to helping the teacher put the course's ideas into operation. In this context the label 'coordinator' can sometimes seem almost ironical when the person concerned is unable to liaise regularly either with advisory staff or with col-leagues over the policies and principles of classroom practice which are at the heart of PNP and which, as PNP coordinator, he or she should presumably be coordinating.

The fragmentation of effort, the lack of linkage between the key agents in the change process, can affect people at all levels. Thus the workload of advisory staff makes it impossible for them always to follow through into classrooms, and nurture there over time the ideas they have promoted. Some heads may feel so overwhelmed by the tide of new developments — first PNP, then the deluge of documents and requirements associated with the Education Reform Act — that they too may feel able to do little more than register that someone has been on a course about something to do with classroom practice. Coordinators may have job specifications so extensive and diverse that their best intentions are subverted. And this is to presume that the various parties would pull in the same direction if they were able: in fact, of course, the lack of structural linkage can be generally exacerbated by conflicts of value and belief about both strategy and substance.

At the end of the line is the class teacher. Unless he or she has encountered the messages about practice directly from an adviser or on a course, the chances are that these messages will have been through a series of filters before the class teacher receives them: head, coordinator, colleagues, summaries of documents rather than originals and so on, perhaps slightly but significantly changing their meaning at each stage as in the manner of a children's game. Usually the class teacher is defined as the recipient of ideas about practice; more rarely as a contributor, let alone a generator. Yet the practice in question touches the class teacher much more directly than it touches any of the other people in the chain — it is, after all, the teacher's own. So not only is there sometimes a lack of linkage between formally designated change agents like coordinators, advisers and heads, but the class teacher as the most vital link in the chain may be missing altogether in such liaison as does take place.

Given the resourcing of PNP, this situation might represent something of a lost opportunity. In particular, the role of PNP coordinator could be looked at afresh in this light. The as yet unpublished study of coordinators which PRINDEP has undertaken as a follow-up to Report 5 (Chapter 5) shows a process of regression at work since the relatively heady and experimental days of 1985–86: coordinators gradually abandoning some of their more innovative cross-school roles and taking on responsibility for a class. Where this is so, it will make even more difficult the kind of linkage which the present study seems to dictate, namely one in which the coordinator occupies a key role in relation to the improvement of classroom practice, liaising closely with advisory staff on the one hand and head and class teachers on the other.

The Inviolability of the Classroom

The second additional point about strategy is this. We noted at the end of

Part 2 how in PRINDEP's study the day-to-day and minute-to-minute aspects of a teacher's classroom practice emerge not infrequently as something of a no-go area. For one reason or another the plethora of messages about good practice from advisers, heads, coordinators and others may stop just short of the classroom door. From that point on many of those concerned are rather less happy to intervene in what the teacher does, even though all would probably endorse the statement at the beginning of this report about its critical importance to the child.

Coupled with this reluctance to engage with the detail of a teacher's practice — and a logical consequence of it — is the tendency for judgments about practice to be based on evidence from observation rather than interaction. Similarly, practice becomes talked about less in terms of operational detail than in terms of broad sentiments and commitments; less in terms of learning *processes* than in terms of what is called 'the environment of learning': a kind of conceptual skirting round of the very act which is at the heart of education. Obviously, in this matter as in all others there are many exceptions. But the instances of no-go recur sufficiently frequently for them to be noted as general tendencies rather than isolated incidents.

Apart from denying class teachers access to vital support in respect of the task of developing and improving their practice, this tendency increases further the isolation and vulnerability that some of them feel. These in turn lead to the erection of defensive shields in the face of scrutiny, advice and new ideas. The paradox is that to explore a class teacher's practice is to make him or her vulnerable. But not to do so is to compound that vulnerability, particularly at a time, such as the present, when teachers are under extreme pressure to change the ways they work.

Improving Classroom Practice: Basic Requirements

To sum up so far: among the many factors in the success of policies and strategies aimed at improving classroom practice, three seem, in combination, to have a particularly powerful influence. Based on the evidence of this and previous PRINDEP studies, change at a more than surface level seems to require:

> messages about the sought or endorsed practices which are clear, unambiguous and precise as to both their *substance* and their *status* (as policy, recommendation, suggestion or option);

> consistency and close linkage between the various change agents having a role in the improvement of practice (advisory staff, head, deputy, coordinator, etc.), not excluding the class teacher himself/herself;

direct engagement by some at least of these change agents in the deeper levels of the day-to-day classroom practice of the teachers concerned.

Conversely, our evidence indicates that change of a token or surface kind, or no change at all, or even practice directly contrary to that sought, are associated with:

messages whose substance and/or status is vague, ambiguous or imprecise;

lack of consistency and linkage between the change agents;

exclusion of the class teacher from the process of defining good classroom practice;

avoidance of direct engagement by the change agents in the actual classroom practice of the teachers concerned, other than at the surface level.

Classroom Practice: Alternative Realities

The reference above to 'surface' and 'deeper' levels of practice beg definitions, and these we now offer.

From Observation to Interaction

In one sense what we mean by these different levels will be readily apparent to anyone familiar with the job of teaching. 'Surface' is just that — what we see and hear on entering somebody else's classroom: the way the room is arranged; the equipment and display; the way children are grouped and the kinds of work they are undertaking; their apparent involvement, interest and enthusiasm; the way they and the teacher relate to each other. Much can be inferred from such cues, particularly by someone combining professional experience and personal sensitivity, and they will always and necessarily provide a basis on which those with responsibility for the work of teachers — heads and advisory staff, for example — monitor classroom practice.

In this sense what is meant by the 'deeper' levels of practice will also be easily recognized. They are what are encountered when after watching and listening one begins to interact with the participants. Thus discussion with the teacher will reveal the intentions underlying what has been observed, and will also show the extent to which what the teacher does has been properly thought through. Discussion with the children will enable one to begin to judge the kinds of understanding they are gaining from the tasks the teacher has set, and the degree to which those tasks are appropriate to their abilities. It will also enable one to penetrate the strategies many children employ to seek the teacher's attention or, conversely, to look busy and avoid it.

Engagement with Practice: Minimum Requirements

Our evidence suggests that while observation of teachers at work is common enough, it is less common for the observer to interact with the teacher and the children, despite the fact that such interaction is a necessary part of any attempt to discover and judge the direction and quality of the children's learning. So when we refer to 'direct engagement' with a teacher's practice at the end of the previous section we mean, as a minimum, *one-to-one interaction with the children and their teacher*. Moreover, the nature of the job undertaken by heads and advisers means that they see but a tiny proportion of the class teacher's practice. Their visits are inevitably short and relatively infrequent. Practice is *sampled*, and a great deal can hang on the quality and typicality of what at the time of the visit happens to be going on. It is this which provokes among teachers such frustration: 'But she's only seen me teach once . . . . He has never even seen me in action . . . . She came in and looked round then went out without even saying anything . . . . How can they possibly claim such-and-such about my practice on that basis?'

One reality that is quite frequently missing from an outsider's observation is that of teaching over a period of time: the way the various individual sessions observed come together to form a whole which is far more than the sum of its parts. If the function of the outsider's visit to a classroom is merely to gain an impression, then the one-off is sufficient. But if the context is that of professional development, with the aim of enhancing and improving the teacher's practice, then a more extended engagement is called for.

There are many more ways of defining what is going on in primary classrooms. In the remainder of this section we propose to concentrate on three others, all prominent in the PRINDEP data, and all of direct relevance to the central PNP concern with the improvement of classroom practice.

Teaching Strategies: For the Children or for the Teacher?

The question of why, as teachers, we employ a particular teaching strategy can always be answered in two ways. One is that it is best for the children, and the other is that it is best for the teacher. Naturally, we presume that the two are related, and that the more comfortable we feel with a particular way of working, the more likely it is that we are being effective in helping children to learn. However, the Level 1 and 2 data remind us that the connection is not an inevitable one, and indeed that it is possible to provide child-centred justifications for almost anything one does.

The most familiar instances of strategies employed to serve the teacher's rather than the child's interests are the 'time-fillers', those activities children are given when the main task is completed 'to keep them quiet until playtime'. However, beyond these is the possibility that more substantial activities may serve, in part at least, a similar function. The data, for instance, provoke questions about the *real* function of some art, craft and topic work; is it offered exclusively in pursuit of educational goals or does it serve in addition (or even instead) to create time for the teacher to concentrate his or her attention elsewhere? Do art and craft activities, by their nature, require less teacher-child interaction than mathematics and language, or do they get less teacher-child interaction because they are deemed less important? Is the quite substantial amount of time they are sometimes allocated less a reflection of their value than of their strategic usefulness to the busy teacher of a large class?

In short, *is one of the functions of some educational activities to create time and space for the teacher to concentrate on others?* If so, how far is this function a legitimate one? We are not asserting that this is universally the case, though our evidence indicates that it does happen. Rather, we are raising it as a question to be addressed honestly, particularly in relation to those classroom activities which take much of the children's time but little of the teacher's.

The Reality of the Broadly-based Curriculum

Questions about the balance of an activity's *strategic* and *educational* functions take us on to the issue of the curriculum as a whole. The 'broadly-based curriculum' is a cornerstone of PNP (and the phrase also appears, though used somewhat differently, in the curriculum chapter of the 1988 Education Reform Act). How far is the principle reflected in practice?

In Report 8 (Chapter 4) we charted systematically five main aspects of the management of curriculum and curriculum development in PNP schools. They were:

the ways in which curriculum posts of responsibility were allocated;

the main strategies for in-school curriculum development;

the range and priorities of curriculum areas under review;

schools' use of INSET to support curriculum development;

schools' use of increased capitation (the PNP development fund).

There we showed how the traditional 'basics' of mathematics and language, and especially mathematics, dominated the league tables of posts of responsibility, development initiatives, INSET, resourcing and so on, and how these tendencies were subtly buttressed by staff gender and status to convey messages to both staff and children about what aspects of the curriculum really matter. The report accepted that our educational system places different areas of the curriculum in a clear pecking order, and, this being so, that it makes sense to resource fairly generously the areas accorded highest priority.

However, the discrepancies in terms of curriculum management and development were sometimes so marked as to raise the question of whether there might be a minimum level of attention, initiative and resourcing below which one might as well provide nothing as a little. Commenting on the principles of depth, balance, relevance, differentiation, progression and continuity with which curriculum breadth is conventionally linked, we suggested:

> If a curriculum can meet all the latter criteria it will certainly in the best sense be broad. But equally, a curriculum will have no chance at all of meeting such criteria unless each of its constituent parts (not just those one or two parts deemed the most important) is supported by an adequate level of curriculum development.

The classroom data of the present study allow us to take this argument further. For the discrepancies in curriculum *management* in the school seem to be matched by discrepancies in curriculum *delivery* in the classroom. We stress that the issue is not one of mere *time*. Different parts of the curriculum are allocated different amounts of time in accordance with both their perceived importance and their nature, and although there may be arguments about the educational priorities such allocations reflect, the principle seems eminently sensible.

The issue, then, concerns not time but *treatment*. The Level 1 and 2 classroom material raises important questions about the seriousness of professional intentions in respect of certain 'non-basic' curriculum areas; about provision for them on a day-to-day basis in terms of layout and resources; about the extent to which children are being adequately challenged and stimulated in these areas; and about the degree to which their learning is being properly monitored and assessed. The Level 3 data, including the systematic recording of activities and interactions over time, will allow us to pursue further this idea of the reality of curriculum breadth and balance, for in the final analysis the version of the curriculum which most truly matters is not that claimed or perceived by the Authority or its teachers, but that experienced by the child.

Practice: Acknowledging Problems, Dilemmas and Compromises

So far we have outlined two alternative 'realities' which need to be acknowledged and explored by those seeking to understand and improve classroom practice. The first was what might emerge from an attempt honestly to address the question of whether some purportedly educational activities may occasionally be undertaken as much for the teacher's benefit as for the children's. The second came from the need to look beyond the rhetoric of the broadly-based curriculum to the consequences for children, in terms of the curriculum they actually experience, of particular strategies for curriculum management and delivery. The third such 'reality' is even more fundamental. It concerns how we conceive of and discuss 'practice' itself.

We argued in the introduction to this report that study of teachers' practice must include engagement with the way they think about their work as well as with what they can be seen to do, and that the latter cannot be properly understood without reference to the former. PRINDEP's study of classroom practice at each of the three levels sought to apply this principle. What emerged was a sense of day-to-day decisions being made in a context of pressures and constraints, some of them intrinsic to the job of teaching, some of them particular to a school, and some of them resulting from LEA policies and expectations. Frequently these were compounded by the isolation which some teachers felt and/or the barriers to outside influence which they erected.

We explored some of the critical decisions teachers had to make and reconcile: concerning what the children should learn on each occasion, which children should receive the teacher's attention at any one time, and how the classroom and the children should be organized to facilitate each of these. We illustrated the way different teachers responded to these requirements, and the compromises they found themselves having to make as a result.

We also showed how consciousness of others' views of 'good practice' was an additional and sometimes powerful influence on teachers' decision-making. Sometimes these views could be accommodated without difficulty and were helpful and productive, but on other occasions they caused problems. For example, some teachers found that the external messages conflicted with their own views; or with their particular classroom circumstances; or even that different messages seemed to conflict with each other, or at any rate proved quite difficult to reconcile.

One of the most critical of these areas concerned the vital question of how a teacher responsible for teaching the whole curriculum to a large number of children so organizes both the curriculum and the children's learning that he/she can give all the children the attention they need. It is a challenge to which no single solution seems wholly satisfactory, and teachers devised various compromises, most of them variations on two linked themes: reducing the level of challenge of activities in lower status curriculum areas so that children could work for long periods relatively unsupervised and allow the teacher to invest attention in what were seen as the more important activities; and/or defining certain children as 'undemanding' and giving them less attention.

This version of practice is one in which dilemmas and compromises play a prominent part. It contrasts sharply with the versions of practice which many primary teachers are given or feel obliged to claim — the one where one operates, or claims to operate, in accordance with a set of 'principles of good primary practice' which are rarely defined, let alone argued through and justified; the one expressed in language of such unclouded certainty that few care to express doubts or propose alternatives; the one where there are only two kinds of problem: those which one cannot admit to because they stem from lack of competence, and those which one can admit to because they are somebody else's fault.

The alternative version of practice reflects rather different assumptions.

First, teaching is a difficult and complex job and therefore the basic condition for professional development must be one in which the open discussion of the difficulties and complexities is encouraged rather than avoided. Such discussion is then seen as a mark of professional maturity rather than of professional weakness.

Second, while some of the problems teachers daily experience do relate to professional expertise and/or the particular circumstances in which they work — the children, the school, colleagues, resources, time and so on — others are intrinsic to the job itself. Teaching has at its core the making of decisions which *by their nature* create dilemmas and require compromises. The fact that these dilemmas exist is a reflection not on the individual teacher, therefore, but on the job itself.

Third, classroom practice improves by progress being made in parallel on three fronts: by sharpening, refining and extending teachers' professional knowledge, understanding and skills; by identifying the dilemmas which lie at the heart of primary teaching, confronting them, analyzing why they exist, and considering how best they can be resolved; and, as a link between the first two, by ensuring that the professional knowledge, skills and understanding one aims to develop relate to teaching as it really is, problems, dilemmas and compromises included, rather than to a tidied-up version of the job from which such inconveniences are removed.

There is always a fine balance to be struck between confronting harsh realities and preserving professional morale, but the standard reassurance, frequently voiced during the months since the 1988 Act, 'don't worry — we do all of this already', is probably no more in the interests of the teacher than it is of the children.

Conclusion

This report has had two main themes: the character of classroom practice in PNP schools, and the Authority's strategies for improving it. It is the first of two such reports stemming from a three-stage study of teaching in sixty schools.

Part 1 surveyed the physical arrangements in the classrooms of nearly forty teachers, reported their accounts of how they dealt with day-to-day matters like grouping, curriculum delivery, planning, record keeping and so on, and recorded their responses to some of the Authority's ideas about how their classrooms and teaching might be organized.

Part 2 presented five of PRINDEP's case studies of a further ten teachers at work, showing how they tackled some of the basic decisions of which teaching is constituted, and identifying some of the critical points at which dilemmas were confronted and compromises were required.

Part 3 explored the uses which might be made of this material by the Authority and schools. One, relatively straightforward, was concerned with the particulars of the data — the variations in organization and practice as recorded, and the role of the Authority's messages about good practice. We trust that LEA and school staff will find the material helpful and instructive at this level. The other way of using the material was more complex and wide-ranging. It raised fundamental questions not only about the most appropriate strategies for improving classroom practice, but also about the very way in which such practice is defined and discussed.

Some of the central points in this last analysis were as follows. First, the present study consolidates the findings of previous PRINDEP reports about some of the main factors facilitating or frustrating change in classroom practice in Leeds primary schools. Second, the study confirms the considerable potential of each of the separate elements and roles in the Authority's PNP change strategy, but suggests that this potential would be enhanced if there were more effective linkage between them. Third, the class teacher is shown to be very much at the end of a line: receiving messages about practice which he or she has had little or no part in constructing and which may be ambiguous and imprecise; undertaking complex and demanding tasks with which some of those outside the classroom fail to engage except at a relatively superficial level; and therefore sometimes forced into a defensive or rationalizing posture in the face of new ideas. Fourth, it is probable, therefore, that both classroom practice and the confidence of the practitioner would gain if these trends could be reversed. Fifth, the modification of strategy alone is not enough. There also needs to be a shift in the way that practice itself is defined and conceived, and in the aspects of classroom life upon which strategies for improving practice focus and operate.

In this context it is worth recalling the present report's suggestion that notwithstanding the undoubted importance of classroom layout and organization, they are but the framework within which the acts and interactions central to teaching and learning take place, and it is the latter which should be brought to the fore in definitions of 'practice' and strategies for improving it. Moreover, this view is supported by earlier PRINDEP data as well as that gathered for the present study. In Chapter 2, for example, we argued that insufficient attention appeared to be given to the day-to-day procedures whereby teachers diagnose the learning needs of individual children and assess their progress.

Diagnosis and assessment are not only essential teaching skills but are also among the most elusive, and it is not surprising, therefore, that their relative neglect in the professional development of experienced teachers is matched by comparable neglect in initial training. It is now widely recognized that this must change, not least because these skills have now taken on a critically important role in the National Curriculum's assessment programme.

Finally, the complexity and elusiveness of classroom diagnosis and assessment serve to underline the importance of the main shift argued for in the latter part of this report, namely, towards a more open acknowledgment of the problematic in teaching: the everyday decisions which have to be made; the difficulty of reconciling ideals and practice; the dilemmas and compromises; the possibility of conflict between the teacher's and the child's interests in decisions about curriculum content, group activities, and the monitoring of learning; and the inevitably imperfect solutions. Though vision in education is essential, it needs to be combined with realism, honesty and a preparedness always to ask questions about the impact on children of what one does. Without the last, ideals and practice will always remain a long way apart.

9
Conclusion

The last part of the previous chapter explored some critical issues concerning primary classroom practice and ways of changing it. It also brought us back to the main theme of this book. In this brief concluding chapter we offer some more general comments on the theme of planned change in primary education as it has been illuminated by our studies of initiatives in one of Britain's largest LEAs.

We do not at this stage offer final judgments on this matter, or on the Primary Needs Programme. At the time of writing we are still processing data, including those from the most intensive part of the study of classroom practice just discussed. Volume 2 will complete the analysis and discussion of this and other material before moving on to set out the project's overall conclusions and recommendations.

The seven studies included here have ranged over the three main *levels* within the local system of education — the LEA, the school and the classroom — and have explored some of the ways these intersect and interact. The studies have also considered various *stages* in the change process, from goals to the strategies devised for achieving them, from the dynamics of change to its outcomes.

The Primary Needs Programme started with one main and three subsidiary or enabling goals. In Chapter 1 we traced these back to three distinct and to some extent competing views of educational priorities: social and material disadvantage in the inner city, children with special educational needs, and the post-progressive view of good primary practice. Subsequently, we followed through particular facets of this composite ideology — the chosen categories of pupil need (Chapter 2); the notion of a 'broadly-based curriculum' (Chapters 3, 4 and 8); and classroom pedagogy (Chapters 6, 7 and 8).

We also showed how the unresolved tensions within the programme's goals caused continuing problems within schools, particularly for the main PNP change agent, the coordinator (Chapter 5); and how the goals' diffuseness and ambiguity tended to encourage confusion and rationalization at the point where heads and class teachers had to translate them into everyday decisions or reconcile them with existing practice (Chapters 4, 6 and 8).

The range of strategies devised to secure the programme's success was extensive. At the LEA level the chief impetus came from an effective alliance between two groups: politicians and advisers. The former were considerably more prominent than their predecessors, and intervened not just in the broad sweep of policy, but sometimes also in its detailed operation. This is very much a characteristic of large urban councils in the 1980s — a counterpart (and perhaps conscious response) to the expansion of the powers of the Secretary of State and the DES during the same period. The other half of the alliance — an enlarged and reorganized advisory service with a clear proselytizing function — used both day-to-day contacts with teachers in schools and a range of central in-service courses to deliver the preferred versions of practice and monitor their implementation (Chapters 6 and 8). Such direct LEA influence contrasted with strategies at school level of a more indirect or enabling kind: refurbishment and increased capitation (Chapter 4) and — perhaps the single most potent strategy of all — enhanced staffing (Chapters 4 and 5).

Our studies provide a detailed commentary on the dynamics of many of these strategies at work: advisory and support staff seeking to shift teachers' understanding and indeed prejudices in respect of the chosen categories of need — material and social disadvantage, special needs, race and multiculturalism, gender and equal opportunities (Chapter 2); advisory staff encouraging teachers to organize their classrooms, pupils and curricula in new ways (Chapters 6 and 8); heads sorting out ways of deploying their established and additional staff to promote curriculum and professional development, identifying their curriculum priorities, allocating resources and setting up review and development programmes (Chapter 4); PNP coordinators undertaking complex and demanding cross-school roles in pursuit of these and other objectives (Chapter 5); and class teachers collaborating not just within the staffroom but also, often for the very first time in their careers, in the classroom (Chapter 7).

Finally, the studies in this volume explore some of the outcomes of these change processes — a difficult task, as we stressed earlier. While issuing the proper notes of caution in this regard, we have also tried not to dodge our responsibilities. Thus, for example, we find: evidence of a much sharper focus on and more systematic treatment of children with special needs, from ethnic minority groups and from materially disadvantaged backgrounds (Chapter 2); schools whose professional cultures have been transformed into arenas for lively discussion, initiative and collaboration; new approaches to the internal management of schools, with heads increasingly looking to other senior staff to work with them in management teams, taking a more sophisticated approach to specialist roles and task delegation, and involving staff at all levels in the decisions which affect their work (Chapters 4 and 5); individual teachers, through TTT, gaining access to alternative approaches to classroom planning and provision, and able to pass on to their children the benefits of more sustained and systematic attention (Chapter 7); classrooms whose appearance, layout and day-to-day organization are more efficient and visually stimulating (Chapter 8).

This, of course, is not a catalogue or summation. These are only examples, and each chapter contains many additional outcomes of PNP which are discussed in much more detail; as we have emphasized, the final assessment must await the completion of the project. But there is already sufficient to indicate the undoubted and positive impact of this initiative on the character of primary education in Leeds.

However, the same process which identified gains also, naturally enough, exposed problems. Thus the debit side of the needs question was the apparent persistence of attitudes among some teachers which might be construed as verging on the racist or sexist; the tendency to make the educational needs of socially and materially disadvantaged children so secondary to providing emotional security that they could occasionally almost be forgotten; the ideologically legitimated neglect of able children; the highlighting of children's problems rather than their potential; and the relative lack of attention given to professional development in the vital areas of needs identification and diagnosis (Chapter 2).

We also found schools in which expensive extra staff had apparently sunk without trace, marginalized because of the threat they provoked to the existing order, or simply underexploited because of a failure of managerial will or imagination; coordinators prevented from coordinating or lacking the personal skills and specialist knowledge to do so convincingly or productively (Chapters 4 and 5); teachers working in the same classroom but in no real sense working together (Chapter 7); classrooms in which change was of a cosmetic rather than a fundamental kind (Chapter 8).

We also found a sometimes counter-productive tension among the various elements in the Authority's change strategy: between messages about good practice delivered authoritatively from above and the aspirations of school staff wanting, and for their own development needing, to work such matters out for themselves (Chapters 4, 6 and 8); between the idea of a change agent in each school (the PNP coordinator) and the roles of other staff with major responsibilities for change and development, not least the head and deputy (Chapters 4 and 5). Beyond these there were the tensions of a strategy whose constituent parts and actors sometimes lacked the common purpose and structural linkage needed to generate change of the scale and character which was needed (Chapter 8).

Again, however, this list is indicative rather than comprehensive, and it is certainly neither possible nor desirable at this stage to do a neat balance-sheet calculation of the programme's net profit and loss. Instead we prefer to end by raising two clusters of issues of a general but fundamental kind whose importance is such that they need both to be signalled here and carried forward into the project's final stage and for further consideration in the second volume.

In Chapter 1 we argued that the proper study and understanding of educational processes require us to attend not just to actions and behaviours but also to their contingent thoughts, ideas and meanings. The first cluster of issues, therefore, is essentially *conceptual*. The goals of the Primary Needs Programme were brief, broad and diffuse, yet they had the force of policy and were coupled with a strategy which was elaborate, expensive and therefore expected to deliver a great deal. The three key concepts, the focus and *raison d'être* of the programme, were *needs*, *curriculum* and *pedagogy*. About each of them, as both concepts and practice, our studies have raised many questions.

The notion of *needs*, as we said at the beginning of Chapter 2, raises fairly familiar philosophical and psychological problems, and these — their familiarity notwithstanding — deserve attention. The definition adopted in this particular context could also be regarded by some as somewhat selective, and that too raises questions in the context of a school's responsibility in a pluralist society to meet the needs of *all* its pupils. Moreover, when in Chapter 2 we applied our 'needs' grid (definition/identification/diagnosis/provision) and noted a tendency for the middle two not to feature very prominently (except in the case of SEN children), we were not making an abstract point but indicating a conceptual weakness that could have serious consequences in the classroom. The omission was the more notable because the programme's aims appeared to acknowledge the importance of the missing dimension in their reference to the 'identified needs' of children.

Similarly, the notion of the 'broadly-based' curriculum was superficially attractive, though progressive only in a rather traditional textbook way, but it begged a number of questions, as the discussion in Chapters 4 and 8 showed. Because *curriculum* as such was not defined, the principle of breadth had little practical meaning, or rather almost as many meanings as there were teachers. Moreover, breadth could be, and was, claimed for activities which by other criteria might seem narrow and unbalanced.

There are at least three forms in which curriculum breadth might be sought, two familiar, the other less so. The first two concern *scope*: the range of subjects and the range of activities within subjects — the definitions of breadth used by HMI (DES, 1985). But breadth in this sense is largely about *content* and any curriculum has a number of *operational* elements, each of which contributes to making a mere specification of content an experienced reality: the way it is planned, taught, managed and evaluated, the physical and interpersonal milieu in which it is set and so on. Each of these featured to some extent in the LEA's in-service support package, some (like milieu and pedagogy) quite prominently; but such elements gain most practical value if contextualized in specific areas of content and by reference to specific groups of children.

Another ingredient commonly missing from curriculum discourse was *differentiation* — the analysis of the kinds of curriculum experiences which are most appropriate for particular children. This underlines the earlier point about missing elements in the conceptual framework for *needs*: pupil diagnosis and assessment, and curriculum differentiation are very much sides of the same coin.

Perhaps the most prominent omission, however, was *rationale*. Why this particular version of curriculum? By what arguments was it to be justified? Or was it presumed that merely to assert its efficacy was sufficient? Again, this is not merely a conceptual point: to omit justification from curriculum discourse is to leave teachers without clear reasons for what they do; worse, it may encourage some of them to believe that in education reasons are not needed — a stance which is not only inappropriate but also leaves them very exposed in a climate of increased public accountability.

The third plank in the LEA's conceptual platform was *pedagogy*. It was without doubt recognized as important in PNP, and in that respect the programme has been an important corrective to a general tendency in British initial and in-service teacher education to neglect close analysis of the skills and processes of teaching. But, again, it has to be asked whether the conceptual map of pedagogy was not rather incomplete, when obvious organizational strategies like grouping and classroom layout featured so prominently but other important aspects rather less so.

Among the latter were the many and subtly different forms of teacher-pupil interaction through which children's abilities and progress can be monitored, and through which their learning can be fostered; and the critical theme of *learning* itself. This reflects a more general problem in educational thinking: the tendency to treat learning and teaching as distinct, and to work out the relationship between them from the wrong end: that is to say, starting with the presumed outcomes of preferred teaching strategies rather than identifying the kinds of learning which need to be promoted and then devising the strategies most likely to deliver these (a problem which is well explored by Bennett *et al.*, 1984).

Moreover, as with curriculum in primary education, so with pedagogy. Where a case was made, it was more likely to be on moral or even aesthetic ('good' primary practice) rather than empirical grounds. Allied to this was a tendency, discussed in some detail in the final part of Chapter 8, for pedagogy to be defined and explored more in terms of idealized external features than the decisions and dilemmas which actually confront teachers on a day-to-day basis.

The three components of the programme's rationale just discussed — needs, curriculum and pedagogy — were conceived of not as isolated but contingent. The broadly-based curriculum allied to flexible teaching strategies would provide the kind of education which would meet the needs of all pupils. At one level this is convincing: pupil needs vary a great deal, so it pays to make education broad and flexible. But perhaps it convinces in the way any truism does, leaving one not very much the wiser. Yet even at such a level of generality there are points to be raised. Quite apart from the separate conceptual problems associated with 'needs', 'curriculum', 'broadly-based' and 'flexible teaching strategies', there is the empirical question of whether the first of these will *necessarily* be met by the other three. The argument appears to reside less in empirical evidence than in a combination of common sense and ideological persuasiveness. It could be suggested, for example, that if needs are different, so must the curriculum be, even perhaps to the extent of being, for some children, very sharply focused, instrumental and therefore by some definitions narrow. If this is so, then the *operational* usefulness of the goals diminishes still further.

In response to these observations it could be argued that a general goal or policy, ipso facto, cannot be expected to deliver operational detail. This seems valid where a general statement of intent is then elaborated in the way that broad aims are translated into specific objectives. But in the present case, though this happened to some extent with 'needs' (as we saw in Chapter 2) and 'flexible teaching strategies' (as we saw in Chapters 6 and 8), there was something of a vacuum as far as detailed explication of the character of the *curriculum as a whole* was concerned. This omission has always been a weakness of curriculum discourse in both primary and secondary education in England. Pressed hard by central government in the late 1970s and early 1980s, many LEAs could at the most only come up with somewhat vapid statements about the whole curriculum (DES, 1977, 1979, 1983), despite their statutory obligations under the 1944 Education Act. The direct intervention of central government in curriculum matters, which culminated in the 1988 Act, should be set partly against this background.

These kinds of questions about how we conceive of pupil needs, curriculum, pedagogy, and the relationship between them, are important in any context, but especially so in view of the particular strategy for educational change and professional development adopted by Leeds LEA. If the strategy had been one of providing resources and support for heads and teachers to work out their own solutions to problems as they independently analyzed them (which is the way some other LEAs have operated, at least until the arrival of the National Curriculum), then Leeds LEA's view of pupil needs, curriculum, pedagogy and other issues would have mattered rather less. It could have been accepted merely as the kind of sentiment which reassures teachers that policy-makers support their endeavours and are not inclined to be eccentric or doctrinaire. But because the Authority adopted a top-down approach to development, in which preferred versions of each of these vital aspects of education were delivered to teachers and expected to be implemented by them, rather more came to hang on the substance of the messages in question and in turn they needed to be scrutinized closely as to their comprehensiveness, validity and justification. Ideas must always be examined, but ideas backed by power especially so.

Conversely, the context and manner in which ideas are delivered affect the way they are perceived and interpreted. Thus ideas transmitted from above in a strict hierarchy will frequently be taken as prescriptions to which no alternative is permitted, even if the underlying intentions are rather more open. Ideas about school and classroom practice delivered to teachers by people who do not work there daily will often be dismissed as other-worldly, even if they are packed with insight and good sense, simply because they do indeed emanate from another world.

This is not to underplay the dilemma over strategy which confronts any large LEA, like Leeds, which wishes dramatically to transform the character of its schools after what it perceives as a long period of stagnation and mediocrity. Political time-scales are notoriously short, and are rarely seen as permitting a softly-softly approach to a large-scale reform in which reputations and credibility are invested. It was clear that the system was seriously underfunded, yet political opponents and the electorate would probably not be convinced that a multi-million pound injection of funds was needed unless it started showing results, quickly and tangibly.

For the LEA, therefore, it was necessary to keep the entire programme under fairly tight control. Like central government in respect of the 1988 Education Reform Act, the LEA set the objectives, defined the agenda and proposed the solutions, all with far less consultation than schools would have liked. Like central government in respect of the 1988 Act too, the LEA put implementation in the hands of people it could trust and influence: an expanded and extremely dedicated advisory team who delivered the new messages about practice through a combination of central courses and a high profile in individual schools, and who vetted schools' proposals for additional PNP expenditure; together with school-based change agents (the PNP coordinators) in whose appointment, unusually for posts at that level, the LEA was also closely involved.

Each of the preceding chapters has raised a number of specific points about PNP strategy — our second cluster of issues — at these and other levels, and we do not propose to repeat them. However, there are certain general points which should be noted here. First, a programme can be effectively monitored and steered only if there are sufficient resources to achieve this, and an advisory team of sixteen covering 230 primary schools and 2400 teachers is, by any standards, stretched thin. Ironically, this same group will now be required to police the implementation of the National Curriculum, and the problem will be compounded.

Second, with or without policing, schools will always go their own way. They are used to a high degree of autonomy; they are staffed by members of a profession in which individualism and the importance of having one's own educational 'philosophy' have always been highly valued; and in any case their circumstances, problems and opportunities are unique. Each school is a powerful and complete culture in its own right.

Third, two aspects of the PNP strategy, far from bringing schools into line, may have tended to encourage their divergence and independence. One is the fact, already extensively discussed, that although the programme's rationale was devised and directed from the centre, its form was such as to allow a wide range of interpretations at school and classroom levels. The other is that the apparent bypassing of heads (see Chapter 4) both in the initial consultations and in the original idea of the PNP coordinator, was almost certain to backfire. The Authority was undoubtedly correct in its perception that heads, more than any other group, were responsible for the character and effectiveness of their schools. But dealing with those heads regarded as inadequate or wayward by working round rather than with or through them is a much more questionable strategy; the more so because as a blanket policy it also excluded some of the LEA's most talented heads (from whom much could have been learned) and some of those most active in union affairs (whose support would have made all the difference).

Fourth, our material tends to endorse the potential of each of the various elements in the strategy adopted: the role of the advisory service, increased expenditure on buildings and resources, extensive INSET, enhanced staffing, the catalyzing influence of the PNP coordinator, and collaborative teaching. However, as we argued in Chapter 8, effective though each of these can be separately, linkage would make them even more so. The critical links, as we see it, are those between advisory staff, heads and co-ordinators.

Finally, we return to a question posed perhaps oversuccinctly at the end of Chapter 6. Where, we asked, is good practice to be found: in policy statements, among advisory staff, in the educational literature, on courses, in staffrooms, or in classrooms? And what is the most productive way to link these: in a hierarchical relationship or a dialectical one? It will now be recognized that our study of change in one LEA tends to lead us to the view that practice is best understood, and effective practice is best defined and fostered, through dialectic rather than prescription. The word is chosen carefully: 'consultation' is often no more than hearing opinions before proceeding as intended; 'discussion' is useful but a little bland; whereas 'dialectic' points up the existence of different and even contradictory viewpoints which *need* to be confronted and resolved.

In each of the areas on which the Primary Needs Programme rightly focused — children's needs, the curriculum, pedagogy, home and school — there are different views of the nature of the challenges and the best way to tackle them, and each of the various constituencies involved in education has a valuable and legitimate perspective. If there are any fundamental truths about such matters, they could well be somewhere near where the various perspectives meet, though it is likely that in education the search for absolutes is fruitless and what we are more modestly seeking is the analysis and the solution which are the best we can devise in the circumstances. In any event a strategy for teacher development which ignores, suppresses or fails to foster other than officially approved viewpoints may achieve some things, but development will probably not be one of them.

This, then, is the sense of 'linkage' which seems most appropriate to the circumstances of an LEA seeking to change its educational ideas and practices: constructive dialogue among the various groups concerned, rather than one group trying to bring the rest into line. However, the principle is not an easy one to implement, and an LEA confronted by a serious problem which needs to be resolved quickly and decisively may feel unable to afford this extent of idealism. The matter is far from being a simple choice between 'top-down' and 'bottom-up' strategies, and the extent of the dilemma here should not be underestimated. The consequences and balance of intervention, direction, participation, dialogue and autonomy need to be very carefully judged.

Appendix A
The Primary Needs Independent Evaluation Project (PRINDEP)

The project was commissioned from Leeds University by Leeds City Council, which also funded it.

The project staff consisted of a central team of University staff, together with a succession of teachers from local primary schools seconded to the project by the LEA, two terms at a time, under the University's Teacher Associate scheme.

The project was based at the LEA's premises in Merrion House. Its programme and all its reports were submitted, under the terms of the contract between the University and the City Council, to the Education Committee's Special Programmes Steering Group prior to dissemination, but the project was essentially an independent one: this independence was also a contractual commitment.

Project Staff

Central Team (University of Leeds)

Robin Alexander (Director, 1986–90)
John Willcocks (Senior Research Fellow / Coordinator, 1986–90)
Kay Kinder (Research Fellow, 1986–89)
Steve Conway (Research Assistant, 1986–87)
Martin Ripley (Research Assistant, 1987–88)
Val Carroll (Research Assistant, 1989)

Teacher Associates (seconded by Leeds LEA)

January–July 1987	January–July 1988	January–July 1989
Gwyneth Christie	Keith Goulding	Elizabeth Emery
Adrianne Harker	Jill Herron	Colleen Torcasio
Robert Shelton	Denise Nathan	
Brian Taylor	Margaret Robson	
Kevin Walker	Veronica Sawyer	

Appendix B
Outline of the Methodology of the Study of Classroom Practice (Chapter 8)

In carrying out the enquiry which forms the subject of Chapter 8, we had to balance the constraints of limited resources with the need for a large enough sample to illustrate something of the range of PNP practice. The number of primary schools in the LEA fluctuates slightly as new schools are built or old ones amalgamate. Between 1985 (when PNP began) and 1989 the figure was always a little under 240. It was decided to conduct interviews and observation in a quarter of these schools, even though it was clear from the outset that in some cases the enquiry would have to be of relatively modest scope and duration.

The final programme was as follows:

> To conduct interviews with the teacher, and observation, in one classroom in each of sixty local primary schools, at three levels as follows:
>
> at Level 1, in forty schools,
>> to make a single visit to observe a classroom, and then to interview the teacher about its organization and daily use;
>
> at Level 2, in ten schools from the PRINDEP representative sample, and in the light of PRINDEP's existing knowledge of the schools built up over three years of fieldwork,
>> to make a single visit to observe a classroom, to interview the teacher about its organization and daily use, to observe her in action in it, and then to interview her again, discussing the teaching session and her long-term planning strategies;
>
> at Level 3, in a further ten schools,
>> using two observers per school, and with the aid of a radio microphone worn by the teacher so that everything she said could be clearly heard and tape-recorded, to conduct over a period of a fortnight twenty one-hour sessions of systematic

observation (ten of the teacher and, simultaneously, ten of a sample of six pupils, each observed on each occasion for ten consecutive minutes); to conduct interviews about the teaching sessions beforehand and afterwards with the teacher and her support teacher(s) if any, and, at the end of a fortnight, to conduct interviews of a more general nature with the teacher and with the head of the school.

The Sample

The forty teachers at Level 1 were chosen from the attendance lists of the LEA's classroom organization course, held (and repeated on several occasions) about six months earlier. This course was the subject of an extended evaluation described in Chapter 6, and the teachers chosen for the classroom practice study were drawn from those whose earlier reactions to the course appeared in that chapter. The selection of the sample from this source ensured that all its members had been exposed to the same account of the Authority's thinking on some important aspects of the Primary Needs Programme, long enough beforehand for them to have been able to incorporate these ideas into their practice if they intended to do so. This explains some of the emphases in the interviews and observation sessions: for example, the importance attached in the course to the display of children's work and other materials is reflected in the detailed attention to display in the observation schedules.

The schools involved at Level 1 were not already known to PRINDEP, and it says much for the teacher's enthusiasm that so many of them made a positive response. In the event the proposed sample of forty was reduced by only two to thirty-eight.

The ten teachers at Level 2 were drawn from the same list of names, but an extra criterion here was that they should each be from a school in which we had already had an extensive involvement through our Fieldwork B. The demands on these teachers were greater, since we were asking not only to observe their classrooms, but also to observe them at work with their pupils. Again, there was a very positive response.

At Level 3 we made even greater demands on ten more teachers, including extensive observation of daily classroom routines, the use of radio-microphones to record everything they said during the observation sessions, and a strenuous programme of interviews over a period of a fortnight. At this level, in line with our usual Fieldwork A practice, the schools were selected for their known interest in particular aspects of PNP. The head of each school was approached and, if she was willing in principle for the programme of interviews and observation to take place in the school, she nominated a teacher who was then invited by us to take part (but was, of course, free to refuse). Although some of the teachers had initial reservations about wearing a radio microphone, there was no difficulty in making up the sample of ten.

The Observation

The observation schedules necessarily differed at the three levels of the enquiry. In general the observation of the classrooms themselves included a consideration of their architectural features, furniture, equipment and display. While at the school the interviewer drew an A5 plan of the classroom under discussion, roughly to scale, and also made a written note of the following:

> architectural features: alcoves, partitions, tiled areas, wall space, etc;

> furniture: its type and arrangement; how it was used to divide the space; location and use made of teacher's desk, if any; floor coverings; activities for which specific space was allotted, etc;

> equipment: its nature, state and location; how it was labelled, etc;

> display: the amount and location; the materials and backgrounds; whose work it was; whether it was self-explanatory; its apparent purpose; its apparent age; the subject areas represented; the relationship, if any, to other displays around the school, etc.

Reference to Chapter 6 will clarify the reasons for some of the emphases in this list.

The observation of teaching was systematic, using a relatively simple set of categories with the teachers at Level 2, and a more ambitious system with the teachers and their pupils at Level 3. This main programme of observation was principally concerned with the teachers' and pupils' use of time and with the frequency and nature of their interactions.

The Level 2 observation schedule required the observer to:

> monitor the teacher's moves, noting the time, the children to whom she had moved, and the curriculum area on which they were working;

> code all interactions to indicate whether they involved individuals, groups or the whole class, and whether they were initiated by teacher or pupil;

capture as much of the teacher's language as possible;

note whether children who had been set to work independently of the teacher were generally on task, and monitor their use of resources.

At Level 3 the two separate observation schedules were used in parallel. During each hour of observation one observer was concerned with the activity and interactions of the teacher, while another monitored six pre-selected target children for ten minutes each. The observed teachers wore radio microphones so that the observers could hear all they said as unobtrusively as possible.

A comprehensive account of the procedures used in the selection and observation of the Level 3 target children, together with summaries of the pupil and teacher observation schedules, will be found in Volume 2, which deals with Level 3 study in detail.

The Interviews

The interviews with teachers also varied depending on the nature and the extent of the observation which accompanied them. The principle upon which the interview schedules were constructed was that the initial questions on each topic should be as open as possible, to allow the teacher the greatest leeway for her own basic interpretations of the themes under discussion. Follow-up questions, or prompts, were asked only if the teacher had not already spontaneously covered the points they raised.

The interviews took place in the teachers' own classrooms or teaching areas. At each level of the enquiry one of their purposes was to contextualize the observation. In an immediate sense this involved giving the teachers an opportunity of explaining beforehand what they had planned for each observation session, and of commenting afterwards on how it had gone. In a broader sense, however, it was concerned with their longer-term planning strategies and the influences which were shaping their current practice, with their thoughts and ideas as well as with their physical activity.

The Level 1 interviews were concerned with the following matters:

basic details about the school, the teacher and her pupils;

the classroom or teaching area: whether it was shared with other teachers; its general use and the function of its various features; how the children were organized in it; how their work was organized, both beforehand and on the spot; how the children's work and progress were monitored;

the classroom organization course and the extent of its influence on the room, the teacher's daily practice, the pupils, and the teacher personally;

problems, if any, in implementing the course's recommendations: problems with the building itself, with colleagues, with the teacher's own beliefs about teaching, etc.;

other influences on the teacher's classroom organization and practice: visits from members of the LEA's advisory team, staff meetings, colleagues, reading, etc.

At Level 2 it was appropriate to include a number of other matters in the interview, since the teacher had been observed in action in the classroom. First she was encouraged to talk freely about the observation session which had just taken place, and then she was asked in detail about:

the planning that lay behind the session;

any difficulties she or the children had experienced during the session;

the place of that day's work in her longer-term curriculum provision;

any guidelines she was following.

Finally, since the classroom organization course had made a number of specific recommendations, the teacher was asked how five of these worked in practice for her and her pupils. The recommendations were:

that children should work independently for extended periods of the day;

that they should work cooperatively;

that teachers should make opportunities for teaching at group level;

that they should plan to work with one or two groups of children for extended periods within a session;

that different curriculum areas should be undertaken simultaneously.

The programme of interviews at Level 3 was necessarily more ambitious since it related to ten observation sessions each by two observers over a period of two weeks. The class teachers were interviewed at some length at the beginning and end of the fortnight of observations, and more briefly before and after each separate stint. Support staff were also interviewed daily, and again at the end of the fortnight; and there was a final interview with the head. Summaries of all the interview schedules will be found in Volume 2.

Glossary of Abbreviations and Acronyms

CIPFA   Chartered Institute of Public Finance and Accountancy

DES   Department of Education and Science [the department of central government responsible for education in England and Wales]

EPA   Educational Priority Area

EPFAS   Educational Psychology and Family Advisory Service [in Leeds LEA]

ESG   Educational Support Grant [central government scheme for direct funding of development and support activity in educational fields of major policy concern]

ESL   English as a Second Language [also abbreviated to E2L]

EWO   Educational Welfare Officer

GRIST   Grant-Related In-Service Training [scheme for funding teachers' in-service development introduced by central government in 1987]

INRS   Individual Needs Recording System [the Leeds LEA procedure for monitoring those children with special educational needs]

INSET   In-Service Education and Training [of teachers]

LEA   Local Education Authority [branch of local government with statutory responsibility for the provision of education in its area]

LEATGS   Local Education Authority Training Grant Scheme [mechanism for funding INSET introduced after the 1988 Education Reform Act]

LISSEN   Leeds In-Service for Special Educational Needs

METRA   A commercial pack based on the direct instruction principles of teaching reading

PNP   Primary Needs Programme [introduced by Leeds LEA in 1985]

POWYS   A computerized annual review system for monitoring a child's progress

PrIME   Primary Initiatives in Mathematical Education

PRINDEP   Primary Needs Independent Evaluation Project [evaluation of Leeds LEA's Primary Needs Programme, undertaken by a Leeds University team directed by Robin Alexander]

SEN   Special Educational Needs

References

ADELMAN, C. and ALEXANDER, R.J. (1982) *The Self-Evaluating Institution*, London: Methuen.

ALEXANDER, R.J. (1979) 'The problematic nature of professional studies'. In ALEXANDER, R.J. and WORMALD, E. (eds) *Professional Studies for Teaching*, pp. 2–14. Guildford: SRHE.

ALEXANDER, R.J. (1981) 'Towards a conceptual framework for school-focused INSET', *British Journal of In-Service Education*, 6, 3.

ALEXANDER, R.J. (1984a) *Primary Teaching*. London: Cassell.

ALEXANDER, R.J. (1984b) 'Innovation and continuity in the initial teacher education curriculum'. In ALEXANDER, R.J., CRAFT, M. and LYNCH, J. (eds) *Change in Teacher Education: Context and Provision Since Robbins*, pp. 103–60. London: Cassell.

ALEXANDER, R.J. (1988) 'Garden or jungle? Teacher development and informal primary education'. In BLYTH, W.A.L. (ed.) *Informal Primary Education Today: Essays and Studies*, pp. 148–88. Lewes: Falmer Press.

ALEXANDER, R.J. (1989) 'Core subjects and autumn leaves: the National Curriculum and the languages of primary education,' *Education 3–13*, 17, 1.

ARGYRIS, C. and SCHÖN, D.A. (1974) *Theory in Practice: Increasing Professional Effectiveness*. San Francisco: Jossey-Bass.

ASHTON, P.M.E. (1981) 'Primary Teachers' Aims, 1969–77'. In SIMON, B. and WILLCOCKS, J. (eds) *Research and Practice in the Primary Classroom*, pp. 26–35. London: Routledge and Kegan Paul.

BENNETT, S.N. (1976) *Teaching Styles and Pupil Progress*. London: Open Books.

BENNETT, S.N., ANDREAE, J., HEGARTY, P. and WADE, B. (1980) *Open Plan Schools: Teaching, Curriculum, Design*. Windsor: NFER.

BENNETT, S.N., DESFORGES, C., COCKBURN, A. and WILKINSON, B. (1984) *The Quality of Pupil Learning Experiences*. London: Lawrence Erlbaum Associates.

BENNIS, W.G., BENNE, K., CHIN, R. and COREY, K. (1976) *The Planning of Change*. London: Holt, Rinehart and Winston.

BERLAK, A. and BERLAK, H. (1981) *Dilemmas of Schooling: Teaching and Social Change*. London: Methuen.

BERNSTEIN, B. (1970) 'Education cannot compensate for society', *New Society*. 26 February, pp. 344–7.

BLENKIN, G.M. and KELLY, A.V. (1987) *The Primary Curriculum: A Process Approach to Curriculum Planning*. London: Harper and Row.

BLYTH, W.A.L. (1984) *Development, Experience and the Curriculum in Primary Education*. London: Croom Helm.

BLYTH, W.A.L. (ed.) (1988) *Informal Primary Education Today: Essays and Studies*. Lewes: Falmer Press.

BLYTH, W.A.L. (1989) 'The study of primary education in England: retrospect and prospect'. In ALEXANDER, R.J. (ed.) *Primary Education and the National Curriculum: Papers from the 1988 Conference of the Association for the Study of Primary Education*. ASPE.

BOARD OF EDUCATION (1931) *Report of the Consultative Committee on the Primary School* (Hadow Report). London: HMSO.

BOLAM, R., SMITH, G. and CANTER, H. (1976) *Local Authority Advisers and the Mechanisms of Innovation*. Slough: NFER.

BURGESS, R.G. (ed.) (1985) *Field Methods in the Study of Education*. Lewes: Falmer Press.

CAMPBELL, R.J. (1985) *Developing the Primary School Curriculum*. London: Cassell.

CENTRAL ADVISORY COUNCIL FOR EDUCATION (ENGLAND) (1967) *Children and Their Primary Schools* (Plowden Report). London: HMSO.

CUNNINGHAM, P. (1988) *Curriculum Change in the Primary School Since 1945: Dissemination of the Progressive Ideal*. Lewes: Falmer Press.

DEARDEN, R.F. (1968) *The Philosophy of Primary Education*. London: Routledge and Kegan Paul.

DEPARTMENT OF EDUCATION AND SCIENCE (1977) *Local Authority Arrangements for the School Curriculum* (Circular 14/77). London: DES.

DEPARTMENT OF EDUCATION AND SCIENCE (1978a) *Primary Education in England: A Survey by HM Inspectors of Schools*. London: HMSO.

DEPARTMENT OF EDUCATION AND SCIENCE (1978b) *Special Educational Needs: Report of the Committee of Enquiry into the Education of Handicapped Children and Young People* (Warnock Report). London: HMSO.

DEPARTMENT OF EDUCATION AND SCIENCE (1979) *Local Authority Arrangements for the School Curriculum: Report of the 14/77 Review*. London: DES.

DEPARTMENT OF EDUCATION AND SCIENCE (1982) *Education 5–9: An Illustrative Survey of 80 First Schools in England*. London: HMSO.

DEPARTMENT OF EDUCATION AND SCIENCE (1983) *Local Authority Policies on the School Curriculum* (Circular 8/83). London: DES.

DEPARTMENT OF EDUCATION AND SCIENCE (1985) *The Curriculum from 5 to 16*. London: HMSO.

DEPARTMENT OF EDUCATION AND SCIENCE (1988a) *Education Reform Act: Local Management of Schools* (Circular 7/88). London: DES.

DEPARTMENT OF EDUCATION AND SCIENCE (1988b) *1987 Primary School Staffing Survey*. London: DES.

DEPARTMENT OF EDUCATION AND SCIENCE (1989a) *Standards in Education 1987–88: The Annual Report of HM Senior Chief Inspector of Schools Based on the Work of HMI in England*. London: DES.

DEPARTMENT OF EDUCATION AND SCIENCE (1989b) *Report by HM Inspectors on a Survey of Support Services for Special Educational Needs*. London: DES.

DEPARTMENT OF EDUCATION AND SCIENCE/DEPARTMENT OF HEALTH AND SOCIAL SECURITY (1983) *Assessments and Statements of Special Needs* (Circular 1/83). London: DES.

ENTWISTLE, H. (1970) *Child-Centred Education*. London: Methuen.

GALTON, M. and SIMON, B. (eds) (1980) *Progress and Performance in the Primary Classroom*. London: Routledge and Kegan Paul.

GALTON, M., SIMON, B. and CROLL, P. (1980) *Inside the Primary Classroom*. London: Routledge and Kegan Paul.

HALSEY, A.H. (ed.) (1972) *Educational Priority. Volume 1: EPA Problems and Policies*. London: HMSO.

HAMMERSLEY, M. (ed.) (1986) *Controversies in Classroom Research*. Milton Keynes: Open University Press.

HENDERSON, E.S. (1978) *The Evaluation of In-Service Training*. London: Croom Helm.

HIRST, P.H. and PETERS, R.S. (1970) *The Logic of Education*. London: Routledge and Kegan Paul.

HOUSE, E.R. (ed.) (1973) *School Evaluation: The Politics and Process*. Berkeley: McCutchan.

HOUSE OF COMMONS (1986) *Achievement in Primary Schools: Third Report from the Education, Science and Arts Committee, Volume I*. London: HMSO.

KELLMER-PRINGLE, M. (1980) *The Needs of Children*. London: Hutchinson.

INNER LONDON EDUCATION AUTHORITY (1985) *Improving Primary Schools*. London, ILEA.

LEEDS CITY COUNCIL (1985a) *Primary Needs Programme*. Education Committee document, 10 June.

LEEDS CITY COUNCIL (1985b) *Primary Needs Programme: Monitoring and Evaluation Programme*. Education Committee document, 28 June.

LEEDS CITY COUNCIL (1985c) *PNP Coordinator: Job Specification*, 26 September.

LEEDS CITY COUNCIL (1986) *Primary Needs Programme: Equal Opportunities for Girls*. Education Committee document, 16 June.

LEEDS CITY COUNCIL (1987a) *Proposal to Establish a Profile of Need and Provision in Mainstream Schools*. Education Committee document, 1 July.

LEEDS CITY COUNCIL (1987b) *Anti-Racist Education: A Policy Statement*.

LEEDS CITY COUNCIL (1988) *Primary Education: A Policy Statement*.

MASLOW, A. (1954) *Motivation and Personality*. New York: Harper and Row.

MERSON, M.W. and CAMPBELL, R.J. (1974) 'Community education: instruction for inequality', *Education for Teaching*, 93, 1.

MIDWINTER, E. (1972) *Projections: An Education Priority Area at Work*. London: Ward Lock.

MORTIMORE, P., SAMMONS, P., STOLL, L., LEWIS, D. and ECOB, R. (1988) *School Matters: The Junior Years*. London: Open Books.

NIAS, J. (1989) *Primary Teachers Talking: A Study of Teaching as Work*. London: Routledge.

NIAS, J., SOUTHWORTH, G. and YEOMANS, R. (1989) *Staff Relationships in the Primary School: A Study of Organizational Cultures*. London: Cassell.

POLLARD, A. (1985) *The Social World of the Primary School*. London: Cassell.

RODGER, I. (1983) *Teachers with Posts of Responsibility in Primary Schools*. Durham: University of Durham, School of Education.

RUDDOCK, J. (1981) *Making the Most of the Short In-Service Course*. Schools Council Working Paper 71. London: Methuen.

SCHÖN, D.A. (1983) *The Reflective Practitioner: How Professionals Think in Action*. London: Temple Smith.

SCHÖN, D.A. (1987) *Educating the Reflective Practitioner: Toward a New Design for Teaching and Learning in the Professions*. San Francisco: Jossey-Bass.

SCHOOLS COUNCIL (1981) *The Practical Curriculum*. London: Methuen.

SCHOOLS COUNCIL (1983) *Primary Practice: A Sequel to 'The Practical Curriculum'*. London: Methuen.

SHAPLIN, J.T. and OLDS, H.F. (eds) (1964) *Team Teaching*. New York: Harper and Row.

SIMON, B. (1981) 'The primary school revolution: myth or reality?' In SIMON, B. and WILLCOCKS, J. (eds) *Research and Practice in the Primary Classroom*, pp. 7–25. London: Routledge and Kegan Paul.

TANNER, R. (1987) *Double Harness*. London: Impact Books.

TAYLOR, P.H. (1986) *Expertise and the Primary School Teacher*. Windsor: NFER-Nelson.

TAYLOR, M. (ed.) (1974) *Team Teaching Experiments*. Slough: NFER.

TIZARD, B., BLATCHFORD, P., BURKE, J., FARQUHAR, C. and PLEWIS, I. (1988) *Young Children at School in the Inner City*. Hove: Lawrence Erlbaum Associates.

WATTS, A.G. (1978) *NFER Reading Test AD*. Windsor: NFER-Nelson.

WINKLEY, D. (1985) *Diplomats and Detectives: LEA Advisers at Work*. London: Robert Royce.

WOLFENDALE, S. (1987) *Primary Schools and Special Needs: Policy, Planning and Provision*. London: Cassell.

YOUNG, D. (1980) *Group Reading Test*. 2nd ed. London: Hodder and Stoughton.

Index